What Should I B

Suddenly, in the twenty-first century, religion has become a political power. It affects us all, whether we're religious or not. We want to make up our own minds about what we believe, but it's difficult to do this. Everyone has to face the dilemma that we all die but no one knows for certain what death actually is. All religions promise to overcome death, but there's no set of religious or philosophical beliefs that ensures that our life is always happy and secure. Moreover, for many of us, what we were taught about a religion severely diminished our self-confidence and left us with a constant debilitating feeling of guilt and shame.

Through all this turmoil comes the calm, clear voice of eminent psychologist Dorothy Rowe. She separates the political from the personal, the power-seeking from the compassionate. She shows how, if we use our beliefs as a defence against our feelings of worthlessness, we feel compelled to force our beliefs on to other people by coercion or aggression. However, it is possible to create a set of beliefs, expressed in the religious or philosophical metaphors most meaningful to us, that allows us to live at peace with ourselves and other people, and to face life with courage and optimism.

Dorothy Rowe is a psychologist and author of thirteen books, including the worldwide bestseller *Depression: The Way Out of Your Prison*. She is Australian and divides her time between London and Sydney.

'An important and moving account of our beliefs in life and death'
**Lewis Wolpert FRS, Emeritus Professor,
Cell and Developmental Biology,
University College, London**

'Dorothy Rowe uses her exceptional gifts of wisdom, common sense and clarity of thought to explain the nature of religious belief and to show us, as only she can, how to confront the problem of death.'

Carmen Callil

'Dorothy Rowe casts a bracingly cool eye on the fantasies which can inform religious belief. An important and robust attack on the self-serving aspects of religion.'

Gwyneth Lewis

'Too often those who write about religion seek to convert, inflame, or condemn. At a time when belief in God has never been more controversial and debated, the sane, balanced and wise voice of Dorothy Rowe comes as manna from heaven.'

**Peter Stanford, Catholic writer, broadcaster
and biographer**

'I am a great devotee of Dorothy's writing but I don't think it's appropriate for me to offer a quote for this particular book, since I am declared Christian – and happy'

Fay Weldon

'Dorothy's book focuses minds, like mine, who do not allow themselves time to think things through'

**Terry Mullins, Chairman of the
North London Humanist Group**

'Dorothy Rowe brings a refreshingly sane voice to the fraught, confusing but vital discussion of our beliefs about life, death and reality. Looking past the content of beliefs, she asks why people believe as they do and describes with wonderful lucidity how deep-seated emotions shape our ideas about life and these, in turn, mold our experience of it. This book is a timely reminder that we choose what we believe and how we believe it, and a passionate, liberating argument for self-awareness.'

Vishvapani, Buddhist writer and broadcaster

What Should I Believe?

Why Our Beliefs about the Nature of Death and the Purpose of Life Dominate Our Lives

Dorothy Rowe

Routledge
Taylor & Francis Group

LONDON AND NEW YORK

Previous editions published by Fontana (1989) and Harper Collins (1991) as
The Construction of Life and Death (also known as *The Courage to Live*)

First published in Great Britain by John Wiley & Sons 1982

This edition first published 2009 by Routledge
27 Church Road, Hove, East Sussex, BN3 2FA

Simultaneously published in the USA and Canada
by Routledge
270 Madison Avenue, New York, NY 10016

Reprinted 2009

Routledge is an imprint of the Taylor & Francis Group, an Informa business

Copyright © 1982, 1989, 2009 Dorothy Rowe

Typeset in New Century Schoolbook by RefineCatch Limited,
Bungay, Suffolk, UK
Printed and bound in Great Britain by
TJ International Ltd, Padstow, Cornwall
Cover design by Lisa Dynan

British Library Cataloguing in Publication Data
A catalogue record for this book is available from the British Library

Library of Congress Cataloging-in-Publication Data
Rowe, Dorothy.
[Construction of life and death]
What should I believe? : why our beliefs about the nature
of death and the purpose of life dominate our lives / Dorothy
Rowe.
p. cm.
Originally published: . Construction of life and death.
Chichester [Eng.]; New York : John Wiley, c1982.
Includes bibliographical references and index.
1. Personal construct theory. 2. Psychology, Religious. 3.
Death–Psychological aspects. 4. Life. I. Title.
BF698.9.P47R69 2009
150.1–dc22

2008019672

ISBN: 978-0-415-46679-0

Wherever it is happening, the revival of religion is mixed up with political conflicts, including an intensifying struggle over the Earth's shrinking reserves of natural resources; but there can be no doubt that religion is once again a power in its own right.

John Gray

The aims of life are the best defence against death: and not only in the Lager.

Primo Levi

As men's habits of mind differ, so that some more readily embrace one form of faith, some another, for what moves one to pray may move another only to scoff, I conclude that everyone should be free to choose for himself the foundations of his creed, and that faith should be judged only by its fruits; each would then obey God freely with his whole heart, while nothing would be publicly honoured save justice and charity.

Baruch Spinoza

CONTENTS

PREFACE

We live in a crazy world. Over the past few years, thousands of people have been killed, or injured, or driven from their homes by other people who believe that they are entitled to kill those who do not share their religious beliefs. At the same time, a president of the most powerful country in the world, while following policies which have fostered these tragedies, believed that the end of the world would soon be upon us, whereupon he and those who share his beliefs would be 'raptured' into heaven, leaving behind the chaos he helped to create. Millions like him believe that the turmoil in the Middle East and the perilous changes in the world's climate are no more than evidence of the working out of God's plan, and that nothing should be done that would impede His plan.

In the last two years a number of militant atheists have ridden to the rescue – or so they thought. They certainly stirred up controversy. Religion is being talked and argued about in a way I have not seen before in my lifetime (b. 1930). In his book *The God Delusion* and in his television programmes which followed, Richard Dawkins asked in great amazement, 'How can people be so stupid as to believe this nonsense?' Christopher Hitchens was hurt and angry. 'How', he asked in his book *God Is Not Great*, 'can people have beliefs which lead them to be unforgivably cruel?' John Humphrys does not see himself as a militant atheist but as a curious, persistent questioner; as he ended his book *In God We Doubt*, where he interviewed three religious leaders, Rowan Williams, the Archbishop of Canterbury, Professor Tariq Ramadan and Jonathan Sacks, the Chief Rabbi, he could only ask himself, 'How can these intelligent, educated men believe such things?'

These three questions may have been rhetorical and not requiring answer, but asked in the hope that the misguided and the wicked would mend their ways. Parents often ask rhetorical questions of their offspring, questions like, 'How can you bear to live in such a mess?', and expect that within the hour their teenage child will transform his room into a model of neatness. The parents' hopes are always dashed, just as the hopes of Dawkins, Hitchens and Humphrys show no sign of being fulfilled.

However, I have decided to treat these questions as genuine questions, requiring an answer that I shall supply. My answer is based on an understanding of how we create meaning, and how out of these meanings comes our sense of being a person, what we call 'I', 'me', 'myself'. Our sense of being a person is no more than a fragile structure of ideas, but it is our most important possession. So important is it to us that we cannot bear the thought that it will vanish with our death. Our greatest fear is that our sense of being a person will be wiped out if we are humiliated, or if we discover that there is a serious discrepancy between what we thought our life was and what it actually is, or if we are treated as an object of no importance. In these situations, the ideas that constitute our sense of being a person fall apart, but we experience this as ourselves falling apart, shattering, disappearing. Our terror threatens to overwhelm us, and so we do whatever we can to defend ourselves against this fear.

The theme of Primo Levi's account of his time in Auschwitz, *If This Be a Man*, is the battle to survive not just physically but as a person. To be a person we have to assert our right to disobey those who claim to have power over us. Levi wrote about those people who tried to survive in the Lager by being totally obedient. For some unknown reason, they were called 'muselmans'. He said,

> To sink is the easiest of matters: it is enough to carry out
> all the orders one receives, to eat only the ration, to
> observe the discipline of work and the camp. Experience
> showed that only exceptionally could one survive for more

than three months in this way. All the muselmans who finished in the gas chambers have the same story, or more exactly, have no story; they followed the slope to the bottom, like streams that run down to the sea . . . Their life is short, but their number is endless; they, the *Muselmänner*, the drowned, form the backbone of the camp, an anonymous mass, continually renewed and always identical, of non-men who march and labour in silence, the divine spark dead within them, already too empty to suffer. One hesitates to call them living: one hesitates to call their death death, in the face of which they have no fear, as they are too tired to understand.

They crowd my memory with their faceless presences, and if I could enclose all the evil of our time in one image, I would choose this image which is familiar to me: an emaciated man, with head dropped and shoulders curved, on whose face and in whose eyes not a trace of thought is to be seen.

If the drowned have no story, and single and broad is the path to perdition, the paths to salvation are many, difficult and improbable.[1]

Perdition is to lose our sense of being a person; salvation is to be the person we know ourselves to be, and not the person other people tell us that we are, or that we should be. It can take a great deal of courage to be the person you know yourself to be, and so, when courage fails, we resort to believing all kinds of improbable things.

We all believe improbable things. We all have fantasies that we treat as truths. And we all have reasons for doing so which are very important to us. Our reasons are a matter of life and death to us.

Each of us has a fantasy about the nature of death. We know that we are going to die, but all we can ever know for certain about death itself is that a living person grows strangely still. So we create a fantasy about what death is. Our choice of fantasy is limited to two ideas. Either death is the end of our sense of being a person or it is the doorway to another life. As soon as we decide which kind of fantasy we will choose, we determine the purpose of our life. If we decide that death is the end of our sense of being a person, we then have the purpose of making our life satisfactory. There is a multitude of ways we can define 'satisfactory', but, unless we can feel that our life is developing in a way we can feel is satisfactory, we cannot face our death with any equanimity. If we decide that death is a doorway to another life, we then have to decide whether this next life will be better than the previous one. If we decide that the next life will be better than this one, we then face the question of whether everybody goes on to a better life or whether only those who reach a satisfactory level of goodness can proceed to this better life. Our strong sense of justice usually impels us to choose the latter. Now we have to decide what the standards are that determine whether we go on to a better life. Once we decide what these standards are, we then have to live this, our present life, in terms of the next. We can conceive of a better life and the means of getting there in an infinite number of ways, but, whatever we choose, the purpose of our life is to gain entry to a better life after our death.

What we see as the purpose of our life becomes a project stretching forward into the future. Death cuts across that project. We find that we have to accept that our body dies, but we cannot accept the idea that our sense of being a person will vanish. If we can create a fantasy that satisfies us that our sense of being a person will continue on, then that fantasy becomes a dearly held belief. Those people who see death as the end of their sense of being a person try to create a fantasy that they will continue on through their children (this is one of the reasons why having children is so popular), or through their work, or simply in the memories of those who knew them. To die and be forgotten is never to have existed. Hence, we have graveyards, memorials, autobiographies, and family photograph albums. Religion is popular because all religions promise to overcome death. Death has no sting because our soul or spirit or self continues on in heaven, or paradise, or in another life on earth.

Our beliefs about the nature of death, the purpose of life, and the means by which the most important part of us will continue on become our religious or philosophical beliefs. We might want to regard our beliefs as absolute truths, but, alas, they cannot be. As neuroscientists now tell us, our brains do not allow us to see what exists around us. Instead, our brains construct a map of this territory, but they do not allow us to see the actual territory. Even when we have one of those extraordinary experiences which seem to show us something above and beyond the world in which we live, what is revealed to us is our idiosyncratic interpretation of that experience. Some people interpret their experience as being a revelation from God; others interpret their experience as being at one with everything that exists. Either interpretation can be marvellously self-affirming. Our individual interpretations are sometimes referred to as being relative truths. Such relative truths can be reliable, that is, the individual once in possession of them never changes them, but they cannot be valid, that is, saying something accurate about the world, unless we go to the trouble of testing our relative truths against what actually is going on. For instance, you might believe that the restaurant which is to open nearby will be the best restaurant ever, but this belief cannot have any validity until you and your friends go to the restaurant and then compare your observations about the food and service. Until you do this, your belief in the worth of the restaurant is just a fantasy.

What we all need to do is to check our maps of the territory with other people's maps, and to check them carefully against our own past experiences. However, doing this is hard work, and often we can be dismayed to find that our ideas are wrong. It is always very tempting to do nothing, and treat our precious fantasies as being absolute truths. We can even be tempted to claim that faith in our fantasies is more important than evidence that might confirm that they are true.

All of these beliefs about life and death are guesses or fantasies, but, if we have constructed these beliefs with a view to which beliefs would benefit us or which beliefs we can live with most comfortably, we can be very reluctant to change them, for to do so would mean changing how we live our life. The philosopher Arthur C. Danto told the story of what happened to one of the first Christian missionaries to China.

Father Matteo Ricci, a correspondent of Galileo and a mathematician in his own right, offered to teach the Chinese ministers what he knew of science. They would be able to predict eclipses, would be able to do wonderful things. In the end, the ministers decided that it would be better not to know these things. For theirs was a form of life that had worked well enough for a very long time, and surely the most that can be asked of a form of life is that it can be lived, that it bestows a degree of rationality upon existence, and that it holds chaos at bay. It is difficult for us to sympathise with these mandarins, since we regard knowledge as liberating. We regard them in somewhat the same light as we view those astronomers at Padua who failed to look into Galileo's telescope. Yet I believe we might appreciate this refusal to acknowledge facts in pragmatic terms. A system that induces rationality is through that fact alone of considerable value. One does not, in science any more than in life, lightly surrender a system of beliefs that facilitates experience, that renders it tractable and smooth.[2]

Religious beliefs render life tractable and smooth only for those who benefit from holding those beliefs. The two great powers, the Church and the State, have always tried to coerce their subjects into holding beliefs which benefit the people in power in the Church and the State. For many of their subjects, their beliefs are onerous indeed. Their beliefs can lead them to denigrate themselves, or to denigrate others. Their beliefs can lead them into a constant state of guilt and martyrdom. When you have become an expert in feeling guilty, you have acquired the necessary talent for becoming depressed.

I should be grateful because the Church keeps me in business, but I am not because I have seen at first hand the suffering of those who believe that they are, in essence, bad and unacceptable, who can never rest from striving to be good, and who believe that, whatever they do, they can never be good enough. They can never take life easy and just be themselves.

To understand why we hold certain beliefs and fear to

change them we need to understand how we operate as human beings. In this book I explain how our sense of being a person arises out of the way our brains create our minds, how our religious and philosophical beliefs are central to our sense of being a person, how we create our beliefs by interpreting the beliefs of others in our own individual ways (there are as many religious and philosophical beliefs as there are people to hold them), how our ideas of being good become entwined with our ideas about life and death, and how our beliefs develop from our earliest childhood. I also explain why some believers get very offended, and worse, if they think their beliefs are being criticised. Whatever the beliefs we choose to hold, holding a religious belief does not of itself make us superior to those who do not share our belief, nor does it automatically make us virtuous, nor does it give us the right to force our beliefs on others and, if they resist, to rob them of their sense of being a person or to kill them.

Beliefs are ideas. Ideas are things that we create, and, as we create them, we can change them. There is no set of religious or philosophical beliefs which ensures that we are always secure and happy. Like everything in life, whatever the belief, it has advantages and disadvantages. However, it is possible to create a set of beliefs expressed in our own individual way, using the metaphors which are rich in meaning for us, with which we can live comfortably with ourselves and with others, and from which we can draw strength and optimism.

Whatever language we speak, each of us speaks in our own individual idiolect, using metaphors and similes drawn from our past experience. In the discussions about religion and philosophy we often do not realise that another person, using an idiolect very different from our own, is talking about something which we actually share. Fundamentalists of whatever religion are easy to understand because they would have us believe that they know what is right and what is wrong. In contrast, those people who focus on what it is to exist as a human being can be talking about much the same things but not realise this because of the differences in their idiolects. However, sometimes we do understand.

When John Crace interviewed Geza Vermes, whom many regard as the greatest Jesus scholar of his generation, he asked Vermes what he believed. Vermes, a former priest who had been born into a Jewish family who converted to Catholicism, took him to his garden that backs onto 700 acres of woodland. Here he said, 'You know, I'm not a great one for synagogues and other places of worship. When I want to listen to that little voice, I go out there for a walk.'[3]

Most of us know what he meant.

My thanks to all those people who talked to me about their beliefs.

ACKNOWLEDGEMENTS

The author and publisher are grateful to the following for their permission to reproduce passages from copyright material as follows:

The Alister Hardy Religious Experience Research Centre, University of Wales, Lampeter for permission to publish extracts from *Living the Questions* by Edward Robinson Copyright Religious Experience Unit, Oxford; A.M. Heath for extracts from *Memoir* by John McGarhern (Copyright © John McGahern, 2005) Reprinted by permission of A.M. Heath and Co Ltd; Faber and Faber Ltd for extracts from *Memoir* by John McGahern and from *The Death of Tragedy* by George Steiner; Georges Borchadt, Inc for extracts from *The Death of Tragedy* by George Steiner. Copyright © 1961, 1980 by George Steiner. Reprinted by permission of Georges Borchadt, Inc., for the author; Graywolf Press for excerpts from *A Lie About my Father* copyright 2007 John Burnside. Reprinted from *A Lie About My Father* with the permission of Graywolf Press, Saint Paul, Minnesota; Grove/Atlantic, Inc for extracts from *Timebends: A Life* by Arthur Miller. Copyright © 1987, 1995 by Arthur Miller Used by permission of Grove/Atlantic, Inc; Guardian Books for permission to use extracts from *Suspicious Packages and Extendable Arms* by Tim Dowling, Published by Guardian Books; The Guardian for extracts from the articles *Face to Faith* by Mordechai Beck, Copyright Guardian News & Media Ltd 2008, *A Funny Kind of Christian* by Giles Frase, Copyright Guardian News & Media Ltd 2008, *A Kind of Magic?* by Ben Goldacre, Copyright Guardian News & Media Ltd 2007 and

Nature the Tinkerer by Peter Forbes, Copyright Guardian News & Media Ltd 2008; Hachette Book Group USA for extracts from *God Is Not Great* by Christopher Hitchens, Copyright © 2007 by Christopher Hitchens. By Permission of Grand Central Publishing; Houghton Mifflin Harcourt for extracts from *The God Delusion* by Richard Dawkins, Copyright © 2006 by Richard Dawkins. Reprinted by permission of Houghton Mifflin Harcourt Publishing Company All rights reserved; The New Scientist for extracts from *Trapped in a World View* by David Peat; Penguin Group (UK) for an extract rom *Black Mass* by John Gray (Penguin Books, 2007, 2008). Copyright © John Gray, 2007; Random House Australia for extracts from *The Rise and Rise of Kerry Packer* by Paul Barry, Published 2007, Reprinted by Permission of Random House Australia; The Random House Group for extracts from *A Lie About my Father* by John Burnside, published by Jonathan Cape. Reprinted by permission of The Random House Group Ltd and for extracts from *The God Delusion* by Richard Dawkins, published by Bantam Press. Reprinted by permission of The Random House Group Ltd; Verso Press for extracts from *If I Am Not for Myself by* Mike Marqusee. Reprinted by permission of Verso Press.

Chapter 1

RELIGION IN THE TWENTY-FIRST CENTURY

Whatever our religious beliefs and whether we want it or not, in the twenty-first century religion has come to dominate our lives. Religions in a wide variety of forms have always existed, and at times in past centuries what you believed was a matter of life and death. This still applies in some parts of the world. However, in the developed world we prefer to see religion as a kind of unguent that gives comfort in times of loss and confirms our worth when danger threatens. Has not God always been on our side? Apart from this, religion did not play a very significant role in the latter part of the twentieth century when the attention was focused on the Cold War and the likelihood of the Mutually Assured Destruction (MAD) that would follow if the USSR and the USA used their nuclear arsenal against one another. When the USSR fell apart and the Berlin Wall came down in 1989, the effects on the world economy brought into being a word new to most of us then but now so common – globalisation. We were assured that such a change in the world economy would bring inestimable benefits. To many people it seemed that the Millennium would usher in a time which would be the best in human history. But when Muslim extremists flew two planes packed with unwilling passengers into the Twin Towers in New York in 2001 everything changed.

In the days following September 11th television news frequently showed interviews with ordinary Americans who expressed their bewilderment with the question, 'Why do these people hate us?' Their ignorance of their country's relationships with Islamic countries was matched only by that of various American government officials who revealed a basic ignorance of the geography of the Middle East and Afghanistan, while the Central Intelligence Agency, the CIA, had little reliable intelligence about this area and contained no Arabic speakers who might be able to operate as intelligence officers in the Muslim world. Complete ignorance of Islam did not stop commentators in the Christian world holding forth on whether or not the Qur'an regarded suicide bombers with great favour. Moderating voices pointed out that Mohammed Atta, who led the attack on the Twin Towers, and his colleagues represented an extreme form of Islam which could be called fundamentalist, and that there were many Muslims who had nothing but goodwill towards those not of their faith.

Fundamentalism is not a throwback to medieval times but is essentially a modern phenomenon. It is not confined to Islam. Like Islam, Christianity, Judaism and Hinduism are divided into a more liberal mainstream and the fundamentalists. In Christianity, evangelicals include both liberal and fundamentalist churches. As Giles Fraser, the vicar of Putney, has pointed out, 'These [liberal evangelicals] are passionately concerned with issues of poverty and social justice, they run soup kitchens, give generous proportions of income to good causes, have taskforces to reduce their carbon footprint, go on demonstrations against the war, and speak out against the use of torture.'[1] However, at present the Church of England is tearing itself apart in the battle between the liberal Anglicans, whose beliefs differ but little from those of humanists, and the fundamentalist evangelicals. When the American Episcopalian (Anglican) church appointed Gene Robinson, who was in a gay relationship, as bishop of New Hampshire, these evangelicals in the world-wide Church were outraged. African bishops threatened to boycott the next Lambeth conference. In Australia the Archbishop of Sydney, Peter Jensen, supported the Global Anglican Future Conference of evangelical bishops to be held in Jerusalem just before the ten-yearly meeting of all the world's bishops in London. He said, 'Some American Anglicans are as committed to their new sexual ethics as to the Gospel itself, and they intend to act as missionaries for this faith, wishing to persuade the rest of us. The problems posed by the American church are not going to remain in America.'[2] As some people said in the 1970s when gays were venturing out of the closet, 'They're making homosexuality compulsory now.'

The sociologist Peter Herriot has shown in his study *Religious Fundamentalism and Social Identity*[3] that evangelical Anglicans fit in all respects the chief characteristics of fundamentalism. The Archbishop of Canterbury, Rowan Williams, is regarded by evangelical members of his church as failing to uphold the truth of the Scriptures. Rowan Williams tries to maintain the unity of his church, but he persists in expressing views which are contrary to the beliefs of the evangelicals. They believe that the Bible is the infallible word of God. In a discussion with Simon Mayo on BBC Radio Five, Rowan Williams pointed out that there was scant evidence for the Magi, and none at all that there were three of them, or that they were kings. All the evidence that existed was in Matthew's Gospel. The archbishop said, 'Matthew's Gospel doesn't tell us that there were three of them, doesn't tell us they were kings, doesn't tell us where they came from. It says they are astrologers, wise men, priests from somewhere outside the Roman Empire, that's all we're really told.' Anything else was legend. 'It works quite well as legend', the archbishop said.[4] Rowan Williams takes a similarly relaxed view of same sex relationships and gay clergy, much to the dismay of the evangelical members who regard homosexuality as the greatest of sins.

In Israel, fundamentalist Jews hold fast to their literal interpretation of the Bible, that God promised the land to the descendants of Abraham, and thus gave Jews a legal title to Palestine. On this basis, land long owned by Palestinians has been confiscated and Jewish settlements built.

Hindu fundamentalism, much like Buddhist fundamentalism, sounds like an oxymoron, but Hindu fundamentalists and their political party, the BJP, want to turn India into a purely Hindu state. In the course of achieving this aim, the fundamentalists make frequent attacks on Christians and Muslims. Even Buddhist fundamentalists have existed. In 1938 leading members of the Nichiren sect in Japan founded a group devoted to 'Imperial-Way Buddhism' and supported the Emperor Hirohito's army. Christopher Hitchens wrote, 'By the end of the dreadful conflict that Japan had started, it was Buddhist and Shinto priests who were recruiting and training the suicide bombers, or *Kamikazi*.[5]

'Fundamentalists', wrote Peter Herriot,

> represent themselves as returning to the pure premodern origins of their faith, as prescribed by their sacred books and as practised by their legendary founders and heroes. In fact, they use modern means to battle against modernity, and arguably are frequently operating at a postmodern level of sophistication in their use of the media . . . Militant Muslims use other people's media to promote their cause. News media around the world carry accounts and pictures of violent crimes which are committed in order to send a message of fear. The deeds of Osama bin Laden, of suicide bombers in Israel and of kidnappers in Iraq tell the world that it is not safe from a vengeful God and his faithful servants. The other major free global organ, the internet, contains much Islamic recruitment material. For example, a dedicated youth site offers an apologia for the radical cleric Sayyid Qutb, together with the text of his most famous book.[6]

In calling the story of the Three Wise Men a legend, Rowan Williams was not denigrating legend. He was well aware that everyone needs stories and legends, what scholars call *mythos* and I call fantasy, just as much as we need *logos*, rational, sensible, scientific thought. Mythos is essentially those myths and legends which are handed down from one generation to the next and revised and elaborated by succeeding generations according to their own experiences. The stories our ancestors told around the fire in their cave are now being retold in fiction, drama and film, in comics and in computer games. The legends of great heroes who survive death by having extraordinary skills or good contacts in the supernatural world are now being re-enacted in games like

> Ubisoft's *Prince of Persia: Sands of Time* (2003), in which the player could rewind time after time after dying, allowing another chance to attempt a previously fatal

manoeuvre. In shooters, the barriers between life and death are even more blurred. EA's *Battlefield* series allows players to become medics who can revive comrades after fatal wounds.[7]

Myths and legends tell us to be brave and steadfast, that good will triumph, and love conquer all. Moreover, as Karen Armstrong, the historian of religious ideas, pointed out,

> The various mythological stories, which were not intended to be taken literally, were an ancient form of psychology. When people told stories of heroes who ventured into the underworld, struggled through labyrinths, or fought with monsters, they were bringing to light the obscure regions of the subconscious realm, which is not accessible to purely rational investigation, but which has a profound effect on our experience and behaviour.[8]

Mythos and logos are not two separate forms of thought. They interact when we are deciding what course of action we shall take. The myth of the hero who rescues those in danger has often provided the motivation for a scientist or an engineer to explore a novel but essentially practical idea. If we are wise, in planning any activity we try it out first in fantasy to see if things will turn out the way we expect. When some practical project fails we can comfort ourselves with the popular fantasy of what I would have done or said had I thought of it at the time. When frustration and defeat lead to anger and the desire for revenge, we can dissipate these dangerous emotions in fantasies of overcoming those who have frustrated and betrayed us. Indeed, the unity of scientific thought and fantasy goes even deeper than this. Not only are we story-makers and story-tellers but our brains work in such a way that nothing is meaningful to us until we have fitted it into a story.

A story has a simple structure. It has a beginning, a middle and an end. Knowing the middle of a story but not knowing either the beginning or the end makes us uncomfortable, even anxious. Suppose you arrive home one evening to an empty house which you knew was locked against all intruders and you find a large parcel sitting on your kitchen table. Before you carry out any steps to ascertain how it got there what rushes through your mind is a string of hypotheses – you must have left the back door unlocked and the postman let himself in, your neighbour must have had a key, or even Santa has come early this Christmas. You have to find the beginning to the story. When your investigations reveal how the parcel got there, you turn to the end of the story. What are you going to do with the parcel and its contents? When the end of the story is in place you relax. The parcel is fully explained. It has a meaning. Mythos and logos both use the form of the story.

We cannot live just with mythos or just with logos. Living just in fantasy we not only make some dangerous errors in our dealing with the world but we are unable to communicate with other people. We have to pay careful attention to the world in order to find meanings which we can share with others. For instance, my generation, born in the 1930s, were faced in our sixties with the choice of learning about computers or not. Those of us who made the effort to acquire this knowledge can now share with younger generations discussions about computers, their benefits and abysmal failures, discussions which have all the excitement and interest of conversations about the weather, but which make us feel at home in the modern world. Those of my generation who decided that they were too old to bother with all this new-fangled nonsense of emails and the internet find themselves living in a world which is increasingly alien, where younger generations seem very different from what they were like when they were young.

Living just in logos and eschewing everything that is not immediately tangible and knowable removes our ability to live with uncertainty. Fantasy is all about uncertainty, the entertaining of a multitude of possibilities. Fantasy is about doubt. Those who try to live only in logos find uncertainty and doubt impossible to bear.

The Bible, like the Qur'an, can be read as a mythos text, full of stories which might not relate to real events and which are best understood in the light of the circumstances under which they were told. Such a reading is full of uncertainties and therefore unacceptable to those who want to see the world in terms of logos. To fundamentalists their book, be it the Qur'an or the Bible, is the Word of God and therefore is infallible, inerrant and internally consistent. God's word is logos, the Knowledge and the Law. In their world nothing happens by chance. Events that benefit them are caused by God; events which harm them are caused by evil spirits, or the Devil, or by their enemies.

Logos is essential when we want to deal with practical problems or to discover the nature of the material world in which we live, but there are very important aspects of our lives where logos alone is inadequate. In logos if something is A it cannot be not-A, but in fantasy A and not-A can exist together along with every gradation between A and not-A. In human relationships we can love the people we hate, and enjoy a friendship with someone we know is our enemy. Siblings can compete ferociously with one another, and then come together in great loyalty when an outsider attacks them. Those people who try to live only in logos not only fail to understand how mythos works but they also fail to understand themselves and other people. They form simplistic theories about why people do what they do. Thus people are supposed to be driven by their genes, or a chemical change, or evil spirits, or the Devil. What people do is never explained in terms of how they see themselves and the world because this kind of theory recognises that people have choices about what they do, and observers can never be certain that their predictions about what people do will prove to be correct.

Fundamentalists see people in simple, binary terms. They are either good or bad. 'Good' people are fellow fundamentalists; 'bad' people are outsiders. Not recognising that other people are fellow human beings who, like all of us, are mixtures of good and bad, means that fundamentalists have no difficulty in seeing their enemies as objects which can be destroyed. Fundamentalists see the world in similar terms. For them the world is in the grip of cosmic forces, the forces of good against the forces of evil. The fundamentalist is a soldier in the war of good against evil. The myth that sustains the fundamentalist world-view is that of a cosmic war. Such a world view requires an enemy. No enemy, and the myth fails.

Had George Bush decided to see Mohammed Atta and the hijackers as murderous criminals, the myth that sustained the hijackers would have failed. Bush could have called the destruction of the Twin Towers and the deaths of so many people the greatest crime the world had ever seen. He could have sworn that all his forces of law and order would capture those who had aided and abetted these criminals, and that these men would be brought to justice and tried. But he did not do this. Instead he reacted in the way the hijackers wanted. He used the cosmic language of fundamentalism. He announced that all of those who had plotted against America were America's enemy and he would lead a 'war on terror'.

Fundamentalists have wars on abstract nouns, usually some version of a war against evil. For instance, when the evangelical Bishop Chukwuma of Nigeria attempted to exorcise the Reverend Richard Kirker of his 'demon of homosexuality', he said, 'We have overcome carnality, just as the light will overcome darkness.'[9] 'War on terror' fits this fundamentalist pattern. Wars on common or proper nouns, that is, the names of real entities, define precisely which people are on each side and when the war ends. The Second World War was between the Allies and the Axis – Britain, the Commonwealth, the USSR and the USA against Germany, Italy and Japan. To be regarded as an enemy combatant you had to have the appropriate nationality. A Mexican, say, visiting England could not be arrested as an enemy combatant solely on the grounds that he once visited Germany as a student. The war ended when Germany, Italy and Japan each surrendered and signed a peace treaty. In contrast, Bush's War on Terror encompasses us all. The fact that I have met at a party two men who have been released from Guantanamo could arouse suspicion and perhaps lead to my arrest if I visited the USA. There is no possible date when terror will surrender and sign a peace treaty. Already the war on terror is merging with conflicts over nationality and over oil. As the climate changes in future decades the war on terror is likely to merge with conflicts over water and habitable land.

George Bush was brought up in the Episcopalian Church but when he gave up alcohol he took on the language and ideas of fundamentalist Christianity. Stephen Bates, who reported on religion for the *Guardian*, told how

> Peter Singer, the Princeton philosopher, has analysed the president's statements and says: 'No other president in living memory has spoken so often about good and evil, right and wrong.' He mentioned the word 'evil' in 30 per cent of the speeches he gave in the first two and a half years in office and furthermore used 'evil' far more often as a noun than as an adjective (914 uses to 182).[10]

How much of Bush's conversion was a matter of politics and how much a matter of belief is debatable. There were strong political reasons for his conversion. Rather than being seen as just continuing the Bush family dynasty, he could claim that he had been called by God to become president. He could draw on the belief widely held by Americans that they are especially favoured by God, and that America's mission was to provide moral and spiritual leadership to the rest of the world. This belief seems to have been derived from the Pilgrim Fathers who 'saw themselves as being in a covenant with God. The Deity would promise redemption to his chosen, special people, infusing them with grace, and they in turn would give him their allegiance and await his revelation.'[11]

It would be impossible for a nonbeliever to become president of the United States. An atheist simply would not get the votes. Stephen Bates noted,

> Six out of ten Americans say religion plays 'a very important part' in their lives and 39 per cent say they have been 'born again in Christ'. Nearly two-thirds of Southerners claim to have had a religious experience that changed their lives (only half of non-Southerners believe they have had the same) and a quarter of households say they have at least five Bibles in their homes.[12]

He went on,

> God, indeed, does seem to intervene an awful lot on the activities of individual Americans, as well as the state itself, in big things and in small. To Him is ascribed

success in examinations, the election of office, the cure from illness, the escape from Hurricane Katrina, even when others, equally Christian did not survive . . . He does not stop the war in Iraq, or the attacks of 9/11, but He's perfectly capable of correcting a skid on a lonely road.[13]

There had always been various fundamentalist religious groups in America but in the second half of the twentieth century fundamentalist groups were growing more militant. Revivalist preachers were drawing millions into their churches with promises of salvation without suffering. Moreover, the preachers assured their listeners, 'God wants you to be rich!' America does not have an established Church as does Britain with the Church of England.

This lack of a religious establishment was and has remained one of the most significant features of American religiosity. Americans change their religious adherence and choose their churches much more easily than their ancestors could in England and Europe. Allegiances shift; churches and parishes rise and fall; churchmen must become much more entrepreneurial to attract worshippers and cannot rely on custom and habit to maintain their congregations.[14]

The entrepreneurial character of the evangelical churches has forced mainstream churches to attempt to sell themselves in much the same way.

In her study of Christianity and politics in Australia, Amanda Lohrey noted,

Mainstream church attendance in Australia is in decline – a mere 9 per cent attend – except for a 10 per cent increase in the Anglican archdiocese of Sydney. For all the recent razzamatazz, the Pentecostalists represent a congregation of between 160,000 and 194,000 – depending on whose figures you accept – out of a population of twenty million. The number of church-going Anglicans is estimated at around 170,000. Compare this to the number of 'no religion' (2,906,000), declared atheists (347,017) and Buddhists (424,839). The Christian-based Family First Party claims to have 2,000 members, far fewer than the average first-grade football club (whose weekend game attendances are also higher than the megachurches). Arguably the most distinctive feature of the Christian Right in Australia is not its actual numbers but its proselytising zeal.[15]

Another Australian writer, Margaret Simons, in her essay *Faith, Money and Power*, pointed out that,

> It is clear that there has been a revival, not so much in religion as in religious enthusiasm. 'There is more feeling in the spirit,' said one pastor I spoke to. There may not be more Christians overall, but there are more active Christians, particularly among young people. As anyone who mixes with the young will already know, Christianity has become a significant part of youth culture. At the same time it has become acceptable and more common for people of all ages to talk about their religion.[16]

The Hillsong Church in Sydney was founded by Frank Houston but he was forced to resign in 2000 when he admitted having sex with a boy some years before. He was succeeded by his son Brian who, along with his wife Bobbie and son Joel, expanded the activities of the church aided by the congregation's donations. In 2004 Brian Houston estimated that Hillsong had an income of 50 million (Australian) dollars on which he was not required to pay any tax. At each meeting buckets with holes in the bottom are passed around so that change will drop through to the floor. What is wanted is notes, credit cards and cheques. Lohrey wrote,

> Here is religion geared to a generation raised on television and the rapid-fire commercial break. Dr Carol Cusack, a lecturer in religion at the University of Sydney, describes Hillsong's style of worship as more attuned to secular values in the community than that of other denominations. It's not new religion, she argues, but 'part of the re-branding of Christianity as fashionable, trendy, not dowdy'. In the Pentecostal churches there is and always has been plenty of dancing – or at least plenty of clapping and swaying and waving of arms – but now it has a new, slick look to it.[17]

The Catholic Church demands that anyone who wishes to become a Catholic should undergo a long period of instruction and examination by a senior priest. To join Hillsong all you need to do is to be saved. Lohrey asked three teenage girls, all enthusiastic members of Hillsong, how a person was saved. One girl replied, 'You get saved basically just by accepting Jesus, by acknowledging that you have sin in your life, you're not perfect and acknowledging that Jesus is the way to make that right, and you say, "Jesus. I want you in my life." And once you've got Jesus in your life, basically you're saved.'

Lohrey asked, 'What about if you die and you've done some bad things – do you still go to heaven?'

'Yeah, as long as you've accepted Jesus into your life.'

Lohrey wrote, 'Here we have the Protestant doctrine of justification by faith alone, as clearly and unambiguously stated as it could be.'

Lohrey asked the girls what happened to people who lived a good life but did not believe in Jesus. The girl explained,

> They love God but they don't understand what Jesus was. They don't understand that he died for our sins so we didn't have to go to hell. If you just believe that Jesus was a regular prophet, then you can't understand that he died for our sins. But in the end it's really not about what you know and don't know, it's do you have a relationship with Jesus. Basically it doesn't matter what you call yourself, or what you've done, if you have a relationship with Jesus, that's it, pretty much.'

'And everyone else goes to hell?'

'Yeah, much as it sucks, you have to understand that Jesus was the only savior.'[18]

Despite the fact that, as an Anglican, John Howard was bound for hell, when he was prime minister he and other Coalition politicians were keen to address meetings at Hillsong. Hillsong's political influence waned when Kevin Rudd became prime minister. Rudd had been brought up as a Catholic and he never hid how important his religion was to him, but he 'condemned the "privatised, pietised and politically compliant Christianity on offer from the televangelists of the twenty-first century'. Christ's vision was for a just world delivered by social action and driven by personal faith, Rudd said. Christianity was a more demanding challenge than merely to be 'the political handmaiden of the conservative establishment'.[19] Simons commented, 'Why protest, why take action, why even vote when all problems come from a lack of relationship with God, and can be solved by prayer.'[20]

Kevin Rudd knows that keeping the Australian economy sound requires more than the belief in the Prosperity Gospel of Hillsong which says that, if you have a relationship with Jesus, he will make you rich. Hillsong is not the only church which preaches the Prosperity Gospel. Most televangelicals do. The extraordinarily popular American preacher Benny Hinn does. On a recent visit to Brisbane he told his audience,

> 'I am going to tell you something. This is a prophecy. You are about to see the biggest transfer of wealth in the history of the world. You are going to see prosperity like you never dreamed of. Money is being transferred from sinners to the righteous.' His voice boomed out: 'Are you righteous?' 'Yes,' we cried. 'Are you righteous?' 'Yes,' we cried a little louder. 'This is money you never dreamed of. Are you righteous?' 'Yes,' we thundered.

'We' included the Reverend Dr David Millikan, a Uniting church minister. He had gone with a friend to see the healings which Benny Hinn performed. What they saw was the marshalling into the healing circle of those people who could easily take up their beds and walk, or, in this case, get out of their wheelchairs, shove them aside, and walk. Seriously ill people were kept far away from Hinn's healing. Millikan concluded,

> I judge Hinn by the measure of the one he claims to have been following. Jesus never promised people wealth, or instant healing. He didn't promise his disciples houses on the coast. Pastor Benny recast Jesus in his own image. He has forgotten that his Lord died, humiliated, tortured, alone and penniless. But how do you sell that?[21]

A gospel of salvation requires that there be sins and

sinners. For Hillsong, the two great sins are abortion and homosexuality. Sydney provides many examples of these sins. Abortion is legal in Australia. Sydney vies with San Francisco as the gay capital of the world. The annual Gay and Lesbian Mardi Gras celebrated its thirtieth anniversary in 2008. Many thousands of people cheered the parade and enjoyed the party. The parade presented a cross-section of Australian society, and included contingents from the police and the armed services.

The religion of most Australians continues to be sport. The greatest sin an Australian can commit is to fail to mow his lawn and keep his car shiny clean, even when there is a drought. By concentrating on how their team is faring, many Australians turn their minds away from the gigantic problem facing Australia right now – climate change. The effects are already being felt across Australia, from the drought-stricken Murray-Darling basin, the bread basket of Australia, to the damaged and dying Great Barrier Reef, and worse is predicted. But none of this matters, does it, if you're sure to go to heaven when you die.

In the USA the Jewish vote is carefully cultivated by both Republican and Democrat politicians, not just because the Jewish lobby is very powerful but also because Israel plays an important part in the widely held evangelical belief in being raptured to heaven before the world comes to an end. According to the website www.biblebell.org, rapture will occur when Jesus returns to resurrect dead Christians, glorify their bodies, and catch them up to heaven to be with God. The same will happen to living Christians, in the same way that Jesus was raptured. Rapture will occur before the wrath of God falls upon the planet. Wars, starvation, frequent earthquakes, floods, droughts, global warming, and fierce storms will show that the end is nigh. At the same time Israel's enemies will become increasingly hostile and aggressive. Anti-Semitism will become rampant. Fundamentalist church-goers in America give considerable financial support to Israel so that God's plan for the end of the world, as laid out in the Book of Revelation, will be fulfilled. They approve of the massive help which successive American governments have given to Israel in order to expand Israel's defence forces. They see the conflict between Israel and Palestine as evidence of the working out of God's plan. Israeli leaders are not looking this gift horse in the mouth, even though they probably know that a key element in God's plan is the conversion or the death of all Jews.

Along with all this, fundamentalists are battling the scientists. Darwin's theory of evolution presents a huge challenge to those who believe that the Bible is infallible, inerrant and internally consistent. Both Christian and Islamic fundamentalists reject the theory of evolution, despite the increasing weight of evidence to support it. Christian fundamentalists developed their own theory, Creationism, which states that the world was created by God a few thousand years ago. Just how many thousand has varied from time to time, from 4,000 years to around 6,000. Fossils, apparently, were God's little joke. Dinosaurs are seen as existing along with Adam and Eve. In an attempt to avoid the derision Creationism has attracted in the past, the name has been changed to Intelligent Design. Creationists insist that the world could not have just come into being. There must have been an Intelligent Designer. They spurn the question, 'Who designed the designer?' God, they say, has always existed.

Sean Carroll is one of the pioneers of evolutionary developmental biology, which is the science of how genes tell organisms to form their shape, both in growth from the egg and in evolution over time. He said of his new book *The Making of the Fittest: DNA and the Ultimate Forensic Record of Evolution*,[22] 'The body of new evidence which I will describe in this book clinches the case for biological evolution as the basis for life's diversity, beyond any reasonable doubt.' In his review of the book Peter Forbes explained the significance of what Carroll had claimed. He wrote,

The most vivid and bounteous evidence we have for natural selection concerns two kinds of genes: those that never change (immortals) and are going strong at more than two billion years old; and those that are no longer used (fossil genes) but live on accumulating more and more mutations. The immortal genes are vital for cell life processes and are almost identical in every living creature.

They have been preserved by selection because most mutations to them would be fatal.

The fossil genes hang around, gathering mutations, making them even more useless. Because they are not used, selection cannot keep them in trim. Moles still have rudimentary eyes but because they are not needed they are furred over. All of the eye genes are still there but they are shot to pieces. We humans have lost the functionality of half of our odour genes. We still have the genes that dogs use to sniff out their world but again the holes, insertions and other damage have disabled them. The elegance of this double whammy – immortal and fossil genes – for natural selection is almost beyond poetry.

Which brings me to so-called intelligent design, the idea that some biological structures are too complex to have evolved under natural selection. Fossil genes are the nemesis of intelligent design. What sort of grand designer would litter his creations with decayed copies of genes which we know are still functional in other creatures? There is a simpler explanation. Fossil genes have decayed because they are no longer under selection pressure. We humans use our eyes more than our noses. As Carroll says, 'the rule of DNA code is use it or lose it.'[23]

Like fundamentalist Christians, those people who describe themselves as being 'spiritual' reject science. Instead they have developed their own science which, like Intelligent Design, does not require the detailed thought and sheer hard work of traditional science. They use scientific-like terms when they are talking about their own discoveries of magical cures. For instance, the magazine *Nova*, an Australian publication distributed by Health Food shops, carried an advertisement for Hexagonal Water Supplies. Hexagonal water has an

> Advanced Oxygenation System. Vitalized Plus water is hexagonal water! Vitalized water awakens, cleanses, energises and revitalizes. Hexagonal Water has 6 apparent functions: hydrates the cells, helps transport the nutrients to the cells, enhances waste removal from the cells,

supports the immune system, improves cellular communication and enhances metabolic efficiency.[24]

This is undoubtedly a great improvement on square water!

Alternative or complementary medicine, as it is known, has an immense market, not only in its products but in its advertising. Fundamentalist Christians and spiritual people ensured that George Bush would not lose support when he put the interests of the oil industry ahead of scientific research. The science journalist Gordy Slack wrote,

> In Washington the Bush Administration's contempt for science and evidence-based policies is everywhere evident, including its inhibition of stem cell research; its censoring of the Clean Air act, climate change, and other environmental reports; and its depleting of NASA's science budget to pursue vanity projects such as sending humans to Mars. If belief trumps fact, in these days of very dangerous truths, we're screwed.[25]

Our need for good scientific research and a careful appraisal of its results has never been greater. There is no simple answer to global warming. Biofuels might reduce our dependence on oil, but a wholesale switch to biofuels could mean that many people would starve. Are the risks involved in nuclear power worth taking in the long run? Questions like these need to be examined and answered at a global level where every country takes part in the debate and then commits to the programme decided upon. Time is rushing by, the climate is changing faster than scientists had predicted, but Bush dallies, refusing to make a meaningful commitment. On December 18, 2007, he did sign the Energy Independence and Security Act which aims to phase out 100-watt incandescent bulbs – but not until 2012. Wal-Mart launched a campaign to sell 100 million energy-efficient bulbs by the end of 2007, but achieved this by October.[26] Why don't we all make a quick trip to Wal-Mart? However, George Bush says there's no hurry. After all, if you're going to be raptured before the world comes to an end, you don't have to bother, do you?

Research and practice have shown beyond a shadow of a doubt that for an undeveloped country to develop there must be access to contraception and abortion as well as education, especially for women. Both the Catholic Church and the Bush Administration reject contraception and abortion. The Church condemns the use of condoms, while the Bush Administration has withdrawn financial support for any non-governmental agency which includes contraception and abortion in its work. Thus the Church and the Administration have ensured the death of millions of Africans from Aids. In villages across Africa there are only children and old people. The generation which would have brought up the children and looked after the old people has been all but wiped out. The consequences of this situation in coming decades are incalculable, but it is likely they will be terrible.

Events in the first years of this century and all the events to come cannot be explained solely as the outcome of religious belief and practice. Many other factors are involved. However, the ideas held by all of us and especially our leaders about the nature of death and the purpose of life will play a significant part in our lives.

As Bush's presidency comes to a close we are left with:

1 A war on terror which shows no sign of coming to an end. No one is safe from the war. As I write, the 2008 Dakar Rally has been cancelled following the death of four French tourists in Mauritania and a threat from a group linked to Al-Qaeda to disrupt the rally. This will mean a huge financial loss for the organisers of the rally, the competitors and their teams, the countries where the rally would have been held, and the media. No terrorist bomb, just the threat of a terrorist bomb, achieved all this.
2 A tardy and very limited recognition of climate change at the Bali conference in 2007, which resulted in an agreement to do something about climate change some time.
3 An eight-year neglect of science and the application of the results of scientific research to alleviate disease and poverty, and to solve the problem of climate change.

At the same time, in Chechen, a new form of an old conflict is brewing.

When the USSR broke up, Chechen people tried to set up their own independent state. Russia claimed sovereignty and sent in Russian forces to quell the rebels. A terrible conflict followed. Grozny, the capital, was destroyed. Putin spared no effort to defeat the rebels. When his forces had established a kind of peace he installed 31-year-old Ramzan Kadyrow as president. Kadyrow, who enjoys considerable power and has his own militia, was an amateur boxer. He is accused by human rights groups of kidnapping, torturing and murdering civilians. He practises Sufism, a mystical form of Islam that emphasises a personal union with God. Being backed by both Putin and God must be a heady mixture. Against him are the rebels. They started out as a largely secular force, but now their main commanders are fundamentalists with ties in the Middle East. They want to create an Islamic caliphate across Russia's North Caucasian region. The Chechen war proved to be a special training ground for Taliban and Al-Qaeda combatants. The rebel leader, Doku Umarov, has announced that he is extending his movement's battle with Kadyrow's forces to include a holy war against the USA, Britain and Israel. He said, 'All those waging war against Islam and Muslims are our enemies.'[27]

* * *

Meanwhile, Britain had a prime minister who, like George Bush, was a devout Christian. Tony Blair's predecessors, Margaret Thatcher and John Major, were conventionally Christian. Thatcher did not need God to tell her how right her views were, while Major's great passion was not God but cricket. In those days it was wearisome being addressed by both Thatcher and Major as wayward children who needed to mend their ways, but at least they never invoked God in this process. In contrast, Blair was forever letting us know that he had religious beliefs which meant that, not only was he always right in his views, but he was especially good, much better than those of us who led our lives without the benefit of being overseen by God. Blair would have laced all his speeches with references to God and his blessings, but his adviser Alistair Campbell warned him, 'We don't do God.'

Traditionally, the British public prefer their leaders to stick to politics and leave religion to the clerics. However, the significant majority of tame backbenchers which Blair had in the House of Commons meant that Blair could ignore the fact that the British public was against joining the USA in a war against Saddam Hussein and Iraq. As Iraq descended into bloody conflict and evidence emerged that Saddam Hussein's weapons of mass destruction did not exist, Blair did not apologise for his part in this debacle. Instead he insisted, 'I only did what I thought was right.' Writing in the *Spectator*, Ron Liddle pointed out that,

> In his otherwise equivocal memoirs, Hans Blix, the UN weapons inspector who pleaded with Bush and Blair to wait a while before wreaking military havoc in Iraq, blames the two leaders' shared religious fervour for their single-minded commitment to the invasion: their unshakeable conviction that they were doing the right thing.[28]

Believing that you did the right thing may explain your error but never excuse it. Hitler went to his death believing that he had done what he thought was right. Thousands of Hitler's supporters believed the same. They explained Germany's defeat by the Allies in terms of being betrayed by their enemies within Germany.

Not long after he left office Blair converted to Catholicism. Pope Benedict XVI might have praised him, but Cardinal George Pell in Sydney took a much sterner line, as he did in everything to do with Catholicism. He wrote,

> Apparently a religious man, Blair remains an enigma at many levels. He has attended Mass every Sunday for many years with his wife and family, and has just become a Roman Catholic. Yet he implemented and personally supported anti-Christian legislation over the years.[29]

Blair's religious beliefs brought what look like lasting changes to British society. He encouraged representatives of the different religious groups to take part in government policy making. Such inclusivity could be beneficial to society if all groups representing the full range of religious and philosophical thought had been included but, when humanist groups asked to be included in Blair's group of policy advisers, they were refused.

Strongly held beliefs can prevent us from seeing the consequences of our actions. Blair put in endless effort, ultimately successful, in bringing the Troubles to an end in Northern Ireland and uniting in government long-time sworn enemies, the Catholics and the Protestants. He must have been told many times by many people that the root of the problem in Northern Ireland lay in the complete separation of the two communities. Catholic children and Protestant children were educated completely separately, and, until they were adults, many never met members of the other community.

Blair spent part of his childhood in Australia and it was an Australian, Peter Thompson, who sparked his interest in religion. Blair should have known how until the 1960s, Australian society was divided into Protestant and Catholic just as in Northern Ireland. The Australian Catholic Church was adamantly against Catholic children attending state schools. This was the Australia I grew up in. Years later, when I was visiting Northern Ireland, I found that I still possessed my childhood skills of identifying Catholics and Protestants within a few moments of meeting. In Australia, by the 1960s, the influx of migrants from Catholic countries put such a strain on the Catholic education system that the Church had to relax its rules about which schools Catholic children should attend. Not only did Catholic children begin attending state schools but many Protestant parents sent their children to Catholic schools which were regarded as having particularly high standards in education and discipline. Within a few short years the hatred, the ignorance and the horrible myths which each side told about the other had disappeared. However, by then racists had other objects for their hatred. They now could despise refugees from the Vietnam War and the other world-wide conflicts which followed. The then prime minister, John Howard, did not extend his Christian charity to those who were not already Australian.

All this Blair should have known. He once confessed a wish that he had studied history, but it seems he made little effort in making up for this deficit. While bringing peace to Northern Ireland, he encouraged the different religious groups in England to open their own segregated schools. He called these 'faith' schools.

Political leaders have always known that, if you have a problem you can't or don't want to solve, one solution is to change the name of the problem. In 1981, when the seemingly endless series of breakdowns at the Windscale nuclear reactor was causing much public disquiet, the name of the reactor was changed to Sellafield. Comedian Lenny Henry, impersonating the newscaster Trevor McDonald, reported that, 'Windscale is to be renamed Sellafield because it sounds nicer. In future radiation will be referred to as magic moonbeams.'[30] In the same way religious schools became faith schools. 'Religious schools' carry connotations of religious wars and of madrassas where small Muslim boys are supposedly imbued with the ambition to grow up to become suicide bombers. 'Faith' sounds soft, sweet, smiling, and happy. People no longer belong to a particular religion. They belong to a faith. Different faiths come together, share with one another, and never indulge in those nasty arguments about who has the best God. (Though there might have been some rejoicing amongst the Catholics when, in December 2007, their numbers, bolstered by an influx of Poles, topped the number of Anglicans who attend church regularly.)[31]

Whatever Tony Blair's religious beliefs were, they never seemed to cause him distress or to require a regular inspection of his failings. Indeed, he never suggested that he had any failings, except, of course, the times when he was too good. His successor Gordon Brown did not carry his religion as lightly as Blair did. Brown was a son of the manse with all that that implies about conscience and a need to achieve. His biographer Tom Bower wrote,

> Quite emphatically, from his youngest years, Brown was under exceptional pressure to excel, and infused with an obsession to work hard, to disappoint no one and to win. 'What is started must be finished,' was a constant parental admonition to the Brown brothers. Failure was inconceivable. From the pulpit the Reverend John Brown preached that many of the young 'are failing to think life

through and are living carelessly and irresponsibly.' They forgot, he said, that regardless of any remarkable achievements on earth, 'after death we must appear before the judgement seat of Christ.' He admonished 'the multitudes' who gave 'little thought of accountability for their conduct and way of life.'[32]

Gordon Brown seemed to give endless thought to accounting for his conduct and way of life, and did not seem to be at the end of such reflection a happy man. The Calvinist conscience can be implacable.

So can the Catholic conscience. As I write, Kevin Rudd is enjoying his first weeks of being Australia's new prime minister. As time goes by, life at the PM's Lodge in Canberra might not be so happy. What we can be sure of is that, in Australia as in Britain and America, religion will continue to play an important part in the politics of the day.

* * *

In the 1970s when I was working in the National Health Service in Sheffield and then in Lincolnshire, psychologists had considerable freedom in deciding how they should work. I chose to have long conversations with my depressed clients. It took time to establish the kind of relationship where we could explore the ideas which might have led my client to become depressed. I soon found that depressed people struggle with the questions which have puzzled philosophers and theologians for thousands of years. They saw these questions not as universal questions but in terms of the circumstances of their lives. Death featured in our conversations, and, following that, my client's religious or philosophical beliefs. It was clear that these beliefs were very different from those held by people who did not become depressed. My clients had always held beliefs which confirmed their sense of unworthiness, and reinforced their pessimism and their fear. Many told me how they had relinquished the religious beliefs of their childhood but now they were wondering whether these old beliefs might not be true. Had they been born in sin as their priest had told them? Had God's grace, about which their vicar had talked so much, failed to fall on them? If God knew of every sparrow that fell, He must undoubtedly know of their wickedness and would punish them. Was not depression their punishment for their sin? If it was God's punishment, should they not accept it, and resist anyone who tried to take it from them?

I knew that psychiatrists never investigated the religious beliefs held by their patients except to establish whether the belief was an example of 'irrational guilt', which psychiatrists saw as a symptom of depression, or whether it was a psychotic delusion. The implications of these beliefs were never explored. My psychologist colleagues were not interested in religious beliefs. They saw the purpose of life as being happy, and their task as therapists to help people give up being depressed and become happy. They did not acknowledge that the purpose of life for many people is not to be happy but to be good. When the psychiatrist Aaron Beck began to develop his cognitive behavioural therapy he expressly forbade his disciples to spend any time discussing religion or philosophy with their clients. I wrote *The Construction of Life and Death* to help people, including psychiatrists and psychologists, to understand how important religious and philosophical ideas are to all of us.

How times have changed! The Royal College of Psychiatrists now has a Spirituality and Psychiatry Special Interest Group. The Royal College's pamphlet *Spirituality and Mental Health* points out that,

> Making a spiritual assessment is as important as all aspects of medical history taking and examination. When making a diagnosis, a psychiatrist should be competent in distinguishing between a spiritual crisis and mental illness, and able to explore areas of overlap and difference between the two . . . In healthcare, spirituality is identified with experiencing a deep-seated sense of meaning and purpose in life, together with a sense of belonging. It is about acceptance, integration and wholeness.

In essence, the pamphlet is based on few assumptions. It recognises that our religious or philosophical beliefs play an important role in the degree of happiness and security we feel, but it does not assume that certain religious beliefs are mandatory, or that spirituality encompasses the magical. In all, it is a very kind and sensible document.

The Transpersonal Psychology Section is part of the British Psychological Society. On its website Transpersonal Psychology is defined as what

> might loosely be called the psychology of spirituality and of those areas of the human mind which search for higher meanings in life, and which move beyond the limited boundaries of the ego to access an enhanced capacity for wisdom, creativity, unconditional love and compassion. It honours the existence of transpersonal experiences, and is concerned with their meaning for the individual and with their effect upon behaviour.

The terms used in that definition, such as 'higher meanings', are not defined. It goes on to say,

> In addition to drawing upon many areas of Western scientific psychology, Transpersonal Psychology seeks insights from Eastern psycho-spiritual traditions, philosophy, theology, religion, phenomenology, anthropology, sociology, and from studies of mysticism and of humanistic and transpersonal therapies. It also focuses upon typologies of spiritual and subtle experiences, and upon their consequences for thought and behaviour.

There are times when I despair of my profession! Psychology is supposed to be a science. Apart from the study of perception and cognition, and the new field of neuropsychology where positron emission tomography (PET) of the brain can show some correlations between certain types of thinking and specific parts of the brain, the subject matter of psychology does not allow the setting up of experiments similar to the kind of experiments used in chemistry and physics. In this kind of experiment, small, even tiny phenomena are studied in great detail. Alas, the results of the research in neuropsychology have been seized upon by unthinking psychologists and journalists and turned into a new phrenology where different bits of the brain are considered to be the cause of complex ways of thinking and acting, all without any acknowledgement that human beings are constantly interpreting what is happening and acting on those interpretations.

Experimentation may be difficult in psychology, but that is no excuse for abandoning the first requirement of scientific research which is to define the words you are using. Terms like 'spirituality', 'limited boundaries of the ego', 'an enhanced capacity' need to be defined, while 'it honours the existence of transpersonal experience' has all the posturing falseness of 'I hear what you say' and 'I'm comfortable with that'. Why not just say, 'Some people report having experiences which seem to them to be about a reality above and beyond the reality they ordinarily experience'?

Unfortunately, the need to give their sense of being a person a heightened significance has led many psychologists, who, after all, are only human, to use abstract nouns and manufactured phrases to imply that they are in possession of truths unknown to ordinary mortals.

The public section of the website of the Australian and New Zealand College of Psychiatrists makes no mention of 'spirituality' or 'religion'. Neither does the government website on depression, *beyondblue*. However, the website of the Australian Psychological Society lists the following interest groups: Christianity and Psychology; Sufism and Psychology; Buddhism and Psychology; Psychology from an Islamic Perspective; Transpersonal Psychology.

The last contains the following unscientific explanation:

Transpersonal literally means beyond the personal, beyond the ego, to include soul consciousness. Mind, spirituality, and higher states of consciousness are a main focus within transpersonal psychology. Within this context, spirituality refers to a universal dimension that is both transcendent and immanent.

Newer fields of psychology, especially transpersonal psychology and ecopsychology, are taking seriously the holistic notion of human beings as comprising mind, body, and soul. These fields propose that people are spiritual beings living a human life that extends beyond our mundane existence and skin-encapsulated ego-self to include direct experience of the environment and the cosmos. They recognise the importance of integrating spiritual with physical and mental reality, that spirituality is but one part of the whole.

It seems now that, if you seek the services of a psychologist or a psychiatrist, it is not enough just to ask in which theoretical model the therapist works. Ask what his religious or philosophical beliefs are.

* * *

It was a tremendous shock to many non-Muslims when Muslims protested violently about matters which non-Muslims took for granted. Brawls amongst football fans were deplored, but the imprisonment in Sudan in 2007 of a teacher, Gillian Gibbons, for letting her pupils call a teddy bear Mohammed was beyond the comprehension of many. Much worse had already happened before that.

Christopher Hitchens described what followed when Salman Rushdie's book *The Satanic Verses* was published.

The theocratic head of a foreign state – the Ayatollah Khomeini of Iran – publicly offered money, in his own name, to suborn the murder of a novelist who was a citizen of another country. Those who were encouraged to carry out this bribed assassination scheme, which was extended to 'all those involved in the publication' of the *Satanic Verses*, were offered not just the cold cash but also a free ticket to paradise. It is impossible to imagine a greater affront to every value of free expression. The ayatollah had not read, and probably could not read, and in any case forbade everyone else to read, the novel. But he succeeded in igniting ugly demonstrations, among Muslims in Britain as well as across the world, where crowds burned the book and screamed for the author to be fed to the flames as well . . . A number of serious attempts were made to assassinate Rushdie by religious death squads supported by Iranian Embassies. His Italian and Japanese translators were criminally assaulted . . . and one of them was savagely mutilated as he lay dying. His Norwegian publisher was shot in the back with a high-velocity rifle and left for dead in the snow, but astonishingly survived.

One might have expected leaders of the other religions, all cultivated, educated men, to speak out against such barbarity. But, as Hitchens wrote,

> Such was not the case. In considered statements, the Vatican, the Archbishop of Canterbury, and the Chief Sephardic Rabbi of Israel all took a stand in sympathy with – the ayatollah. So did the Cardinal Archbishop of New York and many other lesser religious figures. While they did manage a few words in which to deplore the resort to violence, all these men stated that the main problem raised by the publication of the *Satanic Verses* was not murder by mercenaries but blasphemy.[33]

The public discussion about the attack on the Twin Towers was based largely on the proposition that moderate religion was good, extremist religion was bad. Few voices were heard saying that perhaps the problem was religion. Then a trio of atheists burst upon the scene with books that put religious apologists on the defensive. Such a defence was difficult because scientist Richard Dawkins, philosopher Daniel Dennett, and writer Christopher Hitchens were extremely well informed.

Richard Dawkins's book *The God Delusion* was a great success world-wide. Dawkins is one of those scientists who can explain science to the general reader with immense clarity and simplicity. He reveals the world in all its wonder and complexity. Large though his readership from his earlier books was, the success of *The God Delusion* suggests that there are a great many people for whom religion does not have the answers.

Early in his book Dawkins makes clear what his position is. He wrote,

> Human thoughts and emotions *emerge* from exceedingly complex interconnections of physical entities within the brain. An atheist in this sense is somebody who believes that there is nothing beyond the natural, physical world, no *super*natural creative intelligence lurking behind the

observable universe, no soul that outlasts the body and no miracles – except in the natural phenomena which we don't yet understand. If there is something that appears to lie beyond the natural world as it is now imperfectly understood, we hope eventually to understand it and embrace it within the natural. As ever when we unweave the rainbow, it will not become less wonderful.[34]

Dawkins also makes clear that,

I am not in favour of offending or hurting anyone just for the sake of it. But I am intrigued and mystified by the disproportionate privileging of religion in our otherwise secular societies. All politicians must get used to disrespectful cartoons of their faces, and nobody riots in their defence. What is so special about religion that we grant it such uniquely privileged respect? As H. L. Mencken said: 'We must respect the other fellow's religion, but only to the extent that we respect his theory that his wife is beautiful and his children smart.'[35]

In the television programmes made to accompany his book, Dawkins revealed a kind of bewilderment at the obstinacy and certainty of those whose beliefs were clearly irrational. In this he is like many scientists who understand the functioning of the brain as well as the world but do not understand what people actually do. What people do every moment of their life is to create meaning. They are inter-preting what is happening around them and to them. It is these interpretations which determine what people do.

The meanings which people create might be engaged solely in mythos or logos. Usually it is a mixture of the two. Our meanings arise out of our past experience but, since no two people ever have exactly the same experience, no two people ever create exactly the same meanings. Dawkins revealed the limits of his knowledge about how we create meaning in the opening of his book where he described two boys each being overwhelmed by a sudden heightened awareness of the natural world. One boy went on to be-come an Anglican priest and the other a scientist, Richard Dawkins himself. He wrote, 'Why the same emotion should have led my chaplain in one direction and me in the other is not an easy question to answer. A quasi-mystical response to nature and the universe is common amongst scientists and rationalists.'[36] And that is as far as he goes.

Had Dawkins attempted to answer his own question he would have needed to examine his childhood and that of his chaplain, not just the events and circumstances of their childhoods, but how they each interpreted these events and circumstances. Only by ignoring these questions could Dawkins go on and create his theory about memes.

A meme is an idea or a small set of ideas which travels around a community and lodges in the brain of the people it encounters. We are all familiar with the way certain ideas seem to be in the news at certain times. We hear ourselves using particular words or phrases we might never have used before. For instance, over the time that the phrase 'suicide bomber' entered our vocabularies, 'strictly ballroom' became a popular passion. These ideas could be called memes.

When Dawkins was developing his theory of memes, boys who wore baseball caps took to wearing them backwards. This Dawkins saw as a meme in action. It did appear to be so. But had Dawkins taken the time to get to know some of these boys well enough for them to trust him, and then asked each one, 'Why is it important to you to wear your baseball cap backwards?', he would have got as many different answers as there were boys to ask.

One boy might say, 'I do it because my mates do it.' Asked why it was important to do what his mates did, the boy might describe how he felt that his existence as a person depended on him being surrounded by his friends. If his mates deserted him he would cease to exist as a person. Another boy might answer, 'Because it annoys my mother.' When asked why it was important to him to annoy his mother, he might reveal a picture of a mother who noticed her son only when he annoyed her. A boy who had resisted the fashion might explain that he maintained his sense of being a person by resisting fashion trends. Had Dawkins pursued such a line of enquiry he would have come to understand why some people hold fast to certain ideas, no matter how irrational they might be, while other people reject them.

The philosopher Daniel Dennett has written a particularly long book, *Breaking the Spell*, in which he urged his fellow Americans to break from the spell of religion. In a country where television producers believe that a television scene lasting longer than ten seconds would tax their viewers' patience, and therapists write books running to no more than 100 widely spaced pages about how to solve all of life's problems, a book of 412 pages of close print might not find many readers ready to accept the writer's criticism of their beliefs and be prepared to change their ways. But this is what Dennett and his publishers have produced.

Dennett considers himself to be a 'bright'. This is the name he decided upon in the same way that homosexuals decided to call themselves 'gays'. In this context, the opposite of 'gay' is not 'glum' but 'straight'. Dennett protests that the opposite of 'bright' is not 'stupid'. Perhaps, he says, those who believe in the supernatural might like to call themselves 'supers'.[37] However, he overlooks the fact that words have connotations. 'Gay' has the attractive connotations of cheerfulness and charm. 'Bright' cannot help but have the connotation of superiority.

One of the least attractive aspects of religious people is the pride they take in being significantly better than those who do not share their beliefs. Many religious groups, and not just the Jews, have claimed to be God's Chosen People. If children do not have their wish fulfilled that their parents love them most of all their siblings, they can comfort themselves that they are God's favourite. In the same way Calvinists can consider themselves to be amongst the infallible elect, that is, God had elected or chosen them for salvation. However, the belief that you and your group are better than those who are not in your group is a delusion. Culturally and individually people differ, but we all are alike in what it is to be a human being. We each want our life to have significance in the general scheme of things; we want other people to see us and respect us as a person in our own right, and not see us as an object of no importance; we want to enjoy good relationships with our family, friends and neighbours. The belief in being superior allows us to see other people as objects and thus be able to be cruel to them. It is this belief that leads inevitably to conflicts and genocide.

Christopher Hitchens called Dennett's proposal of the name 'brights' for nonbelievers 'cringe-making'.[38] His book *God Is Not Great* is full of interesting and unexpected information culled not just from his extensive reading, but from his personal investigations, including his marriages, of the different religions. His anger at the stupidity and cruelty of religious people is intense. He sees no reason why all of us should not lead pleasant and secure lives. What prevents this, he says, is the beliefs of the devout. He wrote,

> I once heard the late Abba Eban, one of Israel's more polished and thoughtful diplomats and statesmen, give a talk in New York. The first thing to strike the eye about this Israeli-Palestinian dispute, he said, was the ease of its solubility. From this arresting start he went on to say, with the authority of a former minister and UN representative, that the essential point was a simple one. Two peoples of roughly equivalent size had a claim to the same land. The solution was, obviously, to create two states side by side. Surely something so self-evident was within the wit of man to encompass? And so it would have been, decades ago, if the messianic rabbis and mullahs and priests had been kept out of it. But the exclusive claims to God-given authority, made by hysterical clerics on both sides and further stoked by the Armageddon-minded Christians who hope to bring on the Apocalypse (preceded by the death or conversions of all Jews), have made the situation insufferable, and put the whole of humanity in the position of hostage to a quarrel that now features the threat of nuclear war. *Religion poisons everything.* As well as a menace to civilization, it has become a threat to human survival.[39]

When Hitchens wrote of 'hysterical clerics on both sides' this is not simple abuse. He understands what happens to all of us when we try to maintain something as being the truth when in fact it goes against our reason. He wrote,

> How much effort it takes to affirm the incredible! The

Aztecs had to tear open a human cavity *every day* just to
make sure that the sun would rise. Monotheists are
supposed to pester their deity more times than that,
perhaps, lest he be deaf. How much vanity must be
concealed – not too effectively at that – in order to
pretend that one is the object of a divine plan? How
much self-respect must be sacrificed in order that one
may squirm continually in an awareness of one's
own sin?[40]

A much gentler enquiry into religion was made by John
Humphrys in his book *In God We Doubt*. 'Gentle' is not an
adjective usually applied to Humphrys. He is one of the pre-
senters of the BBC Radio 4 programme *Today*, and is both
admired and criticised for his sometimes stern but always
probing interrogation of politicians and those people who
should be accountable to those who put their trust in them.
When Tony Blair was seeking to be elected prime minister
he was keen to be interviewed by Humphrys, but once he
attained his goal and the public's trust in him began to
erode, he refused invitations from the *Today* editors for
such an interview. Blair preferred the comfort and safety
of the chat show *Richard and Judy*. Also kept safe from
Humphrys's probing questions are those religious leaders
who present their words of wisdom on *Thought for the Day*,
a slot from which all humanists and the like are barred.
Weekday mornings at 7.50 is the time when nonbelievers who
listen to *Today* absent themselves from their radio. If
Thought for the Day speakers had subsequently to justify
what they had just said in the way politicians have to justify
themselves, there would be no drop in listener numbers at
that time.

In God We Doubt is based on the BBC Radio 4 series
Humphrys in Search of God, in which Humphrys interviewed
three religious leaders: Rowan Williams, the Archbishop of
Canterbury, Professor Tariq Ramadan, and the Chief Rabbi,
Jonathan Sacks. When I listened to these interviews, I was
reminded of a comment by Gordy Slack. He wrote,

Several years ago I co-edited a collection of interviews,
conducted by the philosopher Philip Clayton and myself,

with top scientists who were also religious. What I drew from my dozens of interviews, was that plenty of great scientists believe in a personal God, they virtually all try to keep God out of their research, and when they talk about the relationship between their science and their religion they can be quite moving. But they don't make a whole lot of sense, at least not a lot more than your average undergraduate stoner.[41]

John Humphrys was far too polite to come to a similar conclusion about his interviewees, but in fact his book is far more subversive than those by Dawkins, Dennett and Hitchens. A good interviewer can get an interviewee to say far more about himself than he intended, and this is what Williams, Ramadan and Sacks did.

Before beginning an interview, a good interviewer has a clear idea of what he wants to discover. Humphrys wrote, 'What strikes me as important is whether it is possible to reconcile a personal God who is supposed to listen to our prayers and take heed of them with a God who proceeds to ignore them.'[42]

(An Anglican vicar once told me, 'God always answers prayers. Sometimes the answer is no.' Wise parents are well aware that, if they want their child to trust them, they need to give a reasonable explanation which the child can understand every time the parent says no to the child. Why doesn't God do this?)

The Archbishop of Canterbury speaks in such a sonorous voice and with such earnestness and patience that a listener cannot help but feel that what he is saying must be true. But, when the sound of his voice is removed and his words are laid out in print, his hesitations and amendments dissipate the weight of truth which his voice might convey. When Humphrys raised the question of, say, the suffering of a mother watching her child die of cancer, the archbishop's first response was, 'We don't know why.' Humphrys persisted in his questions, and then summarised the archbishop's answers with, 'So the best you can offer to the person whose child has died of cancer, the best you can offer those parents, is "Bear up . . . there's a reason . . . your reward will be in heaven"?' What followed was what Humphrys called 'an extraordinary moment' in the interview.

JH: Is that it?

RW: No, that's not what I want to offer at all, because the conversation I'd have in those circumstances isn't the kind of conversation I'd have here. For one thing . . . if someone says, 'Where's God in that situation?' it would have to be answered partly in terms of 'Where are the people who should be alongside those who are suffering, offering what love and healing they can?' Whether in the name of God or not, the act of God is there as well. I'm not saying there's a purpose in the sense that God has said, 'Oh yes, for that goal, for that end I will devise this disaster, or even that there's a reward in heaven.' I'd say there's hope.

JH: Hope of what?

RW: Hope of healing.

JH: When?

RW: In God's perspective, in God's time, maybe within this world and maybe not. And part of the difficulty of living with the faith is the knowledge which you've underlined so powerfully, that for some people in our time frame in this world there is not that kind of healing. It's not there. And that's not easy to face or to live with.

JH: But you can live with it?

RW: Just . . . just.[43]

In his interview with Simon Mayo, Rowan Williams said that over the years his belief in the Virgin Birth had strengthened. However it seems that he is still struggling with the problem which the Australian philosopher John Mackie described in its simplest form thus:

God is omnipotent, God is wholly good, and yet evil exists. There seems to be some contradiction between these three propositions, so that if any two of them were true the third would be false. But at the same time all three are essential parts of most theological positions: the theologian, it seems, at once *must* adhere and *cannot consistently* adhere to all three.[44]

Liberal Anglicans, when commenting on a major tragedy, offer as a consolation that God 'is beside' those who suffer. Many fundamentalists, believing as they do that we live in a Just World where good people are rewarded and bad people punished, take the view that suffering is inflicted by a just God only on those who deserve it. Clients have told me how their vicar, minister or priest has told them that their cancer or their depression, or the death of their child, showed that they were wicked. They should acknowledge their sin and repent.

Tariq Ramadan did not tell Humphrys that suffering was the result of wickedness. Rather he took the view that suffering exists, so put up with it. He told Humphrys, 'This is life, we are going to suffer because at the end of the day life is suffering.' Humphrys asked, 'But why did God want that to happen?' Ramadan replied, 'I don't know why he sometimes makes me happy or sad, but this is life. The only thing I know is that we have the responsibility to do our best with what we do and what we are facing.' He went on, 'Suffering is a gift and a problem . . . We live with this with great difficulty. And sometimes out of our suffering we become better, we become wiser, we become more knowledgeable about life.'

Ramadan rejected Humphrys's suggestion that in the end it is blind faith. He said,

> We are dealing with people who are suffering. What you can do when you are a doctor, when you are a social worker, you do your best to make them suffer less . . . In the end every human being is a reformer. You reform your own self, you reform your family, you reform society, you reform around you. Whatever you can do, do it. But remain humble because, at the end, you cannot change everything and you have to accept the reality of life.[45]

To say that suffering exists because life is suffering explains nothing. Ramadan was saying that you should be humble and not expect an explanation of suffering. Yet you must try to relieve suffering. How can you do this if you have no idea of the cause of suffering? In past centuries doctors treated grave illnesses with blood-letting because they believed they were removing the cause of the illness.

All they were actually doing was weakening the patient's resistance to the disease. Someone who seeks to relieve suffering without knowing its cause could themselves become the cause of suffering. Moreover, believing that something is inevitable becomes a self-fulfilling prophecy. A Muslim mother, on learning that her son was preparing to become a suicide bomber, might not try to dissuade him, but decide that, since her son was going to suffer whatever he did with his life, he might as well suffer in a way which brought honour to the family.

When Humphrys asked Jonathan Sacks, the Chief Rabbi, how anyone who has seen his child suffer and die could hold on to his faith, Sacks replied,

> To my mind, faith lies in the question. If you didn't have faith you wouldn't ask the question. If I did not believe in a just and law-abiding God, I would not find injustice and human suffering worthy of question whatsoever. After all, the universe, if it has no God, is utterly indifferent to my question. It's blind to my hopes and indifferent to my prayers. So, if I have no faith, I cannot ask the question. Faith is in the question . . .

Humphrys commented, 'I have to say that if a politician said that to me, "That's a most difficult question. If I give you an answer it will destroy your faith in the political system, in the democratic process, so it's very important that that question not be answered", I'd think he was having me on.'

I often talk about things I do not believe exist – things like Freud's id, ego and superego, Jung's collective unconscious. I often talk about the abstract nouns 'depression' and 'schizophrenia', but I do not believe that a depressed person has a thing called depression inside him, or that a psychotic person has a thing called schizophrenia inside him. How can we examine ideas if we do not ask questions about them, even, or perhaps especially we do not believe that the idea relates to anything real? Saying that faith is in the question is nothing but an attempt to bamboozle the faithful and silence the critics.

Humphrys said of the explanations he had been given, 'It won't do.'[46] He concluded,

I suspect that on the most primitive level [religion] is not all that different from the little scrap of blanket that so many small children rely on. They need it whenever they get tired or life looks a bit threatening. I say 'need' not 'want' deliberately: every parent who has had a child with a comfort blanket knows what I mean.

I invite you to imagine the impossibly grand figure of the Archbishop of Canterbury – mitred and robed, holder of an ancient and powerful office, head of the worldwide Anglican Church, crowner of monarchs, sitting on the steps of Canterbury Cathedral with his thumb stuck in his mouth, stroking his bearded cheek with a little bit of satin at the edge of his comfort blanket. It's not easy, I grant you, and this image may not do a great deal for the dignity of the primate's office, but the comfort blanket is not a million miles away from what religion has to offer at its most simplistic. Strip from Christianity the notion of proof, evidence and historical events (or non-events) and what drives belief has little to do with the head and a great deal to do with the heart.[47]

For 'heart' read 'emotion'. Emotion is a meaning, an interpretation of what is going on. Anger is 'How dare that happen to me!' Anxiety is 'Something terrible might happen.' Fear is 'Something terrible is happening.' Jealousy is 'That person has something which is rightly mine.' And so on.

* * *

Whatever we encounter, we give it a meaning. We cannot conceive of the opposite of meaning. Calling something meaningless is to endow it with a meaning.

We give something a meaning even when we lack all the knowledge necessary to find what that thing actually means. Presented with something unexpected, we can entertain a number of possible explanations (meanings) until we settle on one. On our way to the door to answer an unexpected knock, we speculate about who our caller is. Opening the door supplies the answer. In situations where we cannot get an answer to our question, 'What is this?', we supply an answer with a fantasy.

Death presents us with a need for such a fantasy. All we can ever know about death is that a living person becomes strangely still. What has happened to the person who that living being was we do not know and cannot know. So we create a fantasy.

Death presents us with only two possible fantasies. Either death is the end of my sense of being a person or it is a doorway to another life. We might spend much time puzzling over which fantasy to choose, but, once we choose, that fantasy determines the purpose of our life.

If we choose to see death as the end of our sense of being a person, the purpose of our life is to make our life satisfactory. How to define 'satisfactory' is an individual choice from an infinite array of possibilities, but, having arrived at a definition, we try to achieve our goal. It is only by feeling that our life has been satisfactory that we can face death with a degree of equanimity.

If we see death as a doorway to another life, we immediately have to decide what that life will be. Will it be better or worse than our present life? If our present life has not lived up to our expectations, we dream of a better future life. For many people the hope of a better life after death is all that sustains them in their present life. However, if we decide that there is a better life after death, we are then presented with the question, 'Does everyone go on to a better life, no matter how wicked they've been?' Our sense of justice tells us that this cannot be so. There must be standards which have to be met if we are to qualify for a better life after death. Having decided what these standards are, we know that the purpose of our present life is to meet these standards. Thus we have to live this life in terms of the next.

No matter how we might try, we cannot ignore death. If there were no death, if we lived for ever, we would not have to choose between different options concerning what we can do. All we would need to decide would be in what order to do things. Death makes us choose how we spend our life. We have to define death, even though we can define it only in terms of a fantasy. Our definition of death becomes a central part of our religious or philosophical beliefs.

A curious paradox of human life is that, while we can

actually live only in the present, we give meaning to the present in terms of our past and our future. 'I am what I am', we say, 'because of what has happened in the past, and I do what I do now because of what will happen in the future.' The causes of our actions lie in our past and the intentions of our actions lie in our future. Thus the world we each construct encompasses not just the immediate present but also a past and a future.

We can find our past intriguing and often ponder on it, but it is our future that engages most of our attention. 'What have I got to do at work today?' we ask ourselves on waking. 'Where'll I go for my holidays this year?' we say, reading January's newspapers. We react with joy to something that engages our interest as a possible goal. The greatest misery is to be without a goal, to see no purpose in living. We create goals, make decisions like 'I must lose some weight/scrub the kitchen/visit Aunt Milly', even though we know that some activities are trivial and Aunt Milly does not like visitors. By setting such goals and working towards them, we know that we are fulfilling some part of the purpose we have given to life. *We know that life must have a purpose because life is finite. If there was no death, if life was infinite, we would need no purpose. We could do this, and then that, and then some other thing. There would be no rush to get things done, no need to work in order to eat. We would not have to think about the future; we could live entirely in the present. But death exists, and it is death that fixes our attention on the future.*

What kind of beliefs about death and the purpose of life can best sustain us in our very uncertain future?

To arrive at an answer to that question we need to understand ourselves and what it is to be human.

Chapter 2

WHAT IT IS TO BE HUMAN

The Creationists' assault on the Darwinians has lasted for many years, but they seem not to have realised that there is now another area of scientific research which is much more of a challenge to fundamentalism than the theory of evolution. This research is by those neuroscientists who study the connections between the brain and the mind. Perhaps it is not so surprising that Creationists prefer not to challenge the neuroscientists. Debating whether the universe came into being without someone having first to design it or whether it appeared at God's command is relatively simple. Understanding the brain is much more difficult. It is the most complex object scientists have ever encountered. Nevertheless, it is now clear that our physiological make-up is such that we are unable to see the world directly. All we can see is the picture or model or map which our brain has created of what is going on around us and to us. As the neuroscientist Chris Frith wrote, 'Even if all our senses are intact and our brain functioning normally, we do not have direct access to the physical world. It may feel as if we have direct access, but this is an illusion created by our brain.'[1]

The picture our brain creates can come from only one source – our past experience. Since no two people ever have the same experience, no two people ever see anything in exactly the same way. Thus it is that we each have our own individual truths. Our truths are guesses, illusions, fantasies. If we wonder whether a certain belief does have a close relationship to what is going on, we can test it by checking it against other observations we have made. We can compare it with other people's observations. We can do an experiment to see if our predictions based on our belief prove to be correct. In short, we can use scientific method in order to determine the validity of our belief. Only by working in this way can we both protect ourselves from harm and communicate with other people. Deciding that the busy road is empty of traffic but not looking to see if you are right can result in considerable damage to yourself. Moreover, all those people to whom you have to explain what you did will think that you are an idiot.

The inconvenient truth for those of us who claim to be in possession of some absolute truth, which must be taken on trust and be believed without question, is that such is our physical and mental equipment we are not capable of knowing for certain that what we know is an absolute truth which exists in all time and space, eternal, transcendent, unchangeable. We can hope, wish, believe that we are in possession of an absolute truth, and we can have very pressing reasons to believe that this is so, but, if we cannot validate our belief, it cannot be anything more than a belief which is a fantasy.

Most of us have discovered that we can have moments of feeling wonderfully comforted and supported by something which is not visible or tangible, moments which take us out of our mundane circumstances and dissolve the barriers between ourselves and the world in all its glory. There are times when our defences against realising what our situation exactly is disappear and we see it with utmost clarity; or we suddenly can see our future plain before us. Sometimes the cramped, boringly and suffocatingly predictable world of our existence suddenly opens up to reveal a vast, glorious expanse of wonder and infinite possibilities. Such experiences can leave us feeling at home in the world. They can strengthen us and give us hope and courage. However, wonderful though these experiences can be, they can never be more than private experiences which we interpret in our own individual way. If we conclude that we have discovered an absolute truth which we must now force on other people, we denigrate our private experience and inflict suffering on others. If we decide that our special, private experience has made us superior to others, we are deluding ourselves.

The vast number of different religions and the different opinions within each religion are examples of the multitude of interpretations which can be given to the nature of death and the purpose of life. The degree of anger and ferocity which believers can use against those who do not share their belief goes far beyond the degree of anger and ferocity we will try to employ when we are in physical danger. It is the anger and ferocity we all will resort to, one way or another, when our sense of being a person is under threat. A believer angrily defending his religion is saying, 'Destroy my faith and you destroy me.'

What is this 'me'? What we call 'I', 'me', 'myself' is infinitely precious to us, yet rarely do we understand what it is that constitutes 'me'. I call 'me' our sense of being a person. Chris Frith calls it 'my sense of self'. He wrote, 'One of the illusions which my brain creates is my sense of self. I experience myself as an island of stability in an ever-changing world.'[2]

To understand this 'island of stability' and why it is an illusion we first need to understand the nature of language. If you speak only one language you may think that your language describes the world as it is. But if you speak, or have to learn, another language you know that your second language describes a world different from the world your first language describes. Reality does not create language but that language creates reality. If you speak English and you have to learn French or German you discover that the French and Germans have words for certain experiences which English lacks. Perhaps English speakers would prefer to deny that they ever experience glee and satisfaction when someone they know and perhaps envy suffers a reversal of fortune, whereas German speakers acknowledge this with their word *Schadenfreude*. Similarly, perhaps English speakers like to think that their memory functions impeccably when talking to other people, and so they have no need for the French phrase *esprit d'escalier*, meaning the things you should have said in a conversation but which you only remember some time after the conversation has ended.

However, if you go further afield to the study of Japanese, or perhaps one of the many languages spoken in New

Guinea, you have to enter a world very different from your own. So different can these other language worlds be that it can be near impossible to translate accurately from that language into English, not just because English lacks the necessary words, but also because it does not have the necessary grammatical forms. Thus sometimes a language very different from our own can provide us with an essential tool which our own language lacks, and which we need to understand an aspect of our experience.

When physicists have worked together they have traditionally spoken in English, French or German. These three languages create a world which is full of things. The names of these things are called nouns. Things do things to other things. Words which indicate doing are called verbs. For a group of words to be a sentence it must contain a verb as well as a noun or two, as in, 'The boy hugged the girl.' However, the Indo-European languages English, French and German much prefer nouns to verbs. Notice how I had to add a second 'things' in the sentence, 'Things do things to other things.' Instead of saying 'The boy hugged the girl' we might prefer to say, 'The boy gave the girl a hug.' In this sentence we create something that does not exist. There is no such thing as 'a hug'. There are only arms hugging. When we create a noun like 'a hug' we can wrongly assume that, since there is a name, there must be in reality a thing to which it refers. We can go searching for this thing. Where do you keep your hugs? In your wardrobe? Under the bed?

This is obviously ridiculous, but in all seriousness, since the end of the nineteenth century, psychiatrists and psychologists have been searching for the things to which the nouns, which they have created, refer. These are nouns like 'depression' and 'intelligence'.

This predilection for creating names for non-existent things has done great damage to certain people who have been unlucky enough to encounter psychiatrists or psychologists who were devoted to these words. Many of the people whom these psychiatrists encountered were exceedingly unhappy. They were despairing, they wept, they felt enormously guilty, and were very afraid. Instead of describing what these people were doing, psychiatrists lumped all their ways of behaving into one word, depression, and said that these people had a mental illness. From then on these psychiatrists talked about how this thing, depression, was lodged inside the person's body. They explained the appearance of this thing in terms of some as yet unknown chemical imbalance, or a yet to be found gene. It is only of recent years that some psychiatrists have started to wonder if this thing, depression, actually exists. Perhaps people behave as they do because of the circumstances of their lives.

In a similar way, psychologists noticed that some people behave more intelligently than others. Instead of studying people behaving intelligently or not so intelligently, psychologists decided that inside each of us was a lump of intelligence. Some of us have bigger lumps of intelligence than others. Psychologists then worked out ways, so they thought, of measuring the size of these lumps. They assumed that people were born with a lump of a particular size, and it did not change over time. Intelligence testing was a boon to many children, but to others it was a curse. As the years passed and the evidence mounted that the assumptions which the psychologists had made were wrong, those psychologists who had built their career on intelligence testing resisted all challenges to their cherished beliefs. Now it is clear that 'intelligence' is no more than an abstract noun which, at its best, is no more than shorthand for referring to people behaving intelligently. We are all born with a large array of potentialities. Which of these potentialities emerges and which withers and dies depends on what our environment offers us after we are born.

Some physicists have wondered whether the languages they work in, with their predilection for nouns, are leading them into error. Writing in the *New Scientist*, the physicist David Peat told the story of how, in 1925, Werner Heisenberg worked out the basic equations of what became quantum mechanics. 'One of the immediate consequences of these equations was that they did not permit us to know with total accuracy both the position and the velocity of an electron: there would always be a degree of irreducible uncertainty in these two values.' Heisenberg devised an explanation for this, but, when he showed his result to Niels Bohr, his mentor, he had the ground cut from under his feet. Bohr argued that Heisenberg had made the unwarranted assumption that an electron is like a billiard ball in that it has 'position' and possesses a 'speed'. These are classical notions, said Bohr, and do not make sense at the quantum level. The electron does not necessarily have an intrinsic position or speed, or even a particular path. Rather, when we try to make measurements, quantum nature replies in a way we interpret using these familiar concepts.

The American physicist David Bohm agreed with Bohr. Bohm pointed out that what went on at a quantum level was not things doing things to other things but a doing, a processing. 'To describe them accurately requires a process-based language rich in verbs, and in which nouns play only a secondary role.' Accordingly, in 1992 Bohm and some like-minded physicists, including David Peat, met a number of elders of the Blackfoot, Micmac and Ojibwa tribes – all speakers of the Algonquin family of languages.

These languages have a wide variety of verbal forms, while they lack the notion of dividing the world into categories of objects, such as 'fish', 'trees' or 'birds'. Take, for example, the phrase in the Montagnais language *Hipiskapigoka iagusit*. In a 1729 dictionary this was translated as 'the magician/sorcerer sings a sick man'. According to Alan Ford, an expert on Algonquin languages at the University of Montreal, Canada, this deeply distorts the nature of the thinking processes of the Montagnais people, for the translator had tried to transform a verb-based concept into a European language dominated by nouns and object categories. Rather than there be a medicine person who is doing something to a sick patient, there is an activity of singing, a process. In this world view, songs are alive, singing is going on, and within the process is a medicine man and a sick person.

The world view of Algonquin people is of flux and change, of objects emerging and folding back into the flux of the world. There is not the same sense of fixed identity – even the person's name will change during their life. They believe that objects will vanish into this flux unless renewed by periodic rituals or the pipe smoked at sunrise in the sun dance ceremony of the Lakota and Blackfoot.[3]

The Algonquin language is a remarkable reflection of what we all experience, irrespective of what language we learn to speak. For the first few weeks of our life all we were aware of was a passing, ever-changing phantasmagoria. As all babies do, we watched this parade with great interest, and we began to notice that certain patterns seemed to recur. We had come into the world already primed to prefer certain patterns, one in particular which later we came to know as a face. We noticed patterns in sounds, particularly one we had learnt before we were born, the sound we later learned to call 'the sound of my mother's voice'. A pattern recurred in what we smelt, and we learned to associate that smell with an easing of the pain which we later learned to call 'hunger'. These patterns emerged and then folded back into the flux of the phantasmagoria. We looked for these recurring patterns, and noted, 'There's one. There's another. And look, there's another one.' There seemed to be an infinite supply of examples of certain patterns. Weeks passed, and we started to create a theory which, from then on, became the basis of our experience of the world. Yet it was a theory which we could never prove to be true. For the rest of our life we acted on it, but in trust, not certainty. When we were about eight months old we created our theory of object permanence. We thought that, perhaps, instead of there being an infinite supply of certain familiar patterns, there was just one pattern or thing which came and went. There is no way of proving beyond all doubt that the things you recognise go on existing when they are out of your sight. You just have to take it on trust that they do.

How can we survive in a world which we see as a passing phantasmagoria? The only way is to note recurring patterns in the phantasmagoria and then try to give each pattern a kind of real permanence. Speakers of the Algonquin languages do that by carrying out certain rituals. Speakers of the Indo-European languages try to pin these patterns in place by giving them names.

Ritual is time-consuming, so it is useful to be able to seem to corral parts of the passing phantasmagoria and give it a solidity and regularity with words, but, if we want to take account of the fact that the world we live in is in a constant state of flux, our language does not let us do it. We talk about 'the brain' as being a thing. So it is when we look at a brain from the outside and see a greyish lump of stuff. When we talk about what goes on inside the brain we talk about things such as neurones and chemicals such as serotonin. However, the living, working brain is not a collection of things but is a multitude of processes, moving, changing, interacting. We talk about 'the mind' as an invisible thing which is in the brain, somehow connected to it, but this is not how we experience our mind. All we experience is a stream of consciousness, a kind of passing phantasmagoria. Yet we talk about two things, the brain and the mind, and we wonder how they are connected. It seems that the language we speak is preventing us from asking the right questions. Perhaps what we need is a language which allows us to talk about being, changing, doing.

This is the kind of language I need when I want to describe how our sense of being a person comes into being. Lacking such a language, I have to resort to metaphor.

Our sense of being a person seems like it is a unit, something we can refer to by using a noun – person, self, identity – or a pronoun – I, me, myself – but actually it is part of a process which is in constant movement and change. This process is the means by which we live in the world, interact with the world, and try to make sense of the world. It is the process of creating meaning, which is what human beings are engaged in all the time. This process could be likened to a swiftly flowing stream of water with its constant movement and change. As the stream flows, part of it forms a whirlpool. When we look at a stream of water we can see the whirlpool and talk about it as if it is a thing. We can say to someone, 'Look, there is a whirlpool.' However, we cannot bend down and lift the whirlpool out of the stream because the whirlpool and the stream are one. If a large rock is thrown into the stream or the stream dries up, the whirlpool disappears. In a similar way the process of living in the world, acting on the world and trying to make sense of the world, which comes into being at some as yet unknown time after conception, is in constant movement and change. At some point early in life the process develops its own whirlpool which becomes the individual's sense of being a person. This sense includes but is far more than consciousness because it contains the memory, including the unconscious or implicit memory, which is an essential part of our sense of being a person. Memory shows us to be in constant change, yet it gives a sense of being a person passing through time.

Like the whirlpool, our sense of being a person is a construction which is in constant change. Moreover, just as a whirlpool can be destroyed by a rock being thrown into it, so the sense of being a person can be threatened with destruction by events. Since the process *is* the process of living, and the purpose of life is to live, the process strives to maintain the integrity of the sense of being a person by constantly monitoring its degree of safety from external assault by aspects of the environment. This monitoring is a stream of interpretations by the process of what is happening. It is a stream of messages along the lines of 'safe, safe, danger, DANGER, safe, danger, safe' and so on. There are many degrees and kinds of safety and danger. What we experience is the creation of those interpretations. We call this kind of interpretations *emotions*.

Emotions do not need words, though the meaning of each emotion can be put into words. All emotions relate to our sense of being a person. Emotions are the meanings we create which concern the degree of safety or danger to our sense of being a person. The positive emotions relate to safety; the negative emotions relate to danger. Feeling happy is the interpretation 'Right now everything is the way I want it to be.' Feeling angry is the interpretation 'How dare everything not be the way I want it to be.' The neural basis of the primary emotions of fear and anger develops very early in a baby's life, while the more complex emotions like jealousy ('How dare that person have something which is rightly mine') require a fully functioning cortex.

List the positive and negative emotions and it is immediately apparent that there are many more negative emotions than positive ones. Danger is seen and recognised in all its various possibilities. The sense of being a person is fragile and needs to be protected at all times. We do this because we know how terrible it is when our sense of being a person falls apart. When we have great confidence in our ability to deal with life, we do not question our sense of being a person. But when something important to us does not eventuate, when someone insults and humiliates us, or when we find that we have made a serious error of judgement, our self-confidence diminishes and we begin to feel anxious. If we cannot find a way of dealing effectively with this situation our fear grows. We feel ourselves falling apart. This is not an empty metaphor. Falling apart, shattering, crumbling, even disappearing is what we actually feel. If we know that what is falling apart is our ideas which no longer fit our situation, we can ride out the storm of uncertainty that must follow until we are able to construct another set of ideas which will better relate to our situation. But, if we do not know that it is our ideas that are falling apart, we have to find some way of holding ourselves together. We create a fantasy which we hope will strengthen and comfort us. Since the fantasy is always about our sense of being a person, it always has within it some interpretation of the nature of death and the purpose of life. Sometimes the fantasy is no more than a kind of transitional object, a comfort blanket, something that helps us get from a dangerous situation to one of safety. Sometimes the fantasy becomes our way of life.

In his autobiography *Words* Sartre showed how in childhood the image he developed of himself and his experience of death combined to form the plan by which he lived his life. Sartre's father died soon after his birth, and so Sartre's mother returned with her baby to her parents' home. Here Sartre was made much of by his grandparents; but as a fatherless infant in a home where his mother was still regarded as a child, Sartre soon came to feel that he was acting a part, that:

> I was an imposter . . . I had been told over and over again
> that I was a gift from heaven, much longed for,
> indispensable to my grandfather and to my mother. I no
> longer believed this, but I still felt you were born

superfluous unless sent into the world to satisfy some particular expectation.

As he was realising this:

I saw death. At the age of five: it was watching me; in the evenings, it prowled on the balcony: it pressed its nose to the window; I used to see it but I did not dare to say anything. Once, on the Quai Voltaire, we met it: it was a tall, mad old woman, dressed in black, who mumbled as she went by: 'I shall put that child in my pocket'. Another time, it took the form of a hole . . . I was playing in the garden of the villa, scared because I had been told that Gabriel was ill and was going to die. I was playing at horses, half-heartedly galloping round the house. Suddenly, I noticed a gloomy hole: the cellar which had been opened; an indescribable impression of loneliness and horror blinded me: I turned round and, singing at the top of my voice, I fled. At that time, I had an assignation with it every night in my bed . . . I lived in terror – it was a genuine neurosis. If I seek its cause, it goes like this: a spoilt child, a providential gift, I found my profound uselessness even more obvious because family ritual struck me as a contrived necessity. I felt superfluous, so I had to disappear . . . I was condemned and the sentence could be carried out at any time.

Sartre's grandfather was a teacher who revered books and writers. Sartre saw that his salvation, his protection against death, lay in becoming a writer and this he did:

My commandments have been sewn into my skin: if I go a day without writing, the scar burns me . . . My bones are leather and cardboard . . . I can see my mad undertaking to write in order to be forgiven for being alive has, in spite of lies and cowardice, some validity: the proof is that I am still writing some fifty years later . . . I had long been afraid of ending up as I had begun, somewhere or other, somehow or other, and that this vague death would be merely the reflection of my vague birth.

As a child he became certain that he would live to complete

his task. At the outbreak of the Second World War Sartre's friends feared that they would die, and many of them did, but Sartre had no fear of sudden death:

> I had forearmed myself against accidental death, that was all; the Holy Ghost had commissioned a long-term work from me, so he had to give me time to complete it . . . I had killed myself in advance because only the dead can enjoy immortality . . . Between the ages of nine and ten, I became entirely posthumous.[4]

Not everyone can, like Sartre, reflect upon and report on the development of their system of beliefs. For some, it appears to be most dangerous to look at the connection between childhood experiences and the adult philosophy of life, and so the person avoids doing this, even when his philosophy of life proves most painful in the living of it. Felicity was one such person. She was a middle-aged woman, gentle, charming, and pretty, looking like she could have stepped straight out of one of those radiant advertisements which extol the virtues of some personal or household cleansing agent. But she kept her distance, both in physical and psychological space, for she believed, without the shadow of a doubt, that she gave off some unpleasant odour. She knew that this was usually the reason why people were unkind to her. She tried to wash away or to disguise the smell, and when she felt that she was not succeeding, she grew very distressed. She was forced to acknowledge what she saw as an indisputable fact to her husband and doctor and later to me, and when each of us said, in our own way, 'But you don't smell', she knew we were lying. She believed that she gave off an offensive odour. There was nothing I could say that would dissuade her.

In her work Felicity was extremely competent, but her relationships with her colleagues were a torture to her. She saw herself as being 'easily swayed by people' and she minded this very much.

> I do something and then get really mad afterward. 'You fool, why did you do that?' I worry about what people think, obviously. I can be talked into anything. People ask me to do something and I just can't say no. And then

I moan at my husband afterwards. If I said no I'd feel I'd have offended somebody. I've found that through life that with the best will in the world you still offend people. Sometimes you say something and it's taken the wrong way and you don't realise until something comes back to you.

I asked her whether she preferred to be liked or respected. She said that she preferred to be liked

because people wouldn't respect me anyway. I always work on the principle that nobody likes me. I always work from there, and I never make the first move in friendship. I'd never ask anybody in for a cup of coffee unless I'd been invited there first. I would never make the first move.

Felicity described her childhood as being quite ordinary, but as we got to know one another better she revealed a far from happy childhood.

I think my older sister, as regards my father anyway, was the favourite. I can always remember asking him something and his stock answer was 'Ask your mother': He'd never give you a decision. And I seem to remember her saying once, I must have been grown up then, she must have said it without thinking, he was dead then, something about, 'Oh your father thought more of you when you went teaching than he had ever done.' Obviously gave me a feeling that I was definitely not – that my sister was the one.

(Felicity was a past-mistress in uncovering an insulting meaning in whatever was said to her, even when no insult was remotely contemplated by the speaker.) When, eventually, we talked about affection, she said,

I suppose we were brought up without a lot of affection. I'd never kiss my mother and father. We had a good home. Mother made sure we had everything, but I hardly ever saw my father. My mother would do more for me. I was brought up during the war. My mother was always busy – organising canteens and poppy days, that sort of thing.

I asked her if her mother had cuddled her as a child. 'Not that I remember', she said. 'What about your father?' I asked. 'Oh, no, no. But don't get me wrong, my mother, we were very close, especially as I grew up.'

However, later she told me of two childhood memories that still haunted her. The first was of when she was four or five and her mother one night left her alone in the house while she went on an errand. On her own Felicity became terrified. She began to cry and scream so loudly that the neighbours came running. Her mother arrived home to find a crowd of people in the front porch, all trying to pacify the terrified child on the other side of the locked door. Her mother opened the door, the neighbours went away, and then her mother belted her to punish her for causing a commotion. The other memory was of when she was fourteen and she and her girlfriend were accosted by two American soldiers. During the war being accosted by American soldiers was an inescapable hazard for every woman and girl who lived where Americans were based, and sometimes the experience could be most unpleasant. However, the men who spoke to Felicity and her friend were just lonely young men who wanted a chat, and so the four of them took a stroll down the High Street. That was the extent of the encounter; but when Felicity got home her mother knew of it, and Felicity was thrashed, first by her mother and then by her father when he got home from work. Next day her mother took Felicity to the barbers and had her hair cropped short. After that, night after night, Felicity would lie in bed and listen to her parents talking together. Each night she was terrified that they had discovered some crime of hers of which she was ignorant and that they would again mount the stairs and punish her.

Many adults who had had similar experiences in childhood would recount their stories in words filled with anger at their unjust and cruel parents. But not Felicity. She had to preserve her parents as good people, and to do this she must see herself as bad. Thus Felicity came to believe that she was someone that no one could like, and, when her intelligence could find no adequate reasons for this dislike arising from her own behaviour and/or from the general disagreeableness of other people, she created the fantasy of an intrinsic, ineradicable, offensive odour. Such a belief, unpleasant though it may be, provided her with a protection against further hurt. Knowing that other people would not like her, she did not have to risk liking them.

When I asked her whether she saw people as basically good or basically bad, she said, 'Basically bad, I think. It just seems to me that nobody likes anybody. I never used to feel that. But now nobody likes anybody. It's just all false.' I asked her about her religious beliefs. She said, 'I can remember as a child trying to think, "How did the world begin in the first place and if it was made in seven days, and there is a God sitting up there, well, where did God come from? Where did the space come from?" You could go mad thinking about that.' The answer Felicity had found in the thrillers and occult novels by Dennis Wheatley.

> It's some kind of good and evil forces which are at war with one another, and I can only think that the evil forces are winning because certainly the world is not improving, is it? I think Mother Shipton's right. She said the end of the world would come in 1982 or 3. Doesn't the Bible say that when the Jews get their own country once more the end of the world is nigh? . . . Put it this way, if there is just a God, then He's not a good God, but if there's a God and there is a Devil, then there is a battle in which God is losing.

Felicity's experiences in childhood and adolescence had led her to create a picture of the cosmos somewhat like that in Zoroastrianism, with Ahura Mazda, the lord of goodness and light, who battled Angra Mainyu, the lord of evil and darkness. Her experiences had robbed her of the belief that life could be good and hope always possible. She preferred not to hope for a better life because she felt that further disappointment would be utterly unendurable. Her pessimism was her defence against being annihilated as a person. The world could only become worse because either God was not good or, if He was good, He could not withstand the onslaught by the Devil.

Despite the many difficulties he had had to overcome, Romulus Gaita believed that God was good. His son Raimond said of him, 'He prayed each day to a God he believed would listen to all prayers when they came from a pure heart.'[5] Raimond wrote a most beautiful memoir about his father. In this he told how Romulus had been born in 1922 in a village in Yugoslavia but always considered himself to be Romanian. His family was very poor, his father died when he was a baby, and at thirteen he fled his family to escape from his drunken uncle. He got himself an apprenticeship with a blacksmith in a distant village. He finished his apprenticeship and, at seventeen in 1939, went to Germany in search of work but was soon forced to work in the munitions factories in the Ruhr. He endured the heavy bombing, and fell in love with the beautiful, sixteen-year-old Christine. It was a tempestuous relationship, but they married and Raimond was born. Soon after, she began to show the first signs of the deep depression which ended some years later in her suicide. Raimond wrote,

> She seemed incapable of taking care of me, ignoring my elementary needs of feeding and bathing. My grandmother told the story that, just before she gave birth to my mother, she dreamed of Jesus who appeared to her bloody and showing the wounds of the crucifixion. When she awoke, she said to her husband, 'This child I am carrying will suffer.' Later she told the story to my mother, and it is hard to believe that it did not affect the way she was brought up. It may account for the haunted intensity of my mother's eyes even at a young age, as though she feared that she was doomed.[6]

In 1950 Raimond and his parents went as assisted migrants to Australia. As part of his migrant contract Romulus was sent to work on the Cairn Curran reservoir in the state of Victoria. Here Romulus met the Romanian brothers Hora and Mitru. Hora became his closest friend, while Mitru entered into an extremely fraught relationship with Christine which ended in Mitru's suicide some years later.

Romulus worked hard and was able to buy a run-down farmhouse and its land. Here Raimond lived a life in the bush of extraordinary freedom, a freedom which must have protected him from the worst effects of his unstable mother who came and went and was unable to mother him in any way. (I have observed in my own life and in the life of certain friends and colleagues that children of unstable or aggressive parents who are able to escape from their home to the bush, or beach, or field do much better in adult life than those children who remain closeted with their parents.)

As a small child Raimond learned that, patient and kind though his father was, he would not tolerate lying. He wrote,

> My father valued truthfulness above most things . . . I have never known anyone who lived so passionately, as did [my father and Hora], the belief that nothing in life matters so much as to live it decently . . . My father and Hora looked upon prudential justifications of truthfulness and other virtues as demeaning of our humanity. They did not value truthfulness for its usefulness. They valued it because they were men for whom *not to falsify* had become a spiritual demeanour.[7]

Romulus was an extremely skilled blacksmith. When he was thirty-five and his marriage over he began writing to a woman in Yugoslavia. Raimond wrote,

> Her name was Lydia. She was in her early twenties, tall, slim, dark and very beautiful . . . I do not remember him more happy. He was young, strong, respected, joyful in his work, at home with the natural as much as the human world, and he was about to marry a young woman who looked like a film star. His work engrossed him, his business prospered, his friendships flourished. It is small wonder that he was always whistling or singing.[8]

Then he met a woman who had known Lydia in Germany. Romulus told her of his plans.

> She listened appalled, with evident pity for him. She told him to lay aside his plans. Lydia was not the woman he imagined her to be. On no account should he trust her. He must write to her and demand she tell him the truth . . . When Lydia finally replied, nothing could have prepared him for what she told him. She had a husband whom she had married only a week earlier, after a long engagement.[9]

Romulus was thrown into confusion.

Morality was for him as substantially a part of reality as the natural facts of human action and motivation, but when Lydia's letter arrived his moral world collapsed. Despite what he had seen and had personally suffered, his moral world was coloured by an innocence which had not been threatened by my mother and Mitru, because he knew them to be as much victims as agents in a drama that was to consume them. His compassionate fatalism could not, however, accommodate Lydia's mendacity. It could accept many forms of folly and weakness and vice, but not a malevolent human will. Of course he had the concept of such a will, but it was weak in him, an abstraction, never a living reality. Believing himself to be directly confronted with it in the person of the woman he loved and had trusted without reservation, his personal disintegration followed not far behind the disintegration of his moral world.[10]

The ideas which are the basic structures on which our whole sense of being a person is built concern morality and the nature of the cosmos. Just as people who live in a region prone to earthquakes learn to build houses that have the flexibility to bend with the movements of the ground on which they stand, so people who have learned to see the cosmos as something which is always changing, construct moral rules which recognise that, while lying, stealing and killing other people are morally wrong, there are circumstances where one must lie, steal or kill in order to survive and/or to protect others. Such a way of seeing allows the person to adapt to unpredictable circumstances. The individual may feel very angry and disappointed, but he does not fall apart. In contrast, children, who come to believe that the rules of morality are absolute and allow no exceptions, and that behind the ever-changing world is an eternal structure, might find this view a comfort and a strength in enduring the vicissitudes of adult life. However, when events challenge and threaten to invalidate these basic beliefs, when the person discovers that he has made a serious error of judgement, just as a rigidly built house crumbles in an earthquake, so does the central structure of the individual's sense of being a person shudder, break and fall.

People, including myself, describe this falling as through empty, bottomless space. It is strange and terrifying. The shards of their old ideas fall with them. They clutch at these scraps, and try to construct from the pieces something that will explain the catastrophe that has befallen them. They search for something that they feel has been there all along but which they had overlooked.

As Romulus fell, clutching at the scraps of his old ideas, he decided that he had so concentrated on God's goodness he had overlooked the forces of evil. Moreover, his pride in his own virtue was overweening. Now he was receiving the punishment he deserved from the evil forces all around him. Raimond wrote,

> Once, on the verandah, I saw his eyes wide with terror, his body trembling because he believed he could see a sheet of flame rise from the concrete and threaten to engulf both of us. He made wooden and iron crosses to ward off evil spirits and, when he cut the bread, he first crossed it with a knife. He questioned me without respite about the meaning of almost everything I did – why had I put the fork, the matches, my shoes just there, why did I stand or sit here rather than there, why did I write, or say or wear this rather than that, and so on, relentlessly.[11]

When the ground beneath our feet vanishes and we fall into infinite space we need people around us who understand what is happening to us. They keep us safe, comfort us, assure us of our worth, and give us time and space to think, and, out of that thinking, to construct another set of ideas which fit more closely our new situation, but also give us courage and optimism. This was not Romulus's fate. He met psychiatrists who, like all psychiatrists then (and many now), thought that he had a mental illness. Romulus went into a psychiatric hospital which, like all psychiatric hospitals, treated patients as objects of pity and derision, and thus destroyed the remnants of the person's self-confidence. Romulus was given electroconvulsive therapy (ECT) and large doses of the drug Largactil. ECT destroys memory, while Largactil prevents thought. Patients who have been given this drug will say, 'It filled my brain with cotton wool.' Raimond later wrote,

> Only someone with an extraordinary sense of the ethical could be so shaken by a sense of evil, and my father was such a person. I believe it is why he seldom sang or whistled again, and that, when he did, it was never with the same innocent pleasure as before.[12]

There is another state against which we defend ourselves and that is the state we call anguish. Anguish is physically painful. Our heart feels that it is being squeezed by a giant hand, our throat constricts, impeding our breathing. Sometimes we can find some ease through crying, but often we cannot cry. The cause of our anguish is some kind of loss, but often it is a loss of which only we know. Sometimes we are able to confront this loss and we are able to survive the pain that such a confrontation brings, but sometimes we are so frightened of the pain that we lie to ourselves about the cause of our anguish. Primo Levi, doubtless no stranger to anguish, wrote,

> Anguish is known to everyone since childhood, and everyone knows that it is often blank, undifferentiated. It rarely carries a clearly written label that also contains its motivation; when it does have one, it is often mendacious. One can believe or declare oneself to be anguished for one reason and be so due to something totally different: one can think that one is suffering at facing the future and instead be suffering because of one's past; one can think that one is suffering for others, out of pity, out of compassion, and instead be suffering for one's own reasons, more or less profound, more or less avowable and avowed; sometimes so deep that only the specialist, the analyst of souls, knows how to exhume them.[13]

Sometimes the lies we tell ourselves to protect ourselves against anguish take the form of a fantasy. When Primo Levi was in the Lager in Auschwitz he formed a close friendship with Alberto. When the Russian army entered Poland the Germans in charge of the Lagers tried to remove all evidence of their existence. Those inmates they could not manage to kill they forced to set off in a column to walk west towards Germany. Anyone who tried to escape from the march or who collapsed with sickness and hunger was shot. Alberto disappeared while on this forced evacuation, but Primo, who was too ill to join the march, survived and eventually returned home. He wrote,

> As soon as I was repatriated, I considered it my duty to go immediately to Alberto's home town to tell his mother and his brother what I knew. I was welcomed with courteous affection, but as soon as I began my story the mother begged me to stop: she already knew everything, at least as far as Alberto was concerned, and there was no point in my repeating the usual horror stories to her. She *knew* that her son, he alone, had been able to slip away from the column without being shot by the SS, he had hidden in the forest and was safe in Russian hands; he had not yet been able to send any word, but he would do so soon, she was certain of it; and now, would I please change the subject, and tell her how I myself had survived. A year later I was by chance passing through the same town, and again I visited the family. The truth was slightly changed: Alberto was in a Soviet clinic, he was fine, but he had lost his memory, he no longer even remembered his name; he was improving though, and would soon return – she had this from a reliable source. Alberto never returned. Forty years have passed; I did not have the courage to turn up again and to counterpose my painful truth to the consolatory 'truth' that, one helping the other, Alberto's relatives had fashioned for themselves.[14]

It can take great courage to accept that the world is not what we thought it was. When we are young, it can mean giving up the comfort and security of what has been shown to be nothing but beautiful lies. So frightening can that prospect be that a young person can decide to lie to himself and tell himself that nothing has changed, just as Felicity told herself that her parents were good and that she deserved the punishments they inflicted on her. When we are older, accepting that the world is not what we thought it was can mean that not only has our identity changed but our reputation. The bitterest of arguments amongst scientists arise when one group of scientists produces research results which throw into doubt a theory which another group of scientists hold dear, having built their career, their identity and their reputation on this theory. The argument purports to be about science, but it is about that most human of matters, the sense of being a person. Scientists, being human, hate to have their favourite theory disproved. Only the wisest of scientists welcome such an event. Richard Dawkins told the story

> of a respected elder statesman of the Zoology Department of Oxford when I was an undergraduate. For years he had passionately believed, and taught, that the Golgi Apparatus (a microscopic feature of cells) was not real: an artefact, an illusion. Every Monday afternoon it was the custom of the whole department to listen to a research talk by a visiting lecturer. One Monday, the lecturer was an American cell biologist who presented completely convincing evidence that the Golgi Apparatus was real. At the end of the lecture the old man strode to the front of the hall and said – with passion – 'My dear fellow, I wish to thank you. I have been wrong all these years.' We clapped our hands red . . . The memory of the incident I have described still brings a lump to my throat.[15]

Dawkins's elder statesman had the wisdom to know that theories are just ideas, approximations to whatever the truth might be. Knowing this, he did not have to react with fury when another scientist showed him that his theory was wrong. If everyone was like this elder statesman the world would be a peaceful place. However, most people are not wise, and not only are people being killed daily in battles over ideas purporting to be absolute truths, but a simple discussion about health can quickly degenerate into hurt feelings and even anger and abuse.

This happened in a conversation I had with a woman about the government's proposed plan to withdraw financial support for the London Homeopathic Hospital. She felt that this was wrong because the hospital did such good work. I remarked that I had been an outpatient at that hospital but found that the treatment I received did nothing to ameliorate the symptoms of my chronic lung disease, bronchiectasis. Her speech quickened as she assured me that I had been given inadequate treatment, I should have seen a better doctor, and so on. I felt I was being pressured into returning for another course of treatment, so I said that, while many people found homeopathy to be helpful, homeopathy would not restore to normal functioning the severely damaged tissues in my lungs, nor could it lead to the re-growth of that part of my lung which had been removed forty-two years ago. Her angry response to this was such that I was pleased we were talking on the phone and that I was not in immediate physical danger.

Ben Goldacre has not been so fortunate. He is the doctor who writes the Bad Science column in the *Guardian*. Here he applies the simple rules of scientific method and experiment to public reports about science and what purports to be science. Devotees of complementary or alternative medicine do not regard him as a friend. He wrote,

> With alternative therapists, when you point out a problem with the evidence, people don't engage with you about it, or read and reference your work. They get into a huff. They refuse to answer calls or email queries. They wave their hands and mutter sciencey words such as 'quantum' and 'nano'. They accuse you of being a paid plant from some big pharma conspiracy. They threaten to sue you. They shout, 'What about thalidomide, science boy?', they cry, they call you names, they hold lectures at their trade fairs about how you are a dangerous doctor, they contact and harass your employer, or they actually threaten you with violence (all this has happened to me, and I'm compiling a great collection of stories for a nice documentary, so keep it coming).[16]

We live in a world where people comment on one another's ideas all the time. It is an integral part of negotiating our relationships with others. Other people's comments about us keep us focused on trying to work out what is actually going on around us and to us. If we live completely on our own without any human contact we develop strange ideas and habits. We need to be able to see ourselves as others see us. However, how we deal with this commentary depends on how we see ourselves. If we feel confident in ourselves, if we can trust ourselves, we do not get offended by other people's remarks about us. We make very clear distinctions between those people whose opinion we value because they are wise, experienced, and do not resort to criticism in order to further their own interest, and those people who want to manipulate or injure us, or are too stupid to be able to formulate a reasoned criticism. With this second group we adopt the attitude, 'Anyone who criticises me is a fool, and I'm not going to waste my time with fools.' If we do not feel confident in ourselves, if we cannot trust ourselves, we do get offended by other people's remarks about us. Because we have rejected ourselves, we expect others to reject us. We become 'sensitive'. Like Felicity we look for insults and find them even when no insult was intended. When we lack confidence in ourselves, we always feel that we are in danger of being destroyed as a person. So we create defences. There are many kinds of defences, but a very popular defence is that of having a set of beliefs about the nature of death, the purpose of life, and the nature of the cosmos, which we see, not as a theory about the world, but as an absolute truth. The great trouble with theories about the world is that there is no theory which can be devised which has advantages but no disadvantages, and does not contain imperfect logic, inconsistencies, and irreducible dilemmas. Believing that life ends in death certainly has limited imperfect logic, inconsistencies, and irreducible dilemmas, but it has the disadvantage that you will fear and resent that your life will come to an arbitrary end.

Whether you see death as the end or as a doorway to another life, if you hold a theory about the world close to your heart, insisting that it is an absolute truth which is part of your sense of being a person, you make yourself exceedingly vulnerable to other people's criticisms. You cannot ignore them. Moreover, at some level of consciousness, you know that your beliefs express a hope, a fantasy, and are not a description of reality. You know that you are lying to yourself. You might respond with anger when other people criticise your beliefs, but your very anger reveals your weakness and your fear.

A person's denigration of himself has its roots in childhood, and long-held ideas are hard to change. Moreover, the defences we create to protect our sense of being a person can easily become, as Tony and Siegfried show, a prison from which there seems to be no escape.

Chapter 3

'HEMMED IN A CLOSED CIRQUE OF OUR OWN CREATING'[1]

We each live in our own individual prison. Freedom consists of choosing, consciously, the prison in which we live, and making our prison large and variable, with flexible walls, a spacious house with wide doors and windows open to heaven and earth. Unfortunately, so many of us reject freedom, for freedom means insecurity, openness to the unknown. Instead, we build our prison as an impregnable fortress, enclosing a meagre, empty space, and shutting out the myriad possibilities of heaven and earth. Moreover, we regard our fortress not as something we have chosen; but as an absolute and immutable fact of reality. Trapped and helpless, we cannot be happy.

Tony

I work as a psychologist and people who are in difficulties come and talk with me. Sometimes I put our conversations on tape, and it is these conversations that are in this book. Or rather, selections from them. No one other than me would want to listen to them in their entirety, with their gossip, dull anecdotes, repetitions, and platitudinous pleasantries. But they contain opinions, ideas, beliefs, themes – all threads that wind through the conversations and mesh into a tight and vital pattern. It is this pattern which forms the individual world in which each of us lives. This structure is the spectacles through which we see reality. Or, as the Talmud says, 'We do not see things as they are. We see them as we are.' Or as Epictetus said, 'It is not things in themselves which trouble us, but our opinions of things.'

Tony was a man of strong opinions. The first time he came to see me, he harangued me for two hours. He was a tall man, heavily built. The cut of his hair and his sweater and jeans matched the leftish views he was expounding with more passion than reason. His most trenchant attacks were made on the monstrous regiment of women who besieged him – his wife, mother, aunts, colleagues, acquaintances, women in general. Only his daughters were exempt. I felt sorry for his wife. I began to feel sorry for myself. So, having said very little all this time, I intervened to remark that perhaps he found it necessary to put on a show of bluster and anger so that I would not see how hurt and vulnerable he was inside. He sank down like a balloon deflating. He said I was right. I had earlier explained to him that our meeting was not a beginning of a series of meetings, since I was about to depart to Australia for two months. Now I said to him that, if he wished, he could get in touch with me when I returned. He said he would do this, and so on my first day back he telephoned me for an appointment.

He came to see me each week and we talked for two hours. He talked at length, but more quietly and with less aggression. He explained this change in terms of what I was like.

'I wanted to stay with you right from the first session because something deep inside me tells me that I can't frighten you off. You see my aggressiveness as questions, rather than getting at you.'

I thought that all I did was to follow my rule that there is no point in arguing with a person until you know what it is that he is saying. With Tony it took me some eight weeks to find out.

We spent a lot of time talking about art, chiefly music since Tony was a musician, and about relationships. He said, 'I would like to find for myself some niche in life, not in society, in life. I'd like to carve out something and say in that I can reside and have my comfort and my being . . . the whole point about a guitar is a love affair. You hold it tenderly, gently – it's such a demanding bugger. It gives an incredible amount, but only if you get it right.'

I asked him why art was important to him. 'Because without it man has no reason to live.'

'So what you are saying, without art you have no reason to live.'

'Right.'

'What would happen to you if you suddenly found yourself in a world where there was no art?'

'I'd find the most convenient and most painless way of committing suicide. Wouldn't you?'

Later he said, 'The thing that interests me is relationships. Relationships with people primarily. Relationship with music, because music isn't a passive thing. It is an action and a reaction . . .'

But while he called a close relationship 'the most important thing' he also called it 'the most difficult thing'. 'There's got to be a positiveness in a relationship to combat the absurdities that we all produce in our lives – the patterns we produce. I find people's patterns in daily living very hard to come to terms with. My wife says, "Why do you go on about it so? Why don't you let it alone?" I say, "Well, look, we're supposed to have a relationship, and you're the only wife I've got." '

When we spoke of love, Tony said that he was always 'desperate for it, with the effect that when I found someone who responded actively and genuinely, I mean, there was nothing that would touch that!' His metaphor for his need for love was hunger. 'A deep relationship is my meat and drink . . . the reason I have a relationship, usually quite hectic, it's because you're ravenous, you're really hungry and you come across somebody and the chemistry works, and it's not often and, Jesus, you're hungry.'

'Do you see the lack of relationships as starvation?' I asked.

'Definitely, I mean, it would be fairer with rationing, at least you would be sure of your weekly ration – in a sense you feel you're living through a drought – there's no rain, nothing comes in to brighten your life.'

The way Tony defined relationships made for very great difficulties.

One day Tony arrived in high dudgeon about a friend who had promised him something and had 'failed to deliver'. I asked him why it was important to keep a promise.

'Promises should be kept because it exposes you, you have put yourself in a position where you are at risk. If you promise somebody something, you are actually laying yourself on the line. You diminish yourself by not carrying out the promise. A lot of people tell me I am too hard, but what alternatives have I got?'

'Why is it important to keep promises?'

'Because you are what you are by virtue of whether you keep them or not. You're laying your own self, you're laying your own integrity, you're laying your own being on the line.'

'You're demonstrating your own integrity?'

'Yes – and concern and love. What are you going to do? Throw all these things away?'

'What you're saying is that, when a person breaks a promise to you, you feel that that's a sign of a loss of integrity in that person, and that that person is showing you less love.'

'That's right. In the end it's those sort of human gestures that somehow determine the relationship. If somebody I don't care about promises me something and doesn't deliver, I'm not too worried, but if somebody I care about does that, I get worried.'

'Does the fact that your friend did not keep his promise suggest to you that he does not care about you as much as he says, or you had hoped?'

'Well, caring about me is only part of it. Caring full stop is the biggest part.'

'I always think "caring" is a transitive verb. You care about someone or something.'

'I don't think so. I see caring as a conceptual thing, that is a caring person. A phrase "a caring person" is a quality of that person.'

'Am I understanding you to say now that your friend projects himself as a caring person, yet where you're concerned, he does something which suggests a lack of caring? The implication in this is either when he projects himself as a caring person it's phoney, or if he is a caring person the caring does not extend to you.'

'No, it's not that. The caring includes me, but I'm not the most important thing about it. All he's done is tell me that he cares when he wants to care, as opposed to being a caring person.'

'So it's something he switches on and off.'

'That's right.'

'And there's no security in that.'

'Exactly. There's no security in it. I find no security anywhere. Very few people give me security.'

Tony went on to describe me as 'a caring person'. This confounded me. I could not see how I could have a quality of caring which existed in me, even if I lived in a vacuum. I know that my eyes have a quality, blue, which remains the same no matter what I see out of them, but caring, for me, is an experience, something I do and feel, and it always relates to something outside of myself. In the language which Tony and I thought we shared were many traps for the unwary.

One day Tony remarked, 'Really, I'm not scared of living.'

'What are you scared of?' I asked.

'People who don't live.'

'Why do they scare you?'

'Because the whole thing's an act. You never get down to anything. You see, I rather expect that close relationships are short-term. I don't see how fires that can burn so intensely can keep going for so long. I see long relationships in terms of stroking. I don't see meaningful relationships in terms of stroking. I see them as heights and depths. Jesus, I don't want to travel, hovering above the ground about six inches. I want to be right up there or right down there. I don't want to be down there, but I know if you go up there, you've got to be down there some of the time. In this life you do not experience one thing unless you experience the opposite.'

He subscribed to the Spanish proverb: 'Take what you like, says God, and pay for it.'

'I've never got away with anything in my life', he said. In relationships nothing ever happened by chance. He would often say, 'For every action there's a reaction.'

Nevertheless, no matter what price he had to pay for close, meaningful relationships, he still believed that 'any relationship benefits from the start from one thing going for it and that's newness. The newness will carry it for a certain length of time, and it is the precise thing that leads on to other people, because you're after new experiences. That phrase from Hesse in *Narcissus and Goldmund*, "Can there be true love without true love's dangers?" That "dangers" could be translated into newness. By true love's dangers it meant that Goldmund was always finding a new girl, and he was somebody who didn't find a lasting relationship. I find I don't need any of that in terms of my daughters – newness isn't a constant in that sort of bond. But I think in sexual love it is a fact. It seems to be for me. But society condemns that out of hand. I'm probably talking about what people have been finding since time began – newness of relationship is nothing new to the artist. I look around and I find it's evident – the new day, seasons of the year, every springtime – in a sense we know what we're going to expect, but so we do when we go into relationships. Certain things one knows are going to be there, but it's the discovery of them, the actual testing of them, that is the attraction, isn't it? I think artists are sometimes brave enough to say this.'

'If you see goodness of relationships as relating to the newness of relationships, then you're going to get into difficulties in long-term relationships, aren't you?'

'Yes. It's more that business of confirmation: perhaps it's that one is never enough. You need more to confirm.'

'You need relationships to confirm something about yourself?'

'Yes.'

'What?'

'That I'm still capable of them, for a start.'

'And so this is a kind of testing yourself out every time.'

'Yes, yes. I think it's the love factor. If anybody goes out of their way to show that they love me, I'm theirs.'

'What you're saying is that you want to confirm that you're still lovable.'

'Yes. Someone once told me that she'd never known anyone as generous with themselves as I was. And I find people tight, bloody tight.'

Tony often criticised his wife for not giving him the kind of relationship he craved. 'She does not care for the depth because of the hurt and the real living that has to go on because of that relationship. Me, I want it all.' I thought that most women would be reserved with a man who would declare, 'I don't think relationships last. It's one of the beautiful things about relationships that they're fleeting things. Like the butterfly, they can only exist for a length of time . . . The day I stop hurting someone I'll be dead. That must be the nature of life. I don't see relationships as being forever, with a person like me, anyway. I think the depth of a relationship is its own self-destruct mechanism. You're sort of living life as if each day is the last. For most women I have no attraction whatsoever. But for a few women I have a very great attraction.'

'What is it in you that they find attractive?'

'That I can deliver. When they look at me and they see what I'm promising and offering, I can make their dreams come true: I can actually deliver – but I can't deliver for ever.'

'Why not?'

'Because I don't think it's something that can be delivered forever. It's an exhausting thing. It has the seeds of its own destruction in it. There's always a sense that I deplete stocks more quickly than I can build them up again.'

'You see your part of the relationship self-destructing because you run out of supplies. But if you find somebody else there could suddenly be a new source of supplies because this person is feeding you.'

'Yes, that's right.'

'So you find another source of supplies which again will run out and then you've got to find somebody else.'

'Yes. That's absolutely right.'

'That's a fairly exhausting way to live one's life.'

He laughed ruefully and said, 'You shouldn't mock the afflicted.'

The way Tony used the words 'close relationship' often rang in my ears like an empty cliché; so I pushed him to say what 'close relationships' meant to him. This was difficult for him to do, since relationships are something we feel rather than define. He spoke of 'concepts, notions of love, of what a relationship intrinsically was. It's being something to someone and someone being something to you. A relationship is not a negation of the self. It seems to me to be a more positive thing and to include a "we". There's still an "I", there's still a "you", but now there's a "we" – which is something which is a really important condition. What goes to make a "we" I'm not sure. It is the fact that you find you relate in terms of ideas, in terms of priorities, in terms of virtues, if you like. The continuation of the relationship is the acceptance of both selves.'

I commented, 'Then a relationship being a "we", what you've been saying all along, in essence, is that in your present life you don't belong to any relationship where you can say "we".'

'That's right. Hence I say I'm starving. My wife tells me she doesn't want that kind of relationship. And then she says "I love you". My God, I don't know what's going on. I can't go to my wife and just hold her. I suspect that's all I want. The rest, the perks, other things, if you feel the same way as the other person you can discard them. In the end you know what the fundamental is. It's that holding someone close – and everybody that I want to hold close doesn't want to be held close.'

So a close relationship was loving, holding, sharing – and doomed. It reminded me of *Tristan and Isolde* or *La Traviata*, but I dared not say so. Tony tried to despise Romantic music. He talked of the beauty of Bach's music which 'has a beauty all of its own and it's really uncluttered by the sentimentalism of Romantic music. It's put in a confined space and within that space Bach makes things work and he doesn't have to say "Look, I'm free" because in the end you've nothing at all. It's terror, freedom.' But such freedom had its charms. He despised sentimentality, but for Tchaikovsky's *Pathétique*, 'I despise it but I still choke up. Indulgence and sentimentality really get me and I suspect I'm both. I still need my Tchaikovsky. I suppose I link that with women and I always feel that women are horribly sentimental, indulgent creatures.' But women were powerful. 'I see the world as being a woman's world, not a man's world. Men are far superior in terms of integrity.'

These words of his are but a faint echo of his tirade of abuse against women which often made him sound like the male chauvinist Aunt Sally that the less discriminating members of the Women's Movement like to demolish. Occasionally

I commented that he sounded like a naive male chauvinist but forbore to point out the tautology of 'naive' and 'male chauvinist' since I gathered from his discourse that he divided the human race into men, women, and special people, and that I had earned a place in the last group.

In our second meeting, when we were trying to decide whether our discussions should have some particular aim, he said, 'It's a question of knocking out stupid or wrong choices or wrong questions. I think if you're on a journey from A to B you never actually get to B. You simply rule out all the hundreds of paths that will take you to places like the sewerage canal. I don't think it matters if you get to B. What matters is that you've tried to get there – whether you've been through the experience.' He returned to this point some weeks later. 'I don't care about results, objectives. What I want to know is, has the bloke done the journey, has he travelled the road?'

'Why is it important to go on that journey?' I asked.

'Because without it you don't know what another person is feeling. You don't know the processes that are involved. You've no concept of compassion, of enquiry, of the finenesses of intellect. You've none of these things. You're only half a person. One of the innate factors of man is surely the enquiring nature of man into himself. Which is what art is all about. It seems to me that there isn't anything more important than finding out the nature of what you are. We bring very little into the world. The need to survive is innate, but surviving can be achieved at the expense of real living. The enquiry after a god does seem to be one of the fundamentals that man has brought into the world. You can put a lot down to fear and ignorance, but you can't put all of it down to fear, superstition, and ignorance.'

Special people were, for Tony, the people who questioned life, who had set out 'on the journey'. He saw himself as a special person, and this was very important for him because, as he said, 'Ordinary people aren't remembered.' Being remembered was very important.

One day I asked him, 'How do you envisage your death?'

He sighed. 'I've no idea. One thing I fear is the same death as my father, of a tumour. Once it had been diagnosed, I had to wait three months, watching him die. I hope very much I don't die like that. Like Roger McGough, "Let me die a young man's death." I'd rather go out in a blaze of something. But I'm not brave. I don't really fancy being thrown out in the middle of a road from the seat of a motor bike. Death doesn't bother me but dying does. I don't want to become less than what I was – like my father. I travelled every day to that hospital. His condition was getting worse, and I'd keep making myself relive him as he was, a vital sort of person – very distinguished looking, attractive to women, a compassionate man, made a lot of mistakes. Really a very nice human being, and I would not allow this paralysed half of a face with a drooping lip – it has impinged on my memory, but I try very hard to stop it stopping me remembering him as I really knew him. Christ, that must be false, that last three months must be false in the sense that they hid the man and what he was. Three months must be weighed against sixty years.'

'How old will you be when you die?'

'Sixty. And I'd prefer it that way. So I've never worried about pensions, you see.'

'What do you feel will happen to you after you die?'

'Nothing.'

'You see death as the end?'

He sighed, 'Yes, in the ashes to ashes and dust to dust sense. One returns to the atoms and particles that one came from.'

I asked, 'How do you see yourself being remembered?'

He was silent. Then he put his hand to his face and cried. 'I don't know', he said, and a little while later he went on, 'Strangely, I find it somehow gratifying that it can move me to tears, real tears. There's so much hate down below. Can't seem to do anything about myself, and yet, I estrange myself, isolate myself, that's the sort of person I am and I don't think I can help doing it. I don't mean to talk in hopeless terms, but it's part of me. Trouble is, I can't cope with the result. Can't cope with the isolation – I can cope with it at a given moment, but when I'm on my own, there are times – I suspect that's no way to try and learn the guitar.' He lit a cigarette and said, 'I went to the clinic last week. He's a nice guy, that bloke.'

'Dr White?'

'Yes. He's a bloody nice guy. One of life's gentlemen, strange and eccentric, but really nice. He gave me all the time in the world and he said, "You know, I can't do very much for you", and I thought, you've given me an hour of your time. What better service could I have?'

'It sounds like what you are saying is that I don't expect people will remember me because I was a loving person.'

'Something like that. They see me as an awkward bastard.'

'And you don't see people remembering you as a great artist.'

'It's a shame. I think actually I could be passably good. I think I've got the capabilities. I think I could, it's possible, if not probable, for me to give a performance of integrity of music that needs that sort of interpretation – for someone to say, "That guy really understood what Bach was about." When you're trying to make this achievement on the one thing that you think will save your life, and then it starts sinking, you know, and then you're left – the last time I had a guitar lesson it was dreadful, couldn't do a thing. I have this problem about doing anything in performance in a solo role. If I'm accompanying, no problems. When it's for myself, I can't do it. I sit there like an idiot.'

He described how, when a publisher had expressed interest in some of his songs, he told the publisher that few people would want to buy them, and the publisher went away. 'So', said Tony, 'out of the jaws of success I snatched failure.'

He told me about a story he was writing. 'When it's legible I'll let you read it. You'll be bored out of your mind.'

'You're telling me I won't enjoy reading what you're writing. That way you're stopping me from telling you I don't like it.'

'That's right. But do you know what I fear most? That someone will say "That's very good", and then put it away in a drawer for twenty years.'

'Why do you fear that?'

'Because it denies me. I don't really mind people saying "Bloody awful". But to be ignored I find terrifying.' He did, however, 'actually want all these stupid people's approval'.

'And when you get it, you'll despise it.'

'That's right – absolutely bloody right.'

Tony talked a great deal about what he expected the other person in a relationship to give him, but he found my question as to what he brought to a relationship a difficult one to answer.

'I don't know, I bring whatever I am into a relationship. I really don't know what I am, I suspect. I'm capable of love. I'm capable of making love. Well, those for starters. I think I give it my best. I always thought in life that people never wanted my best. They never wanted what I could actually do. They never wanted peak performance.'

'What happens to you when you offer people something and they don't want it?'

'Frustrated – intense frustration, and depression I suspect. That's not a very good word, but when your bed becomes your best friend, that time when you suddenly realise you've got problems, bed's the best place. You don't have to think.'

'Have you always felt this about yourself, that people didn't want your best?'

'Yes.'

'So that if you put yourself in a situation where you're going to demonstrate the best of what you're capable, you're putting yourself in a situation where people are going to reject you.'

'Yes.'

'So in a situation where you're going to give a guitar solo your anticipatory image is not one of going out there, playing well, and having people applaud. It's going out there, playing well, and people putting their hands over their ears and walking out.'

'Or the other anticipatory image is that I'm going to collapse. Then my audience will shake their heads, avert their eyes and gently file out. They don't want to be associated with me. Sometimes I feel that there will be people willing me on, but I'll fail them. I'll collapse under the pressure.'

'Whatever you do, the audience is against you?'

'Yes. I do make it very hard for myself, don't I?'

'If you look at the images that successful artists or racing drivers have, it's that they're going to go out there and win.'

'That's right. I've never felt that on a musical instrument. The thing just sits there and laughs at you. I'm deferential to the music. Any piece I've played I'm honoured to have played it. One thing I can't stand is praise when I've done something wrong. I really want to scream at that. It's almost as if I insist that everyone is as aware as I am of what I'm trying to do. In that case, I'm always going to lose, aren't I?' Then Tony quoted from Gerard Manley Hopkins's poem 'Soliloquy' which he had set for voice and guitar: 'Birds build but not I build – no, but strain, time's eunuch – O Thou Lord of life, send my roots rain.'

I commented, 'The way in which you construe the outcome of every situation you make sure you don't achieve anything. You don't even allow the possibility of achieving.'

'The truth is', he sighed, 'that maybe I want to win in my way.'

'What would your way be?'

'Did you see a film called *A Touch of Class*? Well, the first time they made love, he was putting his tie on and he said, "How was it?", and she said, "Okay", and he was really offended.' Tony laughed at this. 'He got more and more irate, and she said, "What did you want me to tell you, that the stars flew round heaven? It was okay", and he was really furious. I know it. If a woman, if she didn't, didn't dare, break up into little bits, I'd be very insulted.'

'So you want people to go absolutely over the moon about your music. Just saying "That was good" isn't enough.'

'No, it isn't. You can't just enjoy it for that minute. You've got to rave about it, otherwise you'll insult the performer.'

Thus it was that while Tony prided himself on being a thinker, he despised those relatives and colleagues who, he said, 'set me up as a guru'. Of course he despised them because they were not capable of seeing how great a thinker he was, or could be, but even more because they had not 'made the journey'. 'I feel I have to fight night and day, almost, to maintain a position I've reached, whereas people who haven't made the journey, by their very not having made the journey, will wipe you out – their inertia breeds apathy and ignorance. They offend my humanity.' He put this in a poem which he gave to me.

YOU
who deny me
with ev'ry breath you breathe
YOU
who offer life itself
and are barren
YOU
who gain power
knowing nothing of wisdom
YOU
who court success
compromising your own existence to succeed
YOU are not my Peers – neither will I recognise you.

YOU
who force me to fight you
or be overwhelmed by triviality
YOU
who indulge your excesses
call me extreme
YOU
who are dedicated to pain's exclusion
profess tolerance
YOU
who revere mediocrity
mock talent
YOU are not my idols – neither will I serve you.

YOU have driven me from your world
because I dared to dream of things substantial
and dared to speak of them.
YOU used me as your Oracle
and when the words revealed your weakness
YOU destroyed me.

'I'm not one for middle roads. You end up nowhere', said
Tony. At the end of one session I ventured the suggestion
that there is something to be said for tolerance in human
relationships. Tony went away and brooded on this and came
back the next week ready to argue the point.

'I thought that intolerance was –', he paused and took a

deep breath, 'probably a very important facet of all this. I'm not sure that I'm willing to give it up that easy.'

'There are too many payoffs to being intolerant, to give it up', I said.

'Mm.' He went on to talk about 'special' people and then said, 'I really don't know what to do with praise. So people don't know whether to praise me or to boo me. If they boo me they get a mouthful back. If they praise me I never accept it.'

'Once you said I could write what I liked about you so long as it was good, bad, but not indifferent. So, if people are tolerant to you that would come across to you that they are indifferent to you.'

'Yes, that's true.'

'How would you feel if you woke up one morning and found you were a tolerant person?'

'I'd know I was different immediately. I see tolerance as a sort of blunting process. I'm very loath to see it as a virtue. Because everything that is written about tolerance is actually evasion or patronisation, neither of which I want to know anything about. So people who are described as tolerant are evading something.'

'If you become a tolerant person you'd be bland and you wouldn't be complaining, fighting against unacceptable behaviour?'

'There's a sort of missionary zeal underneath it all.'

'So when I say to you that if you were more tolerant towards other people you'd find life a lot easier, I'm in effect saying to you, "Become a lesser person, a worse person than you are and you'll find life easier." And, of course, that kind of message no one will accept.'

'If you said that to me I would have to say, "You're putting my soul at risk." '

'If I give you advice "Be tolerant", I'm actually giving you, in your frame of reference, the advice "Be a bad person." '

'Yes.'

'And to give you that advice is, for you, "Put your soul at risk." This isn't a piece of new, brilliant insight on my part. I've had this conversation with a lot of women who've been sitting where you are now and saying to me, "I'm worn out. I do all this housework", and I say, "Why not do less housework?", and as I'm saying that I'm advising them to become a bad person, because it puts their soul at risk not to keep their houses immaculately clean. It's just what we regard as –'

'You can make a parallel, can you?' He was offended.

'Yes. We each have our own list of virtues.'

'Because I despise; not despise, laugh at, the woman who does too much housework. So I'm not happy about the sense of your parallel.'

'All I'm saying is that different people choose different things to regard as paramount virtues as proof of their essential goodness. What would happen to you if you became a tolerant person?'

'I think it would be the end of me. I think my wife admires and loves me in whatever way she has of admiring and loving because I am what I am. I think she really likes an intolerant bastard. She would accuse me of selling out if I went along with every whim of hers.'

'So in a way she needs you to be nasty and you need to be nasty.'

'There is something of that in it.'

'That's the basis of a long marriage, isn't it?'

He was able to laugh at this, but later he said that if he were not intolerant then he would be 'wiped out' by those people he addressed in his poem.

Tony had been brought up 'a strict Baptist' but when he was twenty-five 'I found that the God I'd been used to praying to and corresponding with at varying intervals and levels of sincerity all of a sudden wasn't available to me.'

'How do you feel about God now?'

'My thoughts waver from the neutral which I rarely am to levels of "If you're there you're a bastard". I'm not really sure. There's that first line of Hopkins, "Thou art indeed just, Lord, if I contend with Thee". As soon as you start contending with a God, then He is what you say He is, because you've acknowledged him. I know what I am, but the reason I'm coming here is because I don't know how to cope with it, the results of it, all the time. I can cope with misfortune, perhaps, better than I can cope with the lack of motivation. Most days you get up and the guitar gives you meaning because the guitar starts talking to you, it puts an alternative proposition to you. If I'd have lived a thousand years ago I'd have built an altar in the shape of a guitar.'

'When you were twenty-five you gave up being a Baptist but you didn't give up being religious.'

'Yes, I am a religious person, but my God is a – all sorts of things. He's first of all "to thine own self be true". I don't know whether I kid myself, but I find I've developed some facility for measuring honesty, cutting past all the shit, and guff, and going straight there – which has earned me no kudos at all. But I can't put a title to my God. Having given up titles, I don't know whether I would like to lumber Him with one. I have a great fear of the Christian God – He must be a bastard, what a bloody sick joke, creating this world. There must be some gods up there, sitting around, and He's a baby god among the bigger immortals, and the baby's been given the world to play with, stirring things round in the world, seeing what havoc can be caused. If there is a God, then this God is some sort of holy maniac, an evil maniac. Evil because He allows enough food to keep the dream going. It's the biggest con trick ever played.'

'The dream? The dream of what?'

'That you're getting somewhere. When I talk of evil, that goes back to my Billy Graham days. That bastard! I was really conned. I was one of those that walked forward. I really could shoot myself for doing that. It embarrasses my soul, not my person. How could I be so out of touch with myself?'

'You feel you've been conned by the Christian God?'

'Oh, yes, very definitely. Not just by the people who serve the Christian God.' He went on to berate St Paul for naming the unknown god of the Greeks 'Yahweh'. 'The Greeks had put labels on so many things and still they felt that it didn't matter how many gods they made, there was still something you can't put your finger on. And that is a very uncomfortable situation. The Greeks, because they had a lot of time to think, could actually stand and bear this discomfort, but man nowadays is so rushing round, is so materialistic, that in the end he can't weigh himself down. He's got to put labels on things.'

'How well can you stand the unknown God?'

'With difficulty, with great difficulty intellectually.'

'But how about emotionally?'

He sat very still for a moment and then said, 'Emotionally, I think, badly.'

'Not that you need to know. You need to be close.'

'That's right.'

'The hunger that you talk about, the hunger in relationships. You want to be close.'

'Yes. In the end you know what the fundamental thing is. It's holding someone close. And everybody I want to hold close doesn't want to be held close.' He shaped his arms around the empty air.

'You don't see God as wanting to be held close?'

He thought about this. 'I suppose not. But I've never given it any thought before. After all, a person, a Being capable of living the life of the universe, it would be difficult to get close to. We're talking in terms of infinity. I don't know what infinity is, but it scares hell out of me. There's no way I can cope with thinking about an infinite God. One of the virtues of death is that it will end it. Death actually has a lot of things going for it. I'm not trying to be perverse, but I do find the thought of some people and infinity more than I can bear.'

'If you think in terms of wanting to hold the unknown God and then you think "Life ends in death", then you haven't left yourself a lot of time to know that God. Then if you say that life doesn't end in death you're still lumbered with all the people that irritate you.'

'They don't irritate me. They offend me, mortally offend me.'

'Yes, mortally offend. You've used that phrase before.'

'It's one of my mother's. I find that people to whom I apply that expression do just that. They offend me, the essential me.'

'If you suffer a mortal wound you die. What we've just worked out together is – you could conceive of your life going on after death, but people who mortally offend you would still be there, and their presence stops you from having a life after death. So they have mortally offended you, haven't they?'

'I've never looked at it in that way before. But the first line of the poem I wrote was the indicative thing in terms of humanity. "You who deny me with ev'ry breath you breathe." If people talk crap and are admired for it – to them I say, "By your very nature you're calling me some sort of lunatic. So bloody well shut up, commit suicide, but get out of my hair. I don't want to see you, I don't want to know you." I haven't thought beyond that. Maybe I have in the way you're describing. But consciously I haven't thought about it.'

Later he said, 'If there is a God, then we must be a reflection of His image. God must be evil as well as good.'

'If you see God as being at least as potentially evil as man, then you can't have any trust or security in Him.'

'No.'

'Where do you look for security?'

'In other human beings. So I'm inevitably tripping over.'

'Do you see any security in art?'

'Yes. But not in art alone. I've always seen art as an expression of a relationship rather than as a descriptive piece of something. Art is about doing the same thing in a different way. I suppose the reason I've fallen back on the classical guitar is because the only creativity left to one is interpretation.'

Tony saw himself as a thinker and he wanted to share his thoughts with me, but even he found it difficult to reveal to me, and sometimes to himself, his basic beliefs, the structure which supported and surrounded him. We do not display our set of basic beliefs any more than we display our skeleton. Yet, just as our skeleton determines whether we spread our fine bones in the shape of a hand or a wing, whether we stand upright or pad along on all fours, so our beliefs determine whether we shall act upon the world with mastery, or soar freely and confidently through life, or stand upright against life's buffeting, or plod through life's weary ways. We do not state some of our beliefs, or even bring them to mind, since we regard them as totally obvious and axiomatic. We hide our beliefs from others to prevent them from laughing at our childish faiths, or belittling our deepest fears, or chiding our foolish optimism. Or simply not understanding what was being told.

If Tony could have stated his beliefs simply and directly, all he need have said was: 'There is no afterlife and God is a child who uses the world for His sport. I must fight against the people who offend me otherwise I shall be destroyed. The meaning and purpose of life lies in art and in close relationships. Close relationships do not last. I shall always fail as an artist. When I die I shall be forgotten.'

He did not say that directly, but he did say, 'I sometimes think that the main problem is coming to terms with a world that I don't have any affinity with and being motivated with it. I really can't see why I should do anything rather than spend my life being depressed, and commenting to all and sundry on it.'

Siegfried

(I wrote about Siegfried in 1980, and since then there have been many changes in the psychiatric system. The big psychiatric hospitals have closed and psychiatric wards and clinics in general hospitals have replaced them, while the different mental health professions work together in multidisciplinary teams. Yet, the more things change, the more they remain the same.)

None of the other psychologists in the hospital would see Siegfried. 'It's your job', they said to me, 'You're in charge.' It was not that they were being unkind. They were embarrassed, the embarrassment we feel when someone whom we see as presenting himself as powerful and competent stumbles and falls. For Siegfried was a consultant psychiatrist and in our narrow hospital world consultant psychiatrists should never become psychiatric patients. But, of course, they do.

There are different kinds of consultant psychiatrists. Some see themselves as scientists. These find university departments with small, well-equipped clinics, where the doctors wear white coats and speak a language not known to ordinary mortals. Some see themselves as psychotherapists. They speak modestly of their knowledge of medicine, wear undistinguished suits, and adopt a manner which may range from the friendly avuncular to the self-effacing: they may advance so far that they abandon suits for the simple clothes of current fashion, and desks and chairs for cushions and rugs, and have behind them the comfort of a private practice. But the fate of most psychiatrists lies not in the austere splendour of a university clinic nor in the impressive ambiguities of the therapy room. The fate of most psychiatrists lies in the large psychiatric hospital, known colloquially as 'the bin'.

Most of these hospitals, once called asylums, were built in the nineteenth century to house the 'pauper lunatics', and since such people were an offence to the eye the hospitals were built well outside the boundaries of the town. The towns grew, and now most of these hospitals are within the city bounds, but even though the great gates that once clanged shut and locked at sunset have been dismantled, the old asylum, despite a change of name, has never become an ordinary part of the community. The local populace still fear to go there; it is still a shameful thing to be one of its patients, however briefly; and the staff that work there are thought to be at least a little odd.

Every so often one of these hospitals is in the news – a report of a scandal, some alleged cruelty or negligence – and for a day or two the papers carry pictures of the blank walls, the narrow windows of this unfriendly edifice, and an editorial demanding reform. Every so often a sociologist or one of the multifarious band of psychotherapists gains the attention of the media to expound his views on the sins and inadequacies of what is called 'traditional psychiatry', and once again the consultant psychiatrists of the psychiatric hospitals suffer public criticism. Not all criticism is made public. Various committees, investigating various matters, descend on the hospital. They deplore the buildings, they commend the diligence of the staff, but their questions imply the criticism which becomes quite plain in the report which follows. But when the newspapers have found some other eye-catching scandal, when the sociologist starts another book or the psychotherapist a new therapy, when the committee of inquiry has gathered its papers and departed, the consultant psychiatrist is left, still with the same collection of inhospitable wards, the same demanding old women, the bizarre, posturing old men, the frightened, the inadequate, the flotsam and jetsam of all the sorrows of this world, and it is his responsibility to look after them. Like Housman's mercenaries, 'What God abandoned, these defended', but, unlike Housman's mercenaries, he works, not just for pay, but out of an inarticulate love, or at least concern, for his patients.

Each consultant leads a team composed of junior doctors, nurses, a social worker or two, and perhaps a psychologist. The consultant may enjoy the satisfaction of leading a group of people who work together with enthusiasm and in harmony and he may share the camaraderie of a group of people who see themselves as belonging together, but the consultant, while defining his own role as the person with ultimate responsibility and authority, may define the roles of the other team members in ways which emphasise his separateness from them. Junior doctors, however able, must endure the discipline of the medical profession and be respectful to their seniors. Social workers cannot be entirely trusted since they have allegiances outside the team, while psychologists are dangerously idiosyncratic people who read books critical of psychiatry. The doctor may feel closest to the nurses, but in the hospital hierarchy nurses are inferior people who are capable of only limited responsibility. Of course, they are not as inferior as patients, but then patients are a race that must be kept apart. It was for my own safety that a nurse in a select clinic snatched a clean and shiny glass from my hand with the cry, 'You can't drink out of that. It's a patient's glass.'

There is always the possibility that the consultant may find himself a lonely leader. Support, then, can come from his colleagues. In a psychiatric hospital consultants may fight quite bitterly among themselves, but, once they are attacked by someone who is not a psychiatrist, they react like individual balls of mercury that suddenly roll together and form one globule which, while glinting metallically, quakes and quivers to itself. It is rare for one consultant to be expelled from the group, but when a consultant suspects that, behind a well-mannered façade, his colleagues are colluding to banish him he feels the chill of Siberia.

Support, too, can come from the consultant's family, but

some families have paid a high price for his consultancy. During the children's school years, when even the happiest of marriages can feel a strain, he was a junior doctor, absorbed in examinations and the responsibilities of his work. So his children may have grown up as strangers to him, perhaps with problems of their own, and between him and his wife there may be a gulf that seems to him to allow no bridge.

Thus it is that some consultants who have accepted the precepts and standards of their profession and have worked hard and responsibly find themselves increasingly alone. Some become exceedingly bitter or autocratic, some join the ranks of the great English eccentrics, some seek release in suicide or a slower death by alcohol. Siegfried was one of these. 'If I don't drink', he said, 'I can't get to sleep.' And if one cannot sleep, one cannot work.

We talked a lot about work. One day I asked him why he had decided to become a psychiatrist.

'I'd rather wanted to do general medicine', he said, 'but I didn't do a great deal of work as a student – I was the typical, average, brutal, licentious medical student. I loved charging round the rugby field on a Saturday afternoon and drinking lots of beer afterwards. I didn't get the house jobs, so I looked round for something I thought I'd quite like and in which I could get a consultant job, so it was psychiatry. I think, too, that I had my eyes set on being the boss of whatever I do. People become consultants because they want to be in command. Over the last week I've been giving some thought to that. Why does it matter so much?'

'Why do you want to be in charge?' I asked.

'Conceit again. I think I'm the most likely to get it right. That's a revolting thing to say.'

'I'm asking you for truthful things, not just what sounds nice. This is how you see yourself.'

'I can get people to work for me', he admitted, 'and they accept my decisions. If I went straight back to work from here I'd be the same. I'd be the boss in my department. I don't know any other way of working.'

But boss or not, Siegfried did not enjoy his work. 'I was going to say there aren't many things that I can't tackle, but

I can easily prove myself wrong. But I'm bored. Nothing exciting happens. I'd like to have something to take charge of, to get my teeth into. Boredom and tedium in day-to-day work. Most of which I know will come to nothing.'

'And so for a long time you've known you've been in a job that doesn't extend you, but if you say that to your friends, relatives, colleagues, then this will sound very conceited.'

'And they would say, rightly, "You're fifty-four, you've left it too late." '

Siegfried was not making an empty boast when he said that he found his work did not extend him. His drinking may have affected his liver, but his intellectual powers were unimpaired. The intelligence tests he did in hospital showed him to be of very superior intelligence. Rarely in his life had he been fully extended, and so he knew that 'if I were given a job to do which would really take something out of me I'd come to life again'.

When we are children we discover within ourselves talents, powers, that we know are truly an essential part of ourselves and, being so, can become the source of the greatest meaning we can find in life. We feel impelled to explore our world through our powers, but most of us are stopped from doing this. Poverty, rigid education, the demands that we fill certain roles in society block us so that sometimes we have to forget the possibilities we once glimpsed, or, not forgetting, suffer punishment like the servant in the parable who buried his talent. When, so Jesus said, his lord discovered this, he commanded that the servant be cast 'into outer darkness: there shall be weeping and gnashing of teeth'. The gap between what we know we could have achieved and what we have achieved is usually filled with much weeping and gnashing of teeth.

When Siegfried said, 'I'm not the person I could have been', I asked him what he would have liked to have been.

'Sounds childish – I'd like to have had command of my ship for longer – I was in command for only one week.' (Siegfried had previously served in the Navy.)

The sea and ships meant a great deal to him, but he had chosen to work in a city many miles from the sea, and he saw no opportunity now of developing a life which related to the sea. Instead he worried about whether he should return to his old job. If he did not, 'Would I be the little boy who ran away? We all adopt our persona, don't we? I've adopted the wrong one.'

'It sounds like very early on you've given a rule to yourself, "Never run away from a dangerous situation: always go towards it." '

'Yes. Childish pleasures, very childish in a way. I remember reading on my flimsy when I came out of the Service, "Reliable in action". I enjoyed that. Didn't matter. If I hadn't been, someone behind me would have made sure I was.'

'Why is it important not to run away?'

'That's an extremely difficult question, isn't it? Training to some extent. My formative ages were, I suppose, eighteen to twenty-five. The training I had was that you did what you were told and you did your job. No one said thank you if you did your job, but they said what the bloody hell if you didn't.'

'So it's important to do your job because if you don't people get angry with you, say "What the bloody hell".'

'Less now because by and large I could get away with murder if I wanted to, I could do as little as I care to.'

'So it's yourself that says "What the bloody hell".'

'These habits, they're ingrained.'

'But if you've got this kind of choice, of doing a job well or doing it badly, facing up to difficulties or not facing up to difficulties, what you're saying is that if you face up to difficulties, you're not getting any praise for it, but if you don't face up to difficulties, people get angry with you, and the people are the people inside yourself. What would happen if neither you nor other people thought well of you?'

'The bottle, I think.'

'But the bottle is an escape. What would happen to you?'

'Mm, the most awful things that can happen to anyone. The loss of respect of one's family, one's friends. A man I know, and tried to treat once, the managing director of quite a big firm, and he wasn't a big enough man for the job, and he's more or less in the gutter. That would frighten me.'

'So, amongst your friends who've given you all this advice, the ones who say, "Don't try so hard, take things easy, you set too high standards for yourself, you ought to relax more, you're getting older now, you can't expect to do what you've done in the past", all this kind of advice, while being said with the best of intentions, comes over to you as something extremely frightening because carrying it out would mean becoming the kind of person you've always dreaded being, because if you became that kind of person, you would be the kind of person who had no respect, completely lost.'

'Yes – but one has to be realistic. It didn't break my heart when I found I couldn't run round a rugby field any more.'

'What does break your heart?'

'I haven't achieved very much.'

But Siegfried had difficulty in acknowledging what he had achieved. As he said one day, 'It's going to take me a while to forgive myself, because I'm almost liking it in here. Several of my staff, junior doctors, nurses, have been here to see me. I think it's quite ridiculous. "Dr Maximillien has gone away because he was overworked and depressed." When I go back they'll have to take me as they find me.'

'How do you think they feel about you now?'

'Well, how does a man say this? They think I'm pretty good.'

'You feel they don't think any the less of you because you're in here.'

'No.'

'But you think less of yourself?'

'Yes – what a peculiar thing to say, "They think I'm pretty good".'

'That's not a peculiar thing to say. Why do you think it's peculiar?'

'Oh, the sort of thing one thinks, doesn't say.'

'Why not?'

'Our culture, I suppose. A man doesn't boast. "Think nothing of it, old boy." '

'Why is it important not to boast?'

'I don't know. I don't like to hear someone boasting. I think it's in bad taste. Breach of ordinary good manners.'

'From what you say it sounds like "If I say anything good about myself I'm boasting." '

'Mm, well, there's a reverse kind of boasting I enjoy enormously.'

'What, saying bad things about yourself?'

'In a sense. In my last year at school we had a remarkable science section in Sixth Form and one or two inspired masters. There were four of us and I'm the only one without a Ph.D., but I'm making more money than the others.' He laughed. 'That is a permissible form of boasting because I think there's some element of humour, and if humour comes into it, then almost anything can be justified, can't it?'

'We use humour to say something we don't dare say straight. But it sounds like you've got rules about never saying anything good about yourself. That there's something dangerous about saying something good about yourself.'

'Yes. Well, isn't it a fact saying something good about oneself, to be honest, you have to say some bad things too.'

'To balance up the picture?'

'Yes, and not becoming the most terrible bore.'

'If you only said good things about yourself you'd become a bore. What would people think of you?'

'Go back to being a little boy who has a good opinion of himself – prove he's as good as he thinks he is.'

'So, if you say good things about yourself, you're setting standards, competitions, that you don't have to live up to –'

'That you *do* have to live up to', he corrected me.

So, to say something good about oneself was not to make a statement about some fact of life, but to create an area of doubt, of contest. Prove yourself, or for your sin of hubris the gods will strike you down. Feel guilty about not achieving and frightened when you do.

Siegfried saw his family as being very disappointed in him. 'I'm a miserable old devil most of the time. When I've drunk half a bottle of gin I go to sleep in an armchair. We don't talk much.'

'How much are you able to tell your children you love them?'

'Not much. I find that embarrassing.'

'If you're embarrassed about telling your children that you love them, then perhaps they're embarrassed about telling you.'

'Yes, yes, we're an undemonstrative family. It's inherited from generation to generation, isn't it?'

'It's learned. You can't claim genes for that.'

'Habit.' He put out his cigarette and said, 'I'm taking up a lot of your time.'

I went on to talk about how in some families people are prepared to show anger but not love. He responded with an anecdote which had nothing to do with what I had said and concluded his story with, 'Are we going to meet again?'

'You're wanting to stop now?'

'I think I'm taking up too much of your time.'

'There's no rush. You got anxious the moment we started talking about affection.'

'I don't think I was getting anxious talking about affection. I was, quite honestly, thinking of your time. I am frightened of affection. Over the course of many years I had a lot of girlfriends and got frightened off when they started getting affectionate. Rather a dirty trick, really. When I was quite a small child, and I had a fairly horrific childhood, I've always been rather concerned about the possibility of being emotionally dependent on anyone.'

'What would happen if you became emotionally dependent on anyone?'

'On previous form, I'd tend to back out.'

'But what would happen if you didn't back out? What do you feel would happen if you became dependent on anyone?'

'I'd assume I'd get hurt.'

'The person would turn on you and be angry with you, or would the person go away, rejecting you?'

'Rejection, non-concern, letting one down, unreliable in crises. I think my brothers had the same experience to some extent. The three of us were closely knit. I suppose in a funny sort of way our parents might have been fond of us, but we got nothing from them except a lot of misery and a lot of fright. It's a hell of a long, involved story.'

'But the trouble is that when a child has had that kind of experience which leads him to draw the conclusion to make the rule, "Never love anybody completely and so save yourself from getting hurt", when a child makes up that rule in childhood, it can, at the time, be a sensible rule to make, but when you make up that rule and continue it for the rest of your life, then it becomes quite a bad rule. This is the problem. In childhood we learn a lot of rules which continue to be true throughout life, "Fire burns", "Don't run on busy roads", and then we learn other rules, or we see the necessity of other rules in relationships, and then when we get older, we don't always review these rules and see whether they still apply.'

'There's the simile or metaphor, if you get your hand burnt, put your hand in a handful of tar, but if you get hurt emotionally, there's nothing to slap on to that.'

'But you can build up your own little wall, defensive wall, against getting hurt again.'

'Well, it can be a fairly good wall.'

'As you get older you don't realise that loving and being loved is a reciprocal relationship, and if you don't let any love out, you don't let any love in. The less love you let in, the more you wither, grow cold at the centre.'

'That's when I get back to Beethoven, Mozart, Bach, and Wagner. I just sit and listen to them. It's all very obvious, isn't it? But it doesn't help a great deal. The sad thought intrudes from time to time – "Does it all matter" – if I've cocked up my job, if I've failed in my capacity to make relationships.'

One day Siegfried asked me, 'Have you ever been in love?', and, having ascertained that I knew what he was talking about, went on to say, 'I was in love once. It was a marvellous experience – a real killer, isn't it? But even on that first glorious occasion, there are still limits, aren't there? Making love to someone whom one loves – human contact, the emotion is really very beautiful. But there are still limits. It's always a sad business, isn't it?'

'You're looking to me for confirmation of all this –'

'Yes.'

'Some people have different experiences.'

'Not many.'

'Would you say that all love comes to an end?'

'This first sort of mad happiness comes to an end, and in all probability that particular love affair comes to an end. There are other things which are never quite the same which can be very pleasant – respect, affection, regard. Even things like ordinary good manners. All quite important. Not the same as love's young dream.'

'No.'

'And I had the misfortune to be at sea when I got my Dear John letter too. Bad luck – bloody guardsman, the bastard.'

'And that was the only time you've been in love?'

'In that sense, yes. It was around that time of my life, I think, as far as one can, never to be very, very firmly committed to anyone again.'

'You decided never to be committed –'

'Yes. I think it was a fairly cold-blooded decision. It was reinforced a bit, one of my brothers was killed, and, not surprisingly, my parents took this pretty hard. At the time there was a lot of people dying, anyway, many of my friends, and just after the war my other brother went to New Zealand, not to be seen for many years again. My mother was terribly upset. We went down to see him off and I was puzzled by this, my mother's distress. If someone went back off leave, maybe one would see him again, maybe not. I remember that feeling very distinctly. Not a very healthy one. But a boy in his early twenties makes these sort of firm decisions, doesn't he?'

'You must have been meeting lots of other people you could have loved.'

'I met a lot of people. Made some very good friends. Most of them were male friends – apart from my wife. Most of us were ex-service people, and extremely good friends. If something went wrong, you could count on them.'

At our next meeting Siegfried said, 'I told you something last week that I've never told anyone before. I don't know why I bothered. About having been in love. It was quite ridiculous: I was eighteen and she was twenty-six. I was naive to the point of thinking that going to bed with a girl was as marvellous as it was improper. It's something that does stay with one. Pity I wasn't twenty-six. Would you like a cup of tea?'

Siegfried always referred to his wife in a way which reflected considerable fondness and respect, and I wondered how much he underestimated her affection for him. One day I said to him, 'I've got the impression from what you've said about your wife and children that you see them as not disliking you, but being disappointed in you. There's that sort of gap. When we feel that someone is disappointed in us, we don't feel that we can communicate with that person easily.'

'I think that went sour, and my wife thinks so too, when she had a puerperal depression with the first baby. I had difficulties, too, in that respect. Coming from being a care-free medical student, suddenly a married man with a small child. My wife got very depressed after the first baby. Dealing with someone who is depressed is jolly hard. And there was a chilliness over the years. I thought on a number of occasions of packing in my job and going back into the Services. When the kids were small they were gorgeous. I used to laugh a lot and play silly games at lunchtime with the children. But I got interested in playing hockey and squash and used to call at the hospital club most evenings and had a couple of pints on my way home. Used to rather hope that the children were in bed by the time I got home. It was rather chilly for a number of years.'

'Did you feel that your wife had rejected you?'

'Yes. I felt her sole concern was for the kids. We never went anywhere. We didn't make many friends. This gives an unfair picture of my wife who is really a very nice person.'

'Yes. But this is what happens in a lot of marriages. Things fall apart after the baby's born.'

'At the moment my wife and I are fonder of one another than we have been for a long time. Perhaps with the kids being more independent and she's got a job.'

Siegfried talked a lot about his friends in the Services and in medical school, but now he said, 'My GP described me as a loner. This is not basically so. I have become so over the past few years. I quite like my fellow beings if I can talk to them.'

'But there's not many you can talk to?'

'No. I've a friend, a professor of physics, who's finding the same thing. He and I used to have some good conversations; but those times are past.'

'When a person gets into a position of power that person often finds the position very isolated. Do you find that?'

'On the whole, no, but I've been very lucky. My colleagues in the hospital are as intelligent as I am – perhaps even more so – and we talk to one another quite a lot. One or two of them share my interest in words and in ideas and know far more about music and art than I do. We all have a similar grotesque sense of humour. If I had been there on my own over the past years, then I would have cracked, but we can talk to one another. Being on one's own in a job like that would be awful.'

'What about the other members of your team – the nurses and so forth?'

'Jolly hard to size up, isn't it? I think they quite like us and they believe us to be competent. They know if something goes wrong we'll carry the can.'

'But there's nothing in those relationships which is over and above what is a good working relationship?'

'No, I'm not going to bed with any of them. We're friends in different sorts of ways. It is possible to be friends with someone whose decision you overrule. In fact that hardly ever happens because they know how we run things and what we like to do. We're set in our ways.'

'The kind of picture that has built up in my mind about your life – where there's a well-defined pattern of relationships which are basically good relationships. There's no part in your pattern of relationships where you're under any threat or danger or feel yourself attacked, but they're relationships where you're at a bit of a distance.'

'Yes.'

'And sometimes the distance is created by the style of the relationship, like the relationships with your nursing staff, or –'

'This is in some ways a warmer one than the one at home, in some ways, I think.'

So Siegfried found his closest relationships within the hierarchical structure of the hospital. Siegfried remembered his years of war service as 'the happy times', and there are a lot of similarities between life in the Services and life – for a member of staff – in a big hospital. There is the clearly defined hierarchy which gives each person a specified amount of power and control and which limits the amount of responsibility each person has to take for his own life. In a psychiatric hospital there is the constant sense of battling with inadequate resources against huge forces which might recede but never vanish, which provoke sudden and often terrible crises, all in scenes revealing an amount of human pain and misery which is matched only by the utter ridiculousness and futility of human endeavour. The essential survival kit is a sense of humour, and the camaraderie, the gossip, the in-jokes can become more important than the danger and the pain.

To fit within a hierarchy with some measure of ease we have to be able to accept the basic tenets of that hierarchy. Never having been a member of the Armed Services, I had always thought that to be an officer was a fairly straightforward activity. However, Siegfried, who was still passionately interested in all things military, lent me several of the books he was reading on war history, and, from one, *The Face of Battle*, by John Keegan, I learnt that to be an army officer was to try to reconcile two disparate points of view, a reconciliation as difficult as the reconciliation of the two views which a doctor entering psychiatry has to try to achieve. John Keegan wrote:

> The student officer . . . is simultaneously undergoing two processes of education, each with a dissimilar object. The one . . . aims, if not to close his mind to unorthodox or difficult ideas, at least to stop it down to a fairly short focal length, to exclude from his field of vision everything that is irrelevant to his professional function and to define all that he ought to see in a highly formal manner . . . the other process of education the student officer undergoes is the normal 'academic' one, which aims to offer the student not a single but a variety of angles and vision; which asks him to adopt in his study of war the standpoint not only of an officer, but also of a private soldier, a non-combatant, a neutral observer, a casualty; or of a statesman, a civil servant, an industrialist, a diplomat, a relief worker, a professional pacifist – all valid, all documented points of view.[2]

The student psychiatrist similarly undergoes two processes of education. One is the formal training of a scientist which is concerned with simplifying complex situations, looks for single causes, follows the laws of contradiction and identity, and is based on the assumption of an objective reality which consists of repeating and discoverable patterns. The patterns which concern the scientific psychiatrist are those of the chemical and physiological changes which underlie and explain human behaviour. At the same time the student psychiatrist has to develop 'not a single but a variety of angles of vision'. He must become proficient in those vague and variable disciplines of psychology and sociology; he must grasp the complex ideas contained in psychoanalytic and existential theory; he must learn to explain behaviour, not by looking for a single cause, but by describing a complex, interrelated, changing, and idiosyncratic pattern. These contrasting modes of thought are often simplified to the debate over the contribution of nature and nurture to behaviour, whether a person's 'illness' can be explained by his genetic inheritance or his family life. In practice, psychiatrists tend to favour one view over the other, and Siegfried certainly followed the traditions of British psychiatry in seeing a genetic cause for schizophrenia and depression. He called the critic of those theories, R. D. Laing, 'that crazy Scot – I think it's vicious, that he should go around unloading a burden of guilt onto the shoulders of unfortunate schizophrenics and their parents, making them think that they're responsible for their child's schizophrenia.' He was equally firm that the cause of depression lay in the genes.

We can find good scientific evidence to support whichever view we prefer, but no amount of scientific evidence can protect us from the implications our search for causes has for our own lives. If we hold to the environmental view, we must then feel guilty when our lives and the lives of our children go wrong; but we can feel some hope that we can repair the fault. If we hold to the genetic view, then we do not need to shoulder a burden of guilt; but genetic faults allow no repair. Our genes can be our tragic flaw.

Alcohol is not only a wonderful way of avoiding your own depression, but also, if you drink enough, you can get other people to concentrate their attention on your drinking and so not do anything that will confront you with your depression. Siegfried had good reason not to acknowledge his depression. His family history showed that pattern which geneticists see as supporting their theories of the inheritance of depression, but Siegfried would say, 'I don't think the gene is in me', and remained loyal to that school of psychiatry which, while allowing for the importance of 'social factors', sees the cause and cure of mental illness in the metabolism of the body. Loyalty, obedience, and trust in leaders were very important to Siegfried, no less important in psychiatry than they were in the Navy. True, he was now at the head of the hierarchy, in a position to have his orders obeyed, but the leader in the hierarchy is as much a part of the system as the lowliest minion. The leader can express his individuality only up to a certain point; beyond that he must fit within the framework, the rules of the hierarchy. If the leader can manage to do this, then he can enjoy the delicious combination of the exercise of personal power within the comfort of a group. Siegfried was like very many people in striving to achieve this and, like many people in a hierarchy, he found that one of the great advantages of being in a hierarchy is that one does not have to relate to many, if any, people as equals, but only as subordinates and superiors. When we relate to another person as an equal that person is not in our control, and therefore may behave in ways which we cannot predict and which may in some way hurt us. The relationship of a superior and a subordinate, whether it be doctor and nurse, teacher and pupil, manager and apprentice, parent and child, is a limited relationship, with each member being able, within the rules of the relationship, to predict and control the other member (subordinates can control their superiors, as every experienced nurse knows). Such relationships allow intimacy without risk. But intimacy is not love, and love is a risky business.

When Siegfried and I were talking about love I challenged him on this. 'When you're in love you're not in control of your life, are you? You said something earlier about not wanting to be emotionally dependent on anyone, so that being in love, or loving someone enormously, you really put your life in that person's hands.'

'Yes.'

'All I'm noting is that your decision to become a consultant and your decision not to love deeply again, both of these decisions were based on the premise of "It's dangerous to put your life in other people's hands" or "For safety's sake I want to control my own life".'

Siegfried laughed wryly. 'Inside this husky tough there's a frightened little boy.'

To the adjectives 'frightened' and 'little' Siegfried could have added 'bad', but it was a badness that he was quite attached to. One day Siegfried was talking about a schoolmaster who had encouraged him to read. 'He was a kind and gentle man', he said, 'I envy him.'

'You don't see yourself as kind and gentle?'

'Only sometimes – and it soon vanishes.'

'Are you saying that this schoolmaster was kind and gentle right through, at his very centre, while your kindness and gentleness is just something on the surface?'

'Yes. He would never have threatened to shoot one of his men – and meant it. I did.' At first he looked as though he might feel guilty about this, but as he talked, it became clear that he took some pride in this aspect of his character.

People who are devoted to duty are not always kind, and Siegfried talked a lot about duty. I asked him if duty was an important concept in his life.

'Yes, enormously.'

'In what way?'

'If you accept obligations, you must honour them.'

'What would happen if you don't accept your obligations?'

'You'd dislike yourself even more than you normally would.'

'How much does a person normally dislike himself?'

'That's a good question. Do I know or do you know?'

'But you used it. You implied that normal people or people generally disliked themselves to a certain extent.'

'There are different degrees to which we accept this. Even psychopaths dislike themselves. That's why they kill themselves. They have a faint glimmering from time to time that they can't make normal relationships.'

'But what about people who don't dislike themselves?'

'The ones I know, or I think I know, are amongst the most dislikeable people one could meet.'

'So people who like themselves are disliked by others.'

'I'd put it differently. They don't have many likeable qualities.'

'What you're saying, and this links with what you said about boasting, you said that most people to some degree dislike themselves, and it's right to dislike yourself, because if you don't, you'd be the kind of person that other people don't like.'

'Yes, or more important, the person you don't like is yourself.'

'What you're saying is that for you to live with yourself, you've got to dislike yourself.'

'Got to find a few decencies here and there.'

'But to be able to like yourself you've got to dislike yourself. You've got to see within yourself dislikeable characteristics for you to be able to live with yourself, because if you started to see within yourself wholeness and goodness, see yourself as a good person, then you would be in danger.'

'Put myself on to lithium. Wouldn't you?'

'If I said to you, well, people like Carl Rogers say that all human beings are at centre good, and suppose I tried to follow the Rogerian approach, and got you to recognise within yourself your natural goodness, which was your real self, then that would be unacceptable to you.'

'I think it would. I think his basic thesis is untenable. We're born with very nasty instincts, aren't we? Aggression, fear, reproduction (I suppose the seeds are there), appetites which we're prepared to satisfy regardless of anyone else, these are the basic things we're born with.'

'And you see them as basically bad?'

'We learn to become nice people. We learn this happy gift, when we have it, by being able to give and receive affection.'

'This is something that comes later, through learning?'

'If we're lucky. And our genes colour this too. I don't think we can remove our genes from the total sort of person that we are. If we've inherited brown eyes, diabetes, tendency to dement, I don't see why we shouldn't inherit a basic kind of brain structure, a basic neurone pattern.'

'But what you're describing is a model of a human being as – a child comes into the world –'

'A complete savage.'

Later I said to him, 'There are some people in the world who feel that their value lies within themselves, that they are valuable people to some degree, and they place that value in their essence, their being, and then there are some people who believe that their value doesn't lie in what they are but what they do.'

'Are the two different? You do so because of the sort of person you are.'

'I was watching a programme on Paul Robeson the other night. When he got into his sixties, he started to develop arteriosclerosis and got depressed. His friends who were being interviewed for the programme, one of them was describing how, in the last ten years of his life, Robeson retired to his sister's home and saw nobody, and when his friends would say to him, "Look, you're such a figure in the movement, people just want to come and sit at your feet. They don't want you to do anything", he would say, "No, I won't have people do that. I can no longer do anything. I can't sing, I can't talk. Because I can no longer do anything, I'm of no value." And he wouldn't accept, even understand, that people would look at him and say, "There is a good man and we will gain something just from being in his presence. He doesn't have to do. He just has to be, and we're enriched just by his existence." Robeson couldn't see this at all. He was a man who placed value in what he did and when he could no longer do, he saw himself as valueless. You come across to me as being like that. That you place a lot of emphasis in what you do, and the way you describe yourself as being in essence not a good person, not valuable. You have certain qualities which you see as good; but if one of your friends or one of your patients said to you, "I benefit from being with you. You don't have to say anything or do anything, but just your goodness helps me", that would be something you would find very difficult to understand or accept.'

'Yes, to some extent, I think I see what you mean, but I think status, a doctor, a consultant, not anything particularly good about me.'

'You create a problem for yourself straight off by the way you define a human being. You define all human beings as carrying within themselves something bad, their instincts, and with that kind of definition, if that's how you see your-self, to be good is a constant struggle. You have the feeling that "The moment I relax, then this terrible badness inside me will get out of control." '

'I don' t think so now, because I think that at an early age I saw this badness, unpleasantness, nastier features, and by accident or by luck I disliked them. Difficult to change one's mind after fifty or sixty years, isn't it?'

'If you define yourself as being born bad, with bad instincts, and then you define life as the process of bringing these bad instincts under control and in some way working hard to counterbalance the badness in you, you've immediately defined life as a struggle, and then when you get to a stage where there's no more work for you to do, and you're also getting older and more tired, then you are in a terribly vul-nerable position because you start to see yourself in danger, that all this badness is going to become more apparent, less controllable. Whereas, if you start off with a definition that a human being is born good, "trailing clouds of glory", and that throughout life bad things can happen to a human being which fill his life with misery, but if at his centre he feels goodness, however this might have been got at by the passage of time, then when that person comes towards the end of his life, he's got something good at his centre which resides in him and in which he can reside, then it's possible for him to find some degree of peace and acceptance.'

'Do you find any evidence that human nature was born good?' There was scorn in his voice.

Death, he said, was the end and he did not fear it. What he did fear was what lay between then and now. I asked him how he would be remembered after he died.

'For perhaps for two generations, nothing else.'

'And what kind of memories will people have of you?'

'Pleasant chap, sense of humour, quite good at his job, drank too much.'

'How would you like to be remembered?'

'Mm – I don't know – it would be doing Shakespeare good now to think that here was the greatest poet of all time. What does one need? Nothing.'

'Some people would be quite happy to be remembered in

the way that you expect to be remembered. I was asking if you would like to be remembered in some way different from that, as a great poet.'

'Mm – loyal, I think, a friend one could rely on, basically, "I'm sorry the old devil's dead." '

'That people would regret that you'd died.'

'Yes.'

I asked him whether he believed in God.

'No.' He said this very quickly.

'Have you ever believed in God?'

'I'll tell you of a slightly emotional occasion I had when my uncle got the chop in the Air Force – a man I was really very fond of. He was the only chap I used to write to regularly. I was about twelve, I think. He was a marvellous man. He was very interested in books, and he used to write to me and tell me about books he thought I might like to read. He put me on to Jane Austen when I was twelve. I used to write reviews of the books I read. They must have been terribly bad reviews, but if he thought they were good reviews, he'd send me sixpence or a shilling. In those days that was really something. And then his aeroplane came down a bit too fast. And, up to that time, twelve, thirteen, I'd had some vague sort of concept of God – I sang in the church choir every Sunday. My last memories of any contact with God was that particular night when I called Him all the filthy language I knew.'

'So God was a person for you up till then?'

'Very vaguely. Even then I thought, if He exists, He's a shit.'

'And how do you feel about Him now?'

'If He exists, He's a shit. When that happened, I felt I'd been rather foolish and went through all the filthy language I knew. With regard to God this had been rather a waste of time. This was rather childish, but I felt a bit frightened after I'd said all these things. Thought perhaps I'm wrong. Perhaps I've made Him angry.'

'And that He'd punish you?'

'No, that He'd make it all different.'

'What did you think He'd do?'

'I'd get a telegram to say it was all a mistake and that the bloke hadn't got the chop after all.'

'That didn't happen?'

'No.'

'So getting angry with God didn't do any good?'

'I didn't expect much. One hangs onto straws.'

'And then what happened? Did you continue to go to church?'

'Yes, because we were fairly hard up and at the end of each four months I used to get my choir money. That was a large part of my income and I liked the music and I liked the Bible. One can still read the Bible with great pleasure, surely.'

We talked about the parts of the Bible that we liked and suddenly he said, 'I've got a Louis Armstrong record. Do you like Louis Armstrong?'

'Yes.'

'I thought you would. Louis and the Good Book – he sang a song about Nebuchadnezzar – God didn't approve of Nebuchadnezzar altogether, so He wrote something on the wall. I've forgotten the Jewish, "But Nebuchadnezzar, thou hast been weighed in the balances and found wanting", and Louis says, "Hey there". Having been weighed in the balances and found wanting by God, there isn't anything else that you can say, except "Hey there".'

We laughed and then I said, 'But that's how you feel about yourself – that you've been weighed in the balances and been found wanting.'

'It's not quite as bad as that. I'm a good deal more ordinary than I thought I was, and perhaps not even very exceptional.'

'Do you still feel that if there is a God, then God's a shit?'

'Oh, yes, He must be, yes.'

'Why?'

'He couldn't intentionally and with the ability to do something about it, run the world like this, surely.'

'I'm not arguing the point one way or the other. I'm just trying to see how you see it. Your feeling is that if there is a God, then He's a shit. He runs this world in a terrible way, does terrible things.'

'How can He tolerate man being so intolerable to man? What end can possibly be served by Auschwitz, the IRA, this wretched business we read about this morning? I could do better than this.'

He went on talking about the horrors of our contemporary world in a way which reflected how he saw God as betraying his trust, and I was reminded of Mark Twain's tirade against God:

> We brazenly call our God the source of mercy, while we are aware all the time that there is not an authentic instance in history of His having exercised that virtue. We call Him the source of morals, while we know by His history and by His daily conduct as perceived by our senses that He is totally destitute of anything resembling morals. We call Him Father, and not in derision, although we would detest and denounce any earthly father who should inflict upon his child a thousandth part of the pains and miseries and cruelties which our God deals out to His children every day, and has dealt out to them daily during the centuries since the crime of creating Adam was committed.[3]

Siegfried doubted that I really understood the nature of life. One day, when he was telling me about the other patients on the ward, he said, 'A lot of them suffer from your basic defect.'

'What's that?'

'Optimism.'

'Why do you regard that as a defect?'

'Because you're liable to be disappointed.'

'So it's better to expect the worst and that way you're not disappointed so often.'

'When I climb out of bed thinking, "Oh God", and then something marvellous happens on that day, then I think, "My God, what a marvellous day!" '

'Have you always felt that it's best not to expect good things to happen?'

'Yes.'

'As a general rule of life?'

'Yes.'

'So if you balance it out, if you expect good things to happen, then you get disappointed, so you have that pain; whereas if you don't expect good things to happen and you go along feeling a sort of low-level misery, thinking that everything is going to happen for the worst, and then something good happens, you get this wonderful feeling; but if nothing good happens, you're still on this sort of low level of misery, and a low level of misery is better than the sudden pain of disappointment.'

'Yes, of course.'

When we were talking about love I asked him, 'Are you sorry now that you did not fall in love again?'

'Well, yes. God, isn't it frightening?'

'Why is it frightening?'

'It hurts – I was telling you what a brave man I was, I don't get frightened. My God, I'd be frightened of that. Can happen only once, I think. That first time of overpowering emotion, all the buts and fears that life imposes, one wonders what goes wrong. Like nothing can be too good. You'll trip over something soon, mate.'

'You feel that when life is good, something bad is sure to happen?'

'Yes.'

'Why should it?'

'I don't think I can answer that question. It seems to be a fairly popular habit.'

'You feel this is a fair description of the way the world is?'

'Yes.'

'But if you live in a world, your world, where you see people, including yourself, in essence, right at centre, being in some way dangerous and bad, and in a world where the probability of the way in which things will turn out is more likely to be bad than good, and you see yourself as unable, unwilling to have a close relationship with anybody, and you see the end of life as the end for yourself, and if there is a God, then He's a shit – if you define your world on those parameters, you haven't left a great deal of space for joy and hope have you?'

'No. So I'm back to Beethoven, Bach, Leonardo, Shakespeare, and the Bible.'

'Are they your sources of – what?'

'Beauty – truth.'

'Why is beauty important?'

'It's just there. It exists, to be looked at again and again. Or listened to, again and again.'

We talked about beauty and I tried to relate this to how he saw the human race. 'If you operate with a model of the human being as being essentially evil, then you've got a model which makes it impossible for you to become reconciled with yourself. Freud's model of the human being was the same as yours. In his life he showed great personal bravery, but he saw the human race as damned.'

'I don't think I go along with the idea of the human race being basically damned. Surely Shakespeare taught us this – the essence of tragedy is that a man of decent qualities destroys himself by having a failing in one or two small respects. Macbeth was a superb character, but he destroyed himself, didn't he?'

Siegfried saw the idea of tragedy applying 'to quite a large extent' to his life. He held to the tragic, not the romantic, vision of life, as George Steiner has described it:

In authentic tragedy, the gates of hell stand open and damnation is real. The tragic personage cannot avoid responsibility. To argue that Oedipus should have been excused on the grounds of ignorance, or that Phedre was merely a prey to hereditary chaos of the blood, is to diminish to absurdity the weight and meaning of the tragic action. The redeeming insight comes too late to mend the ruins or is purchased at the price of irremediable suffering ... Where the tragic conception of life is in force, moreover, there can be no recourse to secular or material remedies. The destiny of Lear cannot be resolved by the establishment of adequate homes for the aged ... In tragedy, the twist of the net which brings down the hero may be an accident or hazard of circumstance, but the mesh is woven into the heart of life. Tragedy would have us know that there is in the very fact of human existence a provocation or paradox; it tells us that the purposes of men sometimes run against the grain of inexplicable and destructive forces that lie 'outside' yet very close. To ask the gods why Oedipus should have been chosen in his agony or why Macbeth should have met the witches on his path is to ask for reason and justification from the voiceless night. There is no answer ... And beyond the

tragic, there lies no 'happy ending' in some other
dimension of time and place. The wounds are not healed
and the broken spirit mended. In the norm of tragedy,
there can be no compensation.[4]

Siegfried would allow himself no compensation. He told me
about 'a special envoy sent to see me from the States. This
chap – something of an evangelist – came all the way here to
see me and said, "I want you to fly back to the States with me
now. I'll put you inside for a month. I'll get this cleared up."
Well, bloody hell. He's a nice man, but I can't join a bunch
of evangelists.' To me he used the standard criticism of traditional psychiatrists, 'Your kind of psychotherapy takes far
too much time. It's not on', and when I persisted he com-
plained, 'I think you're doing a terrible thing. You're starting
to make me think again.' He used many diversionary tactics
to stop this happening and warned me, 'I think you do a lot
of good to a lot of people, but aren't you perhaps in danger of
infecting them with your optimism?'

I persisted with my foolish optimism. 'I think that human
beings are neither good nor bad but simply are. Attributes of
good or bad are the opinions that we hold. The universe just
is. Goodness and badness is something we create, our own
ideas.'

'Can I suggest a more fanciful compromise? There is a God
and He's given us a thread of cotton by which we can haul
ourselves up there, if we don't strain too hard and if we don't
break it.'

'How's your thread of cotton holding out at the moment?'

'Pretty tatty. It hasn't broken, I think, but there's a knot
in it.'

'What sort of knot?'

'It's a granny knot, and they come undone.'

Mollie

Do people who cope with life have philosophies which give
them courage, hope, and optimism? To find an answer to this
question I would need to have known these people for some
time to be able to be certain that they did cope with their

lives. Many people present a good front to the world while at the same time leading lives of 'quiet desperation', or supporting themselves by an addiction, or maintaining their own integrity at the expense of their family and friends. Who were the people I knew who, in the face of life's difficulties, coped? The first person I thought of was my friend Mollie.

Mollie was a social worker and I had met her through our work. We soon became friends, and I often visited her home and got to know Bill, her husband, and their children. They seemed to me to be a close, happy family, a family who laughed a lot. This did not surprise me. One of Mollie's clients, a bedridden old woman, described Mollie as 'coming into my house like a ray of sunshine', and this phrase, sentimental though it sounds, did describe Mollie exactly. I knew that this was not a mere professional cheerfulness. I had seen Mollie, at home and at work, in situations which would have irritated me enormously but in which she would simply laugh, brush aside the provocation to anger, and pursue the right and proper course of action. Her life was far from easy, but she looked on each problem as a challenge to be met with courage and mastery. When Bill took a promotion in his firm and they moved away to another city I knew that Mollie would be greatly missed by her friends and colleagues. She and I kept in touch by letter and phone and the occasional visit, but as usually happens in such friendships, time has the habit of rushing by and months elapsed between contacts. I knew that she had been ill at Christmas time, and we had talked on the phone after she left hospital, but summer went by without us being in touch. As autumn approached I thought I would write to her to bring her up to date with my family news and to ask her if I could come for a visit and interview her for my book. She telephoned me the day she got my letter. 'I've been thinking about you', she said, 'I've been wanting to phone you but I know you're busy. I'd like to talk to you. Dorothy, Bill's left me.'

I was so astounded all I could say was 'You're joking.' But she was not. Bill had packed his bags and gone. So I went to visit Mollie. We talked a lot, walking beside the river, over the kitchen table, in the sitting room late at night. Mollie insisted that she should fulfil my request and talk into my tape-recorder about her philosophy of life. I was glad that she did this because what she said showed that the advice I had come armed with to give her, advice along the lines 'Men are bastards. Take him for every penny he's got', was for her quite irrelevant.

What I discovered straight away was that Mollie was not angry with Bill. She was hurt, bewildered, and very sad, but not angry. In the painful days of the break-up she had got angry with him once, and of this she was very ashamed. The problem that occupied her mind was what had she done wrong, how had she failed to meet Bill's needs, had he needs which she had failed to perceive, much less meet.

In the conversations we had had over the years, the concept of meeting another person's needs figured often in what Mollie said. So the first question I asked her in our recorded talk was 'Why is it important to be needed?'

Mollie replied, 'I suppose I don't really feel I'm a complete person unless I'm needed. I've got this need inside me that I've got to have somebody to care about. I find this very difficult at the moment with the children being at the age they are, and they don't – they're ready, nearly, to make their own lives – and I'm suddenly going to find myself without having anybody to do things for. I feel as though, one's always had a purpose in life, and my purpose has been my family and my work, but my family being always foremost. To me, family life is extremely important. I suppose in time it will take on a different meaning, if the children marry and have a family, and then probably I'll start feeling needed again because the role becomes different. You become a grandparent and you're needed because you're a grandparent. But I feel that at this particular stage in my life the role of a parent – apart from providing a home – my role as a parent is probably over.'

'When you say that needing people makes you complete, what would happen to you if circumstances were such that there was nobody in the world that you felt needed you?'

'I think that me being me, I would probably, in that sort of situation, go out and try and find some way of providing – well, for instance, when I first came to live here I felt that I needed to do something – with the children at school and Bill at work – I needed to do something that was giving me some sort of satisfaction, and so I helped people with agoraphobia, and I think that if I had no one at all I would find some particular group where I could try and find a niche; and try and fit into it and help people who were not quite as well off – not money-wise, but not well off in being able to cope. I think this is where I would probably channel – well, not my affections – to satisfy my own needs, really – to feel that I was doing something useful, really.'

'Why is it important to do something that is useful?'

Mollie thought about this. 'I think that if I don't do something that's useful, if I didn't do my job, I'd just find that sitting at home, just doing housework, doing the sort of normal chores that women do – they have to be done, it's mundane, you have to do them, it's expected of you as a female that you look after the house and see that things are clean – but I do feel it's – I like to feel that I'm helpful to somebody, to be of use in some way, to feel that I'm giving something to somebody, and I think that that would probably give me some satisfaction in myself, make me feel better.'

'Is it the most important thing in life to give to someone else?'

'Yes. I feel that I have this need to give and to be needed to give.'

'What would happen if – suppose you ended up as a patient on a chronic ward with multiple sclerosis, how would you feel about yourself then?'

'I think at first I would probably feel like a lot of people feel – "Why has this happened to me?" But I would hope that I would be able to overcome this and be able to – well, you would, in that sort of situation, identify with your fellow patients and probably be able to gain strength from each other. I would expect that this would happen on that sort of ward. You would be able to help each other, support each other, really you're all in that ward knowing that your days are really numbered. You would all know that you were all there for a certain length of time, and I would be able to contribute something to the other people that were there and not become too engrossed with myself. And probably seek support. I think I found it when I was in hospital earlier this year. One tends, when you're in that situation, to be suddenly thrown into a group where you all feel that you're in it together, and you're all facing an operation or not knowing what the diagnosis is going to be, and you do tend to support each other. You do tend to have this feeling, well, you need each other at that particular time, even though you've never known each other before you walked through the hospital door.'

(Later I pressed Mollie more on this question of what would happen to her if she was completely alone. 'That would be terrible', she said, 'I would crack up.' Horrible though this fate might seem to her, Mollie was not one of those people who believe that their very identity would dissolve were they removed from the gaze of other people. In another context, speaking of her work, she said, 'I'm not just Bill's shadow. I'm not one of those women who only exist as their husband's wife.')

I used Mollie's mention of death to ask her what death meant to her.

'It's not something I've really thought about', she said. 'The only time I've thought about it was when I was very poorly and I thought that it might have come when I was in hospital this time. My general reaction was "Well, I don't suppose anybody would really miss me." Was it going to make them feel "Oh dear" – and had I made them feel that – I don't know, it's difficult to say, but there were times when I felt so very, very ill that I really thought I was at death's door – but I can't really put into words how I saw it or how I really felt, apart from thinking "I wonder if they'll really miss me if anything happens to me now?" '

'Did you hope that they would miss you?'

'Yes. I hoped that I had made some impression on them, that they would miss me.'

'You wanted them to go on remembering you?' (This reminded me of Mary, about whom I had written in *Choosing Not Losing*,[5] who did not want her family to remember her after her death since this would upset them, and upsetting people was the thing that Mary feared most. But, of course, if they did not remember her, it would be as if she had never lived.)

'I felt that I'd want them to think I'd contributed something.'

'To what?'

'Well, particularly with my own family, I'd have hoped that they thought I'd contributed something, and they'd remember me with affection.'

'There would still be love coming towards you even though –'

'I was dead, yes. I can remember feeling very much alone at that time, lying in hospital, relying very much on my fellow patients for support and hoping. Because you do feel terrifically isolated, and when you go into hospital – I think this is a fear that a lot of people have – are you going to come out again, and the longing that you have, you begin to think that you are never going to see your own home again.'

'So, when you think about death, you think that when people go on loving you, you sort of go on existing.'

'No, not go on existing, I suppose you hope that you've made enough mark in your life that people will think of you, and think, "Oh well, I remember her because of this –" or "I miss me mum – no one makes a coleslaw quite like her" – or things like that.'

'Do you believe in life after death.'

'I think there are some spirits after death. I do feel that.'

'In what way?'

'I can't say in exactly what way except that I have had a sitting with a spiritualist who told me that my father was always watching over me and I do believe that this probably happens. I do believe that there are people who probably give us strength, because very often when you face a crisis in your life, I think it's often been said that you get strength from somewhere to face up to it. I think when my father died I coped reasonably well. I was the one that did the catering after the funeral, even though I was one of the main mourners, and I felt that, I don't know, you feel as though you're given something – in certain situations one is given strength from somewhere, whether it is some sort of spirit that gives you this, I don't know, but I think that it could be.'

'Do you feel that your father is watching over you now?'

'I think that probably he is, yes, I think he is.'

'What does he think of it all?'

'That I can't answer. Can't really say. But knowing my father as I knew him, I don't know how he is now, but as I knew him, I would think that he would be supporting everything I would be doing.'

'So that in some way he's giving you strength now?'

'Yes.'

'He's on your side?'

'Yes.'

'That's a nice thing to know. Earlier this evening when you were saying you're not getting much help from your kids I was thinking that, apart from your friends, you're not getting a lot of support, but you're getting more support than I was aware of.'

'I think – I don't know, I can't say for sure this is happening, but I do feel that my father would be there, saying, "I'll stand beside you, no matter what you did." Yes.'

'Do you feel that when you die, you will still be available for people who need you?'

'I would hope I would be. I would hope I would be of some use. Once again, it's something very mystifying because we don't really know what happens, but I feel I'd like to feel that I was being of some help in this way – as giving my family, and friends, the help, the strength they needed.'

'So you see it in terms of being in some way connected with this world? Not in terms of going to heaven?'

'I find that difficult to answer. I think that everybody has a spirit. I can't answer that – I can't get in tune with that.'

'I asked you that because I was going to ask you about your religious beliefs. I've got the impression, from other conversations that we've had, that you believe in God.'

'Yes, I do.'

'How would you describe God?'

'I can't describe Him, really. I think He's up there, and that very often, rightly or wrongly, one sort of says, you need some help, and one expresses one's thoughts to God and you ask for help. I think an instance of what happened to me last Sunday was interesting because when Bill came in the morning to take the children out – he didn't come into the house – he just said, "I'm taking the children", and I was standing feeling very hurt, very injured, and he drove off, and I felt so very, very sad, and I sat down and I said, "Please, please, God, make him come back and show that he cares a bit", and I said this half a dozen times, and at twelve o'clock he drove back and he came in the house and he said, "I'll ring the insurance company about the car. You'd better sit down, you look a bit pale." He got the insurance papers and then he went off again, and I just felt as though I'd asked for this and it had been – He's answered, and I just couldn't believe it because that Sunday I felt everything was against me, that I was losing out, that everything was going right for Bill and nothing was going right for me. Most peculiar that.'

'You felt that was an adequate answer to your prayer? You didn't think that God should have made him come in and say "Mollie, please, take me back"?'

'Well, at that stage, no, that wasn't what I was asking. I just wanted him to show that he had some concern for us at that time. That was my main thought, that he'd been so cold and aloof, that if only there was just one glimmer of light to show that he had some caring in him which I thought he had lost completely.'

'So you weren't asking for a lot.'

'No. For I felt when he drove away first that he was so cold and aloof – he was going and I was left, and I thought, "Well, that just proves he doesn't care two hoots." He's gone.'

'When you describe God as someone you can turn to for help, and when you describe yourself, you say you want to be a person who can help – it sounds that the terms by which you describe the most important part of yourself are the terms by which you describe the most important part of God. Do you see God as being entirely good?'

'No, not always. Because one cannot always come to terms with the things which happen. Therefore you don't always accept that. No, I don't think God is entirely good because you can't always justify why things happen. Many's the time when you go out to visit clients and you look at them and you think "Goodness, fancy that happening. How tragic. Is there a God?" '

'How do you answer that?'

'Well, the only way I can answer that is by saying like I say sometimes about myself, "I wonder what I've done to deserve what's happening to me" – because I've tried to – one of the things I've always tried to live by, it sounds a bit silly, but I try to do unto others as I wish to be done by – and I wouldn't go out of my way to hurt anybody deliberately, and I've always been like this. I think this is one thing that I've always felt – that I – it's just one of my moral codes – I wish to do unto others as I wish to be done by, and yet there are times when one has to face up to certain things, particularly in the sort of job we're doing – when I've had to take someone's children into care and I've thought, "Gosh, what would I have felt like if somebody had come and done that to me?" What torment would I have gone through and how I would have hated that person for doing that. But in my everyday life I would try, I think I do try, to understand and care for people. But I don't know. What's that saying, you can't be all things to all men.'

'But, when things go wrong for you, you look into yourself and say "What have I done wrong?" '

'Yes. This is bad, I realise that, but I do. I sort of say to myself, "I must have done something awful." The times I've said that over the last few weeks. What have I done?'

'You don't feel that this is random bad luck?'

'Well, I suppose not because of Bill's attitude. I don't feel he was having such a bad life that he had to turn against me, so therefore it must be something, I feel, that I've done to make him resent me so much, and hate me, not want to know me. Because I can't live with unhappiness, with aggro. If I have chastised the children I've always had to go to them before they've gone to sleep to tell them that I love them, but they had to be told they were naughty.'

'Do you tell them you love them so that they will go on loving you?'

'Oh, no, no. I just want them to know that I love them, even though I've had to be cross with them. They've got to learn that there's right and there's wrong. And so therefore I find it difficult that somebody – like Bill's turned against me – I find it difficult to accept.'

'When you became ill, did you see that as something that was a message that you were doing something wrong or was that just bad luck?'

'Well, no, I never looked at it in that way at all. It just happened and it was something that I had to go through with – something's gone wrong and it's got to be put right. I didn't look at it as bad luck. I just thought it's happened. It was a traumatic experience and I didn't relish the thought of going into hospital.'

'So you didn't feel that that was some kind of personal failure like with Bill?'

'A personal failure – with Bill – yes.'

'What do you think you should have done with Bill?'

'I think I shouldn't have been so complaisant – I should – although he's not the sort of person you can argue with. When I look back now, I really don't know, apart from trying to talk to him. I feel that probably he didn't feel I gave him enough encouragement. I don't really know what he wanted and I don't honestly know now what he wants. I do so much soul-searching, trying to decide what I've done because all I've ever wanted was for him to be happy, and yet he never was contented because he was always searching for something more. He could never sit down and think "I've got my health, I've got my family, good job, what more do I want? Aren't I lucky?" And yet he did resent the fact that I could do this. He felt that because I wasn't saying "Where do we go from here?" that I wasn't ambitious. It's a funny thing, life, isn't it?'

'When we want to help somebody, we have to be able to work out what kind of help that person needs. It seems that you're finding that you don't know what kind of help Bill needs.'

'No.'

'In general, in work, in relationships with your friends, and with your children, do you feel that, on the whole, you know what people need?'

'Yes. That's why I found it so difficult to accept where I've gone wrong, because one can usually assess what a person is actually looking for, but Bill's always striving for the one step ahead, in any case. I must have fallen down somewhere as a wife, because I can't believe it's all his job that's made him like this, unless it's this drive that he's got that's made him become emotionally flat, and that his work and all the other extra activities that he's done have taken over, and this driving force within himself has flattened his emotions and relationships have to go by the board. That's the only way I can think that he – that's the way I'm trying to understand it, but then am I looking too deeply when all it is in black and white is that he doesn't love me any more. At the moment I feel destroyed, destroyed in myself because I can't – I've always – if ever I've hurt anybody, if I'd felt I'd offended them, I would go up to them and say "I'm sorry". I'd try to do something about it. Whereas with this I feel I can't do anything about it, and because I can't find out about it, I wish it was something I can't do anything about, yet in some way I do blame myself. It's something I shall never find out about – I suppose I shall never get to the bottom of the reason why.'

Mollie never doubted her ability to make friends. Ever since she was a little girl starting school she had had lots of friends who sought her out and who cared for her. She could always feel reasonably sure that she could perceive the other person's needs and so she could help that person. She had thought that the support and love she had given her husband, even when his career ambitions made little sense to her, had been what he needed, but now all she could do for him was to feel pained and baffled by his evident unhappiness. He had withdrawn from family life and gone to live elsewhere. Mollie wondered if he had another woman, but she wondered this, not out of jealousy, but out of concern for him. For Mollie, being on your own is the greatest terror and deprivation, a fate she would wish on no one and certainly not her husband. All she wanted for Bill was for him to be happy. Now he had refused her love and help, and he had told her that he no longer loved and needed her. Such a rejection attacked her very reason for being. But even in the midst of her distress she did not feel totally destroyed. In her work she knew that she was loved, needed, and competent. She did not doubt her ability to make friends, to join a group where she would be loved and needed. She felt that her father was with her in spirit, supporting her, wishing her well, loving her. She knew that God to whom she had turned all her life for help was up there still listening, guiding, supporting her. She felt, too, that while the meaning was still obscure, eventually she would see this experience as in some way beneficial. Tragedies only appear as tragedies because God's purpose is not clear to us. 'Perhaps there is a reason', Mollie said, 'We just can't see it.'

'If there weren't any tragedies', I said, 'there wouldn't be anyone who needed help.'

Mollie laughed.

Eric and Christine

When I began asking people about their beliefs about life and death I was surprised to discover just how many English people had some sort of belief in reincarnation. I, in my ignorance, had thought that this belief was confined to those who had grown up in the orbit of the philosophies of Hinduism and Buddhism. Now I found that there were many people who interpreted their lives in terms of the karma that had accompanied them into this present life. They might not have used or even known the word 'karma'. Instead they would say, 'I must have committed some horrible sin in a previous life to be punished like this.' 'This' was a life of heavy blows accompanied by the misery of depression. The person would feel overwhelmed by guilt and, finding no adequate cause for such guilt in this life, attributed the cause to sins of an earlier life, or they would look back at the series of misfortunes they had endured and, instead of attributing them to life's random unfairness, hold to some notion of justice by accepting responsibility for crimes committed in a previous life. Thus the mixture of the Western notions of sin, guilt, and punishment and the Eastern notions of death and re-birth produced a philosophy of life that was black and heavy in the extreme.

Not everyone interprets karma in such a way. My yoga teachers, Eric and Christine, interpreted it in a positive and joyful way. I had known Eric and Christine for four years, ever since I began attending their classes. They would talk about their philosophy in class, and, as I met them socially in other circumstances, I knew that what they said in class was not a facile recitation of some of the tenets of yoga but rather represented the way they lived their lives. They were past retirement age, but both looked much younger. They had had, and were still having, their share of life's woes, yet they remained courageous and cheerful. Karma, it seemed, could be interpreted optimistically. So I asked them if I could visit them with my tape-recorder, and they agreed.

First of all I asked Eric, 'What do you believe will happen to you when you die? How do you see your death?'

He replied, 'For me, I see waking up in another place, whatever that may be. What happens over there I'm not very clear. From what I've read there are numerous things that can happen, but I think probably it will be something like a period of rest and then a chance to look back on what I've done in this life – re-run the tape, learn from it, and in due course, I don't know how long that would be, I shall come back. It's an opportunity for me to build on my experience of lives to date and, I hope, move on from where I am now. What, I mean who I come back as I'm not at all clear and I don't think that matters. Whether I come back as Eric moved on, or as an entirely different personality of which only my inner spirit is the same, continuing entity, I don't know. I don't think it matters.'

Christine said, 'Don't you think you come back with some part of your personality the same, because otherwise – I mean, look at a group reincarnation – I think we come back in groups. For instance, I think we've probably done exactly this before. Although I may not be a woman next time and Eric may not be a man. I think we've swapped over many, many times.'

'Oh, I'm sure', said Eric, 'I'm sure for myself that I've been a woman because I feel very sympathetic to women and I think I understand them better than I understand men. I expect we shall swap and change as our experience requires.'

I asked, 'Eric, do you see it as a progressive thing in that you're in some way refining yourself or part of yourself so that you're moving along, or do you see it more as a cyclical thing?'

'I would hope it was a progressive thing, but I quite see that just as in one's ordinary life, this life now, one can slip back, not make much progress, I find when I look over my life I find I've gone in fits and starts. There are periods when I feel I've progressed and got on, and periods when I've either marked time or even slipped back a bit, and then that's followed by a period that I would call progression. I think that's what happens in one's series of lives. There are lives when perhaps you mark time and lives when you even slip back a bit, but in general, taken over a sequence, I would hope that I've progressed.'

'Do you see this reincarnation going on forever and ever or do you see the progression leading to a final stage?'

Eric replied, 'I think that given time one will reach the end of that, what happens after that I'm not sure. It may well be something like the Buddhists say, that one merges with the greater consciousness and loses to some extent one's individuality. I don't know, but I would have thought that it wasn't endless forever and ever.'

'How do you feel about the loss of your individuality?'

'It used to bother me terribly', said Eric, 'and I found it very difficult. Now I can see that it doesn't matter. Looking at myself today, that's a long way off.'

'So you still see your individuality – something that is intrinsically you – still coming back again.'

'Yes', said Eric, 'I find myself more and more attracted to Buddhism – Buddha discouraged all forms of speculation, and I'm coming round more and more to thinking that this is it, that one has to get on and do the best one can according to one's life. But I can't help seeing that as part of this progression of life. That eventually we'll end up somewhere, but at the moment I'm not bothered where that is. I'm content to enjoy the journey without worrying about where I'm going.'

'Do you have any recollection of past lives?' I asked.

'No', Eric replied, 'I've no memories that way. We know a lot of people who have very clear memories of what they were. The only thing that I can say is that I have one clear picture of a place. This may be something I've just imagined, but I feel it's a long distance memory. But, I don't know. The mind's such a funny thing. You can kid yourself into believing what you want to believe. This is something that's been with me all my life, a picture of a place, a snapshot almost. It's a cloister bathed in sunlight, nobody about. I can't even see myself or what I was. I've never come across it. I've a feeling it was very long ago so it may not even be there now. That's no proof, but I recognise that I could, long ago, have seen a picture which attracted me.'

I asked, 'How far back in your present life have you held these beliefs?'

'From my late twenties', he said, 'that's thirty years, thirty-odd years.'

'What sort of beliefs did you have before then?'

'Well, I was brought up in the Church of England. My parents were C of E nominally. My grandmother was very strongly Church of England, and eventually I ended up in the choir. I couldn't sing but I looked very nice. Later in my life when I went to college, I took up chemistry and for some time I didn't become atheistic, but I became very agnostic. I thought that there probably wasn't much else but molecules and atoms. And then, after I met Christine, I came in contact with a little fellowship called the Order of the Cross, which is a mystical fellowship. It was founded in 1904 by a chap who had been a Congregational minister, and he had a series of memories from past lives which were all connected with the Christian belief. Implicit in his teaching was reincarnation and implicit also was being a vegetarian. I've been a member ever since. I'm one of the trustees of the Order. On top of that I've always read more widely than that and I've become very interested in yoga and the Hindu beliefs and Buddhism and Taoism and Zen. I find myself very much attracted to that.'

I asked, 'Can you see the roots of that going back to your childhood at all?'

'No. My family were orthodox Church of England. My father and mother were not regular church-goers. No, none of those things were known about. To my grandmother that would have been paganism. I didn't really accept these ideas until I came across the Order's teaching. The older I got the more sensible it seemed, and I would find it impossible to throw over that idea since it seems to me the only idea that gives meaning to what you see around you in life – law of karma and being responsible for one's actions so that what happens to one is not a result of outside forces or germs or accidents or other people cheating you, but what happens to you is one's own direct choice and responsibility. The central core of my philosophy is that one is responsible. If I fall downstairs, it's not just that I fell downstairs, but for some reason or other my consciousness allowed me to fall downstairs. In other words, the lack's in me. If I suffer from some disease it's because I've allowed that disease to take hold of me, or it is to teach me something. I go along with one of the Stoics who said I look upon everything that happens to me in life, whether it is good or bad, as an opportunity of learning. And I think that's a marvellous way of looking at things. Everything that happens, whether it's bad, whether it's tragic – the biggest tragedy you could imagine only stays a tragedy if you cannot draw a lesson out of it and learn to do differently in future.'

'When you say "You learn something from it", you could be saying "Something happened and I drew some conclusions from it", or are you saying "Some things happen to me because there's a power beyond which is using these things to instruct me"?'

'Both. Isn't that the same thing? If you said there is a power beyond me – that may not be some guardian angel pushing me, or even tripping me up, but the workings of the law of karma. You see, I see life as an interlocking web, a network in which – almost like great marshalling yards where there's an enormous amount of lines with branches and points which we travel through. Now, if we have to stop at a station to pick something up, which might be good or might be bad, it's because that's the way the points are set for us. We have set the points. The working of the law of karma is the resultant of our actions, our words, even our thoughts. So, every moment as I'm sitting here thinking, my very thoughts are setting the points ahead of me, like ripples going ahead of a boat, and eventually I have to sail through that course. Now my thoughts at the moment aren't going to make that much difference, but if I go out and kick the cat [and in that household there were a lot of well-fed cats] I've made a major reshuffle of points, and sometimes that new track I'm having to take because I've done something that was basically an infringement of another creature's life, then I shall have to do two things. Either I shall have to know what it's like to be kicked for no reason at all or I shall have, at some time, to make it good – helping someone else or some other creature that's in a bad way – to balance the books. Every time I do something which is morally wrong – and don't start asking me what's moral. Let's say there are moral, amoral, and immoral standards. If I do something which is a good action, I put something on the credit side of the ledger. If I do some wrong deed I put something on the debit side. Sooner or later these have got to be balanced, and if there's a red entry, a debit, then I've got to cancel it by a credit entry.'

I asked, 'How do you see your entries standing now?'

'Well', said Eric, 'one has to endure, suffer is what the Buddhists say, the law of karma, until one can become so unattached to the results of one's action that one escapes from the law of karma, then it no longer has an effect upon you. And this is the probable, of course, that whatever we do, and for whatever altruistic motive, most of us – one in a million is unattached, the rest of us are attached for a greater or lesser degree. Until one can do that one is bound to the law of karma and to the wheel of re-birth. One's incarnations stop when one can genuinely become non-attached to everything. It doesn't mean that one has no place, but that one can do things from the real, true meaning of altruism. One does it because one wants to help, because it is good and not for what one is going to get out of it. One may not have a material reward but one tends to feel good – now that's a reward. It means you're still attached.'

'Are you saying you're still feeling a good deal of attachment?'

'Of course I do', said Eric. 'Don't we all? If I didn't I'd be a saint. And there are a few saints. One hears of them, mostly in India, who are genuinely unattached, and that's why they're saints. They can do good without knowing that they're doing good. People get benefits just from being in their company. I've got a long way to go.'

I told Eric and Christine about the people I had met who interpreted karma in such a fearful way. 'You don't give me any sense of fear', I said.

'Oh, good heavens, of course not', said Eric. 'This is a great misunderstanding. People talk about karma as if it was something bad. But there's good karma.'

'If you assess yourself as a bad person', I said, 'then if you believe in karma you would see your reincarnation as not being the best.'

Eric replied, 'There are very few really bad people. There are very few good people. We're all a bit of a mish-mash in the middle. You know, some of the most cruel and monstrous people in history have had a good side to them – they loved their dogs or their children, or they kept a garden, yet they could do monstrous things. 'There's nobody who is wholly good or wholly bad.'

'So when we're born we're a mixture.'

'Yes, of course, because if we were wholly good we wouldn't be born, we'd have come to the end. The fact that we are born shows that we are a mixture. I think it's the only thing that gives meaning to life, and I don't think it's a thing to be frightened of. All it tells me is "Eric, you are responsible." You can't blame the government, your father and mother, your upbringing, a germ because you caught a cold, you've got to blame yourself. When I say blame myself, that's the wrong term, because I can look back and see the good things that have happened to me and think "Eric, you gave those to yourself." Because we're not punished for our sins or rewarded for our virtues, but we are punished by our sins and rewarded by our virtues. If you look at it that way you've something you can get on with. What's the use of complaining about something when you know it's your own fault. The thing is to make sure you don't do that again.'

'So you see yourself as possessing virtues and also possessing the ability to do better next time', I commented.

'Oh, yes', said Eric. 'You've got to. I've always – a lot of my colleagues in the Order are very hesitant about doing anything in case they make a mistake. I always say I can think of very few decisions that one can make in life that if it is not the right decision cannot be put right or turned to good. There's very, very little in life, except, perhaps, swallowing cyanide that's irrevocable. Nearly everything else, if you find you've made a bloomer, you can either retrace your steps or go off at a different angle. You try to tell people that, oh dear, don't you dare do that, they say, just in case.'

I asked, 'How did your grandmother present religion to you – as something that was painful and threatening –'

'No, not at all. She was a nice old girl. Not one of those fundamentalists that said if you didn't go to church you'll go to hell. Not at all. She just invited me to go along and I liked her and went.'

'It was a pleasant experience?'

'Yes. I used to enjoy it. I think probably because of my long history in the church. For instance, if I hear a Gregorian chant, it does something to the hair on the back of my neck. And I'm sure this wasn't the first life that I've been involved in religion. And I think it was probably in the West, in Christianity, and I think that in this life that's what I'm breaking free of. No proof, of course, just a feeling.'

'Do you have any belief in a personal God, or a transcendent God?'

'Well, yes and no. My own belief is that the whatever, the great mystery, is not an old man sitting on a cloud. It's something which we cannot have the slightest understanding of until we merge with it, and our understanding will become its understanding. At the same time I'm absolutely certain that because we have finite minds and finite understanding, that this infinite does on occasions present itself in a finite form which we can understand. Hence some of the visions that some of the mystics have seen, which have been of tremendous meaning for them but has been presented in the visual form that they would expect, so that Christians see Christ, Buddhists see the Bodhisattva, Hindus see one of their three hundred and thirty thousand gods. I feel that this is really the way in which, for purposes of watching and helping a human soul, the whatever presents itself in a limited form which one can contemplate. You see, there are very few people who can contemplate a mist, an all-over mist. You've got to be fairly well on the path to be able to do that. And therefore I think that this is one of the reasons why mankind through history has created symbols – a Cross, a Virgin Mary, or a Kali or a Shiva or a Buddha – something which they can sit and look at and which can mean something to them and they can relate to. So, as Jung said, man needs his symbols, and those are very potent symbols. Many people will have to employ them for many lives to come, until you can start and have some relationship with something that is informulate. People have to reach a stage where they can see beyond a symbol to what it symbolises and place no actual sacredness or intrinsic power in a symbol, but only see that that power comes from the reality which the symbol symbolises.'

We talked about death and Christine in her usual enthusiastic way said, 'I love it here.'

'You don't want to go?' I asked.

'I want to see what it's like on the other side, but I want to come back again. It's a nice place, in spite of all its peculiarities.'

'You don't fear that you might come back to some terrible place?' (I had often pondered upon why I had awoken to self-consciousness in the 1930s as an Australian in Australia and not as a Jew in Warsaw or a Russian in Leningrad.)

'You'd have chosen it', said Christine, 'when you're up there, when you're looking down from your rest place and you're reviewing your life and saying, "Well, really, this soul needs such and such an experience", and therefore you would choose, say, Australia.'

'You feel we choose our suffering?'

'I'm quite sure we do. A conscious choice, knowing what is necessary', said Christine.

'A degree of understanding', said Eric.

'I think sometimes one has it chosen for one', agreed Christine.

Eric said, 'I feel it's a little like school. When you were a youngster, you hadn't much idea of what school is about, your parents push you there and say that's where you're going. When you've got more understanding of what you've got to do, the things you've got to learn, when the time comes for you to go to university you choose yourself the university. I think it's a bit like that with reincarnations – souls of little understanding are directed, but as one gets older, spiritually speaking, one is consulted and eventually one makes one's choice oneself – this is the experience I must have to round me off. Sometimes one chooses a very difficult experience.'

'This implies some knowledge of the future', I said.

'Yes, sure', said Eric. 'There is a pattern which is changing. It is laid down. We know that in three years there'll be a General Election, unless we have a nuclear war. The pattern is fixed over a large area. Life is to a large extent predestined, not in everything, but in a lot. Whether we've got free will or predestination, we still have to get on and live it. We act as though we've got free will because that satisfies our ego. "I am the master of my fate." That sounds good and gives one a nice feeling. I'm getting round to seeing that there's no free will. That doesn't mean anything mechanical.'

'We have free will within a circumscribed position', said Christine.

'The more I think about it', Eric said, 'the more I think it is more circumscribed than what we think it is. All our choices are determined by our character which is determined by things like what our parents were like, how we grew up, and so on.'

The question of free will and determinism in human behaviour was one which Eric was currently pondering upon, trying to relate personal responsibility to the causal connections of the law of karma. He enjoyed working on problems like this, but now was not the time to discuss the different arguments. Instead Christine went on to tell me about herself.

'I'd been into isms and ults all my life. My mother was a primitive Methodist and I started life being dragged along to chapel three times on a Sunday and I didn't like that one little bit. But I think I always had the feeling that I needed something because I went through the whole lot, Congregationalist, Church of England, even got to the point of signing on to be a Roman Catholic. But all the time I had this feeling that this wasn't quite what I wanted. My own teacher was a member of the Order of the Cross and that's how I got into it when I was about sixteen or seventeen. The idea of karma and reincarnation just seemed so obvious that I couldn't think why I hadn't thought of it before. Like Eric, I've got more and more drawn to Buddhism over the years of doing yoga and meeting so many of the marvellous Indians who are such marvellous people and so full of fun. That's what I like about them. They find the whole of life as one huge joke.'

'How do you see your next life?' I asked.

'I haven't the faintest idea', said Christine. 'I hope it's where it's warmer. I'm jolly sure this is the first time I've been in a damp, cold country.'

'Where do you think you've been before?'

'I think India. I remember when I was at Art College, donkey's years ago, having my eyes tested for colour blindness because they said that no Westerner would ever put the colours together that I always put together – pinks and oranges and yellow – no, India, China, Japan have always fascinated me.'

'Have you any memory of such places?' I asked.

'No. One thing I'm sure of, I was never in a convent or a monkery or whatever you call it.'

'Christine, in class you come over as more – well – childlike and magical than Eric – like you don't have to worry your head about it.'

'No', said Christine, 'that's a feminine attribute. Men are terribly logical and they'll work things out and get there in the end whereas a woman goes whoop and she's there, and not knowing how she got there between whiles: I can't argue with you or discuss as Eric does in a logical way, but I *know* without having to be bothered with all the logic, and how could I be wrong?' She laughed.

Eric said, 'I think actually she's touched on the right word there – the magical side of life. I think we both feel that Life has magical properties, there's far more to it than we know about. Don't you think so?'

'Oh, yes, absolutely', Christine said.

'It's becoming more certain to me – it's always been that way for Christine, me having spent my life in science and industry, always been hampered in seeing the poetic side of life, but I must say of recent years, since I left industry, I've become much more that way – haven't actually seen fairies at the bottom of the garden, but they're probably there if I could look well enough.'

'How do you see that as fitting into your philosophy?' I asked.

'What, the fairies?'

'Well', said Christine, 'don't you think that everything – animals, plants, landscapes, stones – everything has got its particular being and –' She looked at Eric.

He said, 'I just want to refer back to what I said earlier. I'm sure that just as the great mystery has to make itself recognisable if it wants to approach an individual, so I think it has to take on a form which we associate with it.'

'Have you read *The Magic of Findhorn*?' Christine asked me.

'No', I said. I knew nothing of Findhorn.

'Oh, you must, Dorothy. It's a gorgeous book. Have you put the kettle on, Eric?' Eric went out to make the tea and Christine told me about Findhorn. 'Now you have to take it with a slight pinch of salt. It was written by an American when he was absolutely sky-high about Findhorn. Findhorn is a community in the top right-hand corner of Scotland which was founded about sixteen years ago by Peter and Eileen Cady who went there willy-nilly, they had no idea why they were going there and over the years it has become a community, a spiritual community which I feel is one of the most important things that is happening on this planet in this generation. It's a marvellous place. Eric and I went there a couple of years ago and our immediate reaction was to come back, sell up, and go back there to live. It's a fantastic place and the Cadys are fantastic people, and it started by them growing a garden. A friend who was with them, Dorothy Maclean, was one of those people who could contact the spirits of the plants, and it was through Dorothy and Eileen that Peter was able to produce a garden. They grew huge cabbages and roses, marvellous on soil that was not much more than sand and pebbles. And then after some years came David Spangler, another American, who altered the direction of Findhorn slightly. He said that by the time he arrived Findhorn had ceased to be a place to grow gardens and became a place to grow souls. David had a tremendous influence on the development of Findhorn and has written some fantastic books.'

I asked Christine, 'Do you see magic as a word to cover all these things – do you see that as good or bad?'

'Oh, good.'

'Entirely good?'

'No, not entirely good. It can be used – if it's used selfishly, it can be bad.'

'So the badness comes from the usage. You don't see the badness as being outside in the magic forces themselves?'

'No. It's the way one uses it, I'm sure.'

When Eric returned with the tea Christine said, 'I don't see magic as a thing, do you, Eric? It's just sort of force fields.'

'That's right', said Eric. 'Good magic is the power of positive thinking, bad magic is the power of negative thinking.'

Over tea I asked them, 'How easily do you think you could change your beliefs?'

'Oh, I couldn't', said Christine, 'I think they could be enlarged.'

'It depends', Eric said. 'I think if something came along and was presented to me in such a way that it made sense, I would embody that in my belief and cast out things which did not fit. That happens all along.'

'Yes, I think it's a growing thing', Christine said.

'Looking back on my life', said Eric, 'I've changed out of all recognition. I'm sure I could change if I was convinced that something came along that was better. I can't see, quite honestly, a complete and utter reversal. I can see an expansion and extension.'

'When you were a small child', I asked, 'did you feel you were a good person?'

'Just cannot remember', said Eric.

Christine said, 'I can remember very plainly. It's taken me a good deal to overcome one aspect of my mother's treatment of me. She was the most incredibly beautiful woman, and she always used to say in my hearing what a pity it was she had such a plain daughter, and it took me until, well, even now it overcomes me sometimes – that I was hideous and it took me a long time to realise that I wasn't all that bad. However, I think I've got a bouncy nature.'

'Did you think it was just outside that was bad and inside you were all right?' I asked.

'I've always been quite pleased with myself inside', said Christine. 'That's not quite true. I've always known that I was all right inside. Other people might not think I was but I knew I was.'

Eric said, 'Right up into my twenties I had the most colossal inferiority complex. If somebody said good morning to me I used to blush and stutter and hardly could say good morning back.'

'That's something I cannot understand', Christine said.

'Well, it was', said Eric. 'Why it should be I don't know.'

'Well, it was your mother, dear. She kept you right smack under her thumb. You had to do just as you were told.'

'I found it very difficult to stand up for myself', said Eric.

'But even if you could not stand up for yourself, did you have some areas where you felt all right?' I asked.

'Oh, I think so', said Eric. 'I've always been pretty sure of my own abilities. I hope that I've got a reasonable assessment of my own abilities. I don't think of myself as completely good. There are areas where I could be very much better, but I've always been fairly confident of myself intellectually and practically, the use of the hands.'

'Eric's never said he couldn't do a thing', said Christine.

Eric agreed. 'Even if I'm not sure how a thing could be done. I've always said yes, I can do it, and then found out – and have always found out.'

'How far back in your childhood can you remember feeling that?' I asked.

'Oh, far enough. I've always been extremely good with my hands.'

'This links with earlier when you were showing a feeling of confidence that whatever situation you were presented with, in whatever life, you could use this situation in some way to improve yourself, and you were always capable of improvement because you had the confidence that you could do this. If you make a mistake you have the confidence that you can repair it. You can do better next time.'

'Yes', said Eric. 'My difficulty always arose in my relationships with other people. I always felt embarrassed in public, but I seem to have overcome it. One of the formative things in my life was when I went into pharmacy. I was apprenticed to a pharmacist and he taught me the art of salesmanship. That got me talking to people.'

We finished our tea and Christine remarked, 'I think that life is completely fascinating. I get frightfully fed up with it occasionally and I get depressed sometimes, don't I? I get gloomy rather than depressed –'

'Who doesn't?' said Eric. 'We'd be fools if we said we never get down.'

Christine said, 'But I usually reach a point in my gloom when I come to see the funny side of it and start to laugh, but, by and large, I think life's marvellous.'

'Yes', I agreed, 'I always feel that there are so many wonderful things to do.'

'Isn't it a blessing that you have plenty of lives in which to do them all?' said Christine.

I said, 'But when I get terribly tired I think "Oh, I couldn't go through all this again." '

Christine laughed. 'Oh, yes you can. Of course you can.'

Chapter 4

VERY DIFFERENT POINTS OF VIEW

Tony, Siegfried, Mollie, Eric and Christine were all English. They were contemporaries, had received very similar educations, and all were brought up in the Christian Church. Yet they each arrived at a very different set of religious or philosophical beliefs from the ones they had been taught in childhood. Eric and Christine would have said that they shared the same beliefs, yet in a conversation with me where I encouraged them to describe their beliefs in some detail, many differences were revealed. Their beliefs grew out of the way they had interpreted the experiences that had befallen them, and now their beliefs influenced the way they interpreted their current situation.

It is often said that we create gods in our own image. In patriarchal societies the Christian God is pictured as a patriarch, an old man with a flowing beard, who inspires awe and fear in his followers. Jesus would have looked very much like those young men whose mere appearance can suggest to security officers that they could be terrorists, yet, as Christianity travelled west, Jesus acquired blond hair and blue eyes. When individuals describe their God He proves to have attributes which reflect in some way the person's own attributes. Tony's Christian God was a combined image of all those people who had betrayed him and whom he could not forgive. He said, 'I have a great fear of the Christian God – He must be a bastard, what a bloody sick joke, creating this world. There must be some gods up there, sitting around, and He's a baby god among the bigger immortals, and the baby's been given the world to play with, stirring things round in the world, seeing what havoc can be caused. If there is a God, then this God is some sort of holy maniac, an evil maniac. Evil because He allows enough food to keep the dream going. It's the biggest con trick ever played.' For Siegfried 'God is a shit', someone who 'allowed Auschwitz, the IRA, this wretched business we read about this morning'. As much as he hated his God, he hated himself even more. Mollie needed to be needed, and so did her God. If she was asked for help, she would give it, and so did He. Eric and Christine had abandoned the idea of God as a superior kind of person in favour of a myth where each was the central character. Eric had chosen the myth of the lone hero who goes in quest of a treasure beyond price. On his journey he learns from his suffering and never loses sight of his goal, his equivalent of the Holy Grail. Christine's myth has the features of an Indian myth as played by Bollywood, bright and colourful, with lots of music and dancing, and many happy people. The scene changes with her succeeding reincarnations, but the colour, the people, the music and the dancing go on.

There have been frequent reports of research which shows that people who have a religious belief are happy and do not get depressed. Clearly this research did not include people like Tony and Siegfried. They had not abandoned their belief in God, yet both of them were deeply depressed. They simply doubted that their God was looking after them in the way that Mollie's God was looking after her.

All reports of scientific research should be scrutinised carefully, but with research in psychology the scrutiny should always include the questions, 'Who benefits from the results of this research?' and 'Who funded this research?' These questions should also be asked about research in the other sciences, but in chemistry, physics, geology and biology you cannot produce the results you want unless what you want is actually the case. When the pharmaceutical companies produce research which does not show that their drug is better than all others in the field, they hide these results and hope that, when the drug is sold to the public, nothing untoward will happen. However, when your subject matter is people it is easy to get the results you want. This is how you do it.

First, select a group of people who are likely to express the views you want them to express. If you want to show that religious belief protects people from getting depressed, choose your subjects from a church congregation. Do not include people who are depressed or who have suffered major disasters. Do not have a control group of non-believers because this could show that non-believers are as happy as believers. Second, do not have open-ended, individual interviews which encourage the interviewees to reveal more of themselves than they might otherwise be prepared to do. For instance, many people tell themselves that they are happy, and try to ignore the sadness and fear which their circumstances provoke. Use a questionnaire drawn up by yourself with questions crafted to produce the answers you desire. Third, do not include a lie scale in your questionnaire. Let your interviewees 'fake good', as we all do when we are talking to a stranger. Fourth, publish your results in a journal which does not require a peer review. Finally, issue a press release headed 'Religious belief keeps you mentally healthy'.

The beliefs which Tony and Siegfried held were not a result of their depression. These were beliefs which they had acquired in childhood and adolescence. Tony, needing close relationships, tried to find these in his Baptist family, and failed. As his story about Billy Graham showed, he came to hate himself for wanting to be close to the people he despised. Siegfried lost his faith in a benevolent God when his beloved uncle died. He did not stop believing in the existence of God altogether. He needed his choir money, and, as he listened to the sermons and sang the hymns, he continued to be presented with the problem of why God decided not to save his uncle. Was God powerful but uncaring? Or was He a just God who was punishing Siegfried because Siegfried was so wicked? Siegfried chose to see himself as a bad person, deserving of God's punishment. Tony did not need God's punishment. He punished himself. 'Out of the jaws of success', he said, 'I snatch failure.'

When we turn against ourselves and hate ourselves our sense of being a person comes under great threat. However, amongst the feedback mechanisms which hold the structure of the sense of being a person together, is one very powerful mechanism which becomes conscious in the form of a personal pride. Often the very attribute which is the cause of a person's shame becomes the object of the person's pride. Tony and Siegfried took great pride in what they saw as their wickedness. Tony took pride in his intolerance, Siegfried in his capacity to hate himself and to expect the worst. They used their pride to ward off any possibility of a close relationship, even though Tony knew that without a close relationship he could not survive as a person, and Siegfried was drowning in loneliness. Their fear of being hurt again was far greater than their hope of a happier life. Their vision of their gods maintained their view of themselves and their life.

The pride Mollie, Eric and Christine took in themselves was a realistic pride and was derived from how they saw themselves in relation to other people. They were modest in their assessments of themselves, but it is clear that they got along well with themselves. Mollie never doubted that other people would like her and that she could always make friends. When I asked her what would happen to her if she became a patient on a chronic ward with multiple sclerosis, she replied, 'I think at first I would probably feel like a lot of people feel – "Why has this happened to me?" But I would hope that I would be able to overcome this and be able to – well, you would, in that sort of situation, identify with your fellow patients and probably be able to gain strength from each other. I would expect that this would happen on that sort of ward. You would be able to help each other, support each other, really you're all in that ward knowing that your days are really numbered. You would all know that you were all there for a certain length of time, and I would be able to contribute something to the other people that were there and not become too engrossed with myself. And probably seek support. I think I found it when I was in hospital earlier this year. One tends, when you're in that situation, to be suddenly thrown into a group where you all feel that you're in it together, and you're all facing an operation or not knowing what the diagnosis is going to be, and you do tend to support each other. You do tend to have this feeling, well, you need each other at that particular time, even though you've never known each other before you walked through the hospital door.'

When I asked Christine whether as a child she had thought

she was good, she replied, 'I can remember very plainly. It's taken me a good deal to overcome one aspect of my mother's treatment of me. She was the most incredibly beautiful woman, and she always used to say in my hearing what a pity it was she had such a plain daughter, and it took me until, well, even now it overcomes me sometimes – that I was hideous and it took me a long time to realise that I wasn't all that bad. However, I think I've got a bouncy nature.'

Eric saw life – or succeeding lives – as an education, but one where he was bound to succeed. He said, 'I go along with one of the Stoics who said I look upon everything that happens to me in life, whether it is good or bad, as an opportunity of learning. And I think that's a marvellous way of looking at things. Everything that happens, whether it's bad, whether it's tragic – the biggest tragedy you could imagine only stays a tragedy if you cannot draw a lesson out of it and learn to do differently in future.' He saw no reason to pretend that he was stupid when clearly he was not. He said, 'I've always been pretty sure of my own abilities. I hope that I've got a reasonable assessment of my own abilities. I don't think of myself as completely good. There are areas where I could be very much better, but I've always been fairly confident of myself intellectually and practically, the use of the hands.' Christine commented, 'Eric's never said he couldn't do a thing.' Eric agreed. 'Even if I'm not sure how a thing could be done. I've always said yes, I can do it, and then found out – and have always found out.'

As we see ourselves, so we see our gods, and our world. Mollie, Eric and Christine had confidence in themselves and they valued themselves. They saw their world as a place where hope and achievement were always possible, and their religious beliefs reflected this view of themselves and their world. Moreover, in all the interviews each person revealed not just their degree of self-confidence but how they each experienced their sense of being a person.

In my work as a clinical psychologist I had long conversations with many people who were deeply depressed, or who had a tenuous grip on a reality which they could share with others. When one of these people talked to me about how the world around him had become unreal I knew what he meant.

At those points in my life when I had lost all confidence in myself, I struggled, and sometimes failed, to convince myself that what was around me was actually real. I could find no way of being absolutely certain that what I saw was indeed there, or that the person I was talking to was the person I thought that he was. In my late twenties I solved this problem by deciding that I would act *as if* the world around me was real, and I continue to do so until this day. On the whole it works fairly well because I have confidence in my judgement, and, to make sure that my judgement is good, I try to keep things organised and under control. I know that I am not alone in living like this. I am an introvert, and half the human population is composed of introverts.

However, when I began my long conversations with people who were psychiatric patients, I could not understand what people meant when they said, 'I don't know who I am', or, 'Inside there's nothing but an emptiness', or, 'I play different roles, but inside there's no one at home.' When they talked about how they reacted to a disaster and said, 'I felt I was disappearing', I could not conceive of a situation where my 'I' would disappear. Shatter, yes, but disappear? Never. If everyone else in the world vanished, I would be lonely but I would still exist. I would listen to a person talking about their inner emptiness and not doubt the person's sincerity. I just could not empathise with that feeling of emptiness or disappearing, or with the way these people preferred to stay with unpleasant people rather than be on their own. It was my client Peter who gave me an image which I could, with difficulty, grasp.

One day when we were discussing his family, he spoke of his attachment to his Celtic background and said, 'One does feel that because one has grown up in this sort of format, that it is valuable, and that one's sense of self, one's own identity, will disappear if one removes the casing, the setting in which one lives.'

This doubt about the existence of his sense of being a person was something that bothered Peter a great deal. Here he went on to say, 'One time I had a clear identity which depended on my past, my relationships, my physical being within certain perceptible reference points. Underlying this was the fact that one had a fairly good knowledge that one only existed in oneself in one way. However, there was a time when I was staying with a great dear friend of mine, and when I left I went to the end of a long drive to catch a bus, and there was nowhere I had to go, nobody was expecting me anywhere. Therefore, if I didn't turn up anywhere, nobody would notice. I had just left some friends, I was estranged from my parents, and the marriage I had no longer existed, and I came to a sort of T-junction, a physical T-junction of a driveway and a road, but also in a sense a sort of, not an emotional T-junction, a life T-junction, and it didn't matter which way I went. Physically it wasn't important, it was neither here nor there, but from the point of view of how I felt, I felt sort of isolated and non-me. I felt as though I didn't exist, because my existence depended upon other people's recognition of me and my perception of me.'

'What you're describing', I said, 'is that you saw yourself in other people's eyes, like other people were mirrors of you and if there weren't any mirrors there –'

'Yes', he said, 'I suppose you could put it like that. It's not how I saw it. I saw it, and I'm not deliberately playing with words, but I'm trying to say how I saw it at the time, was that my reference points of existence were other people – that I reacted to them and they reacted to me. In my vocabulary this would not be a mirror thing, though one could argue that it is. I saw it as a fact that I functioned in conjunction with other people and I had nobody to function with. Then I had great doubts about my own existence and I think also a great sense of loneliness because if one had nowhere to go where one was expected – I mean there were lots of places I could go where people would say, "How nice to see you, Pete", and this would have been fine, but this wasn't the point. The problem was that I had nowhere to slot into, something that existed, so I felt isolated and I felt lonely and I felt, thought, I didn't feel that I didn't exist, but I felt that I didn't exist. I said that deliberately in that way because it was a double sounding thing. I knew physically that I had my feet on the ground and the sun was shining and there were leaves on the trees –'

'And you were there to think "I don't exist"?' I asked.

'Absolutely, yes', Peter said, 'but the sort of identity thing had disappeared. It was most extraordinary. I think I've felt that to a greater or lesser extent at various times in my life, but that was particularly clear and harsh, in the hard sense of being very pristine and sharp-edged, and that was the most extreme sense I've had of it. I felt there was no setting. I could have fallen under a bus or changed my name and gone to South America and nobody would have noticed and this was very odd and very frightening. Very depressing.' Peter was a member of the other half of the human population. He was an extravert.

I have been writing and talking about introverts and extraverts for many years now.[1] I find that many people know exactly what I am talking about because they have always been aware of how they experience their sense of being a person. However, there are many who struggle with these concepts. When someone says to me, 'I don't know which I am. I think I'm a bit of both', I always find that the person has concentrated on what he does, not on what he experiences. Introverts and extraverts often do the same things, but for very different reasons. Some introverts are very sociable, and some extraverts are very shy. Some extraverts are very ambitious while some introverts concentrate on simply doing what they do as well as they can. Both extraverts and introverts can be very tidy, or live happily with disorder, and there are few people so controlling as an extravert who delights in bossing other people around. What distinguishes extraverts from introverts is not what they do but how they experience their sense of being a person. Extraverts experience their sense of being a person in relationship to other people, while introverts experience their sense of being a person in terms of developing clarity, organisation and control. Extraverts see annihilation of their sense of being a person as being completely and utterly alone, while introverts see such annihilation as being overwhelmed by chaos. In the conversations I had with Tony, Siegfried, Mollie, Eric and Christine it is easy to see who the extraverts are and who the introverts.

In these interviews I was not setting out to discover who were the introverts and who the extraverts, but this became clear simply from what each person said about themselves. Extraverts are people persons, and nothing was more important to Tony, Mollie and Christine than other people. Tony called a close relationship 'the most important thing'; he also called it 'the most difficult thing'. He said, 'There's got to be a positiveness in a relationship to combat the absurdities that we all produce in our lives – the patterns we produce. I find people's patterns in daily living very hard to come to terms with.' He spoke of 'concepts, notions of love, of what a relationship intrinsically was. It's being something to someone and someone being something to you. A relationship is not a negation of the self. It seems to me to be a more positive thing and to include a "we". There's still an "I", there's still a "you", but now there's a "we" – which is something which is a really important condition. What goes to make a "we" I'm not sure. It is the fact that you find you relate in terms of ideas, in terms of priorities, in terms of virtues, if you like. The continuation of the relationship is the acceptance of both selves.'

Christine believed firmly in reincarnation in groups. She said, 'Don't you think you come back with some part of your personality the same, because otherwise – I mean, look at a group reincarnation – I think we come back in groups.' Mollie talked of forming a group with the other patients on her ward, as well as emphasising just how important her family was to her. She was also very clear about what would happen to her if she was alone in the world. She said, 'That would be terrible. I would crack up.'

Excitement and stimulation are very important to extraverts. In her yoga classes Christine was bright and chatty, and we all laughed and chatted, while in Eric's classes we were, like him, quiet and meditative. Tony was very clear about how important excitement was to him. He said, 'I rather expect that close relationships are short-term. I don't see how fires that can burn so intensely can keep going for so long. I see [meaningful relationships] as heights and depths. Jesus, I don't want to travel, hovering above the ground about six inches. I want to be right up there or right down there. I don't want to be down there, but I know if you go up there, you've got to be down there some of the time. In this life you do not experience one thing unless you experience the opposite.' Similarly, 'I see tolerance as a sort of blunting process. I'm very loath to see it as a virtue. Because everything that is written about tolerance is actually evasion or patronisation, neither of which I want to know anything about. So people who are described as tolerant are evading something.'

I commented, 'So when I say to you that if you were more tolerant towards other people you'd find life a lot easier, I'm in effect saying to you, "Become a lesser person, a worse person than you are and you'll find life easier." And, of course, that kind of message no one will accept.'

'If you said that to me I would have to say, "You're putting my soul at risk." '

'If I give you advice "Be tolerant", I'm actually giving you, in your frame of reference, the advice "Be a bad person." '

'Yes.'

For introverts the top priority is not relationships but having a sense of achievement, and this means using their abilities to the full. I was required to write a report about Siegfried, and this meant I would have to give him an intelligence test. He scored very highly. Perhaps it was only in the Navy that he was able to use his intelligence to its full extent. Now he said, 'If I were given a job to do which would really take something out of me I'd come to life again.' Eric made very clear how important achievement was for him, not just in this life but in all his lives.

Extraverts need other people to like them. Introverts need other people to approve of them. Not everyone's approval is important, just the approval of those of whom the introvert approves. Siegfried approved of his senior officers and so, 'I remember reading on my flimsy when I came out of the Service, "Reliable in action". I enjoyed that. Didn't matter. If I hadn't been, someone behind me would have made sure I was.' He might not be achieving anything now, but he did not disagree when I said, 'So, amongst your friends who've given you all this advice, the ones who say, "Don't try so hard, take things easy, you set too high standards for yourself, you ought to relax more, you're getting older now, you can't expect to do what you've done in the past", all this kind of advice, while being said with the best of intentions, comes over to you as something extremely frightening because carrying it out would mean becoming the kind of person you've always dreaded being, because if you became that kind of person, you would be the kind of person who had no respect, completely lost.'

Eric's need for approval by those he approves of is implied in his description of how he could make progress in each lifetime. He said, 'I would hope it was a progressive thing, but I quite see that just as in one's ordinary life, this life now, one can slip back, not make much progress, I find when I look over my life I find I've gone in fits and starts. There are periods when I feel I've progressed and got on, and periods when I've either marked time or even slipped back a bit, and then that's followed by a period that I would call progression. I think that's what happens in one's series of lives. There are lives when perhaps you mark time and lives when you even slip back a bit, but in general, taken over a sequence, I would hope that I've progressed.'

Eric did not doubt his ability to keep his emotions under control. Control of emotions is important to introverts because unbridled emotion seems like chaos. The more intense the emotions, the calmer an introvert is likely to be. Siegfried had had too many experiences of being overwhelmed by painful emotions and wished never to repeat this experience. When Siegfried and I were talking about love I challenged him on this. 'When you're in love you're not in control of your life, are you? You said something earlier about not wanting to be emotionally dependent on anyone, so that being in love, or loving someone enormously, you really put your life in that person's hands.'

'Yes.'

'All I'm noting is that your decision to become a consultant and your decision not to love deeply again, both of these decisions were based on the premise of "It's dangerous to put your life in other people's hands" or "For safety's sake I want to control my own life." '

Siegfried laughed wryly. 'Inside this husky tough there's a frightened little boy.'

In typical introvert fashion, Eric sought clarity. He said,

'For me, I see waking up in another place, whatever that may be. What happens over there I'm not very clear. From what I've read there are numerous things that can happen, but I think probably it will be something like a period of rest and then a chance to look back on what I've done in this life – re-run the tape, learn from it, and in due course, I don't know how long that would be, I shall come back. It's an opportunity for me to build on my experience of lives to date and, I hope, move on from where I am now. What, I mean who I come back as I'm not at all clear and I don't think that matters. Whether I come back as Eric moved on, or as an entirely different personality of which only my inner spirit is the same, continuing entity, I don't know. I don't think it matters.'

Eric's fantasy about what happens in the interval between one life and the next is a re-working of a fantasy that many introverts have. When we review our life, past mistakes seem like chaos. We long to be able to go back again and get everything in order the way it should be.

Through all these conversations runs one vital thread, that of trying to be good. However each person defined 'good', it was related directly to the person's religious or philosophical beliefs. William James defined a religious belief as 'the belief that there is an unseen order, and that our supreme good lies in harmoniously adjusting ourselves thereto'.[2] Whether we believe that the unseen order is the order of the universe or of God and his heavenly choirs, our personal notion of 'good' is derived in part from that order and from the definitions of 'good' used by our parents and teachers. We try to be good in the way that we define 'good'. If you define 'good' in terms of a life devoted to service to others, or in terms of surpassing your father's ruthlessness in making money, then good is what you must try to be.

Chapter 5

BEING GOOD AND THE JUST WORLD

I was waiting to reverse my car out of its parking space in the car park of a shopping centre. Through the rear window I could see a ramp for pedestrians leading down to the entrance road of the car park. A young woman with a little boy of about four was coming down the ramp. The boy broke away from the woman and ran across the road. She caught up with him beside the driver's door of my car. All I could see was the little boy's arm in the grip of an adult hand. The other adult hand came down hard in three smacks on his upper arm. A woman's voice said, 'You are a bad boy.'

Welcome to the world of good and evil.

This was not the woman's intention, I am sure. Her sudden fear at the peril the little boy had put himself in turned to anger, and so she smacked him. Had she been less fearful, and thus less angry, she might have remembered to say, 'That was a bad thing you did.' Then she would have given him the chance to think about what he had done and resolve never to do that again. But she did not, and instead presented him with the idea that he was, in essence, bad.

If this proved to be the only occasion on which the boy was told he was bad, the incident would very likely fade from his memory, but, if his relatives and teachers repeatedly said to him, 'You are a bad boy', he would come to believe that, just as he was a boy and he had blue eyes, unchangeable characteristics with which he was born, so he was bad and he could not change. If he was sent regularly to church, synagogue or mosque the message that he was a sinner would have been impressed on him with great authority. At a Buddhist shrine or a Hindu temple a child might not be told that he was a sinner, but he would be told that he was inadequate and ignorant, and he had much to learn. Whatever the religion, the child is told that his task in life is to become and remain good. It may be that he is taught that it is within his power to become good; or that good works alone will not save him if he does not have faith; or that, no matter how intensely he believes and prays, his essential wickedness remains and that the gates of Hell are always gaping wide to receive the unwary sinner. It may be that the child is taught that, no matter how much he strives to be good, he can never be sure that he has reached the standard of goodness required to be born into a better life.

If children were presented with just one definition of 'good', their task of learning to be good would be hard enough, but between and within religions there is a wide range of definitions of 'good' over which theologians have argued for hundreds of years. Moreover, individual clerics within one religion do not agree on what 'good' is. In his memoir about his father, John Burnside told how, in his teens,

My relations with my mother were breaking down. She had found a packet of Durex and a copy of *The Communist Manifesto* crammed into the sweet, dusty gap behind the more acceptable books on my shelf. A week or so later, she came downstairs in the small hours when my father was on night shift, and found me in the living room with a girl she didn't know. A Protestant. Not much was going on, but she stood behind the half-opened door, in her nightdress, and said in a hurt, firm voice, 'I think you'd better get that girl a taxi home. Her parents will be worried.' After she found the subversive book – lent to me by my history teacher at my all-Catholic school, as it happened – and the *prophylactics*, she called the priest in. Had it been Father Duane, he probably would have made her see that the things weren't nearly anywhere near as bad as she had imagined; instead, the new priest, a peely-wally Englishman with sandy hair and yellowish freckles, came and sat in the front room, ignored the plate of home-made buns and chocolate digestives my mother had put out, and talked about obedience and chastity, while I sat in my father's 'big seat', next to the dead television, nodding from time to time, while the town darkened.[1]

Children listen, or not, to their teachers and clerics defining 'good', but they have already experienced the differing definitions of 'good' held by their parents. These definitions have grown out of the parents' experiences and the conclusions they have drawn from them. Parents demonstrate to their child through their actions what they regard as good and bad, but they also, from time to time, give the child a summary of their definitions of good and bad as a kind of formula for being good/being successful/being liked/getting by. Their summary contains lies and self-deceptions, many of which the child sees even when the parents do not, and it is always out-of-date. The world in which the child lives is not the world the parent knows. The battles which the parent had to fight are not the battles which the child will have to fight. Nevertheless, the parents present their summary as their definition of how to be good.

John Burnside's father was one of that generation of working-class men who fought in the Second World War, and who found on their return that the fine new post-war world, which politicians had promised would be their reward for what they had done for their country, did not eventuate. John Burnside wrote,

For my father, and for whole generations of working class men, cruelty was an ideology. It was important, for the boy's sake, to bring a son up tough: men had to be hard to get through life, there was no room for weakness or sentiment. It wasn't what he would have chosen, but he didn't want me to look for something I couldn't have. What he wanted was to warn me against hope, against any expectation of someone from my background being treated as a human being in the big, hard world. He wanted to kill off my finer – and so, weaker – self. Art. Music. Books. Imagination. Signs of weakness. A man was defined, in my father's circles, by what he could bear, the pain he could shrug off, the warmth or comfort he could deny himself.[2]

Tess Burnside, John's mother, fitted her husband's idea of what a good woman should be.

> The consensus opinion of my mother was that she was a simple and decent woman. She attended Mass faithfully every Sunday, accompanied by her children, but not by her husband. She was polite, God-fearing, conventional, a woman who kept the best china she had been given as a wedding gift for when the priest came to call. For her, what mattered was family, and she did all she could to conceal my father's excesses from the world. I grew up admiring her from a distance: she was the one who taught me to read and write before I started school, the one who scrimped and saved to buy me 'educational' toys, the one who kept things together when it would have been easier, and more merciful, to let them fall apart. All she wanted was a little common decency in her life. She was one of those people who dream of a bookcase full of leather-bound classics and a vase full of freshly cut flowers on the hall table. Of course, there was no hall table, because there was no hall. Obviously, there were no leather-bound books.[3]

It was not his mother but his father who dominated John Burnside's life, a cruel, neglectful, rejecting father. As children often do when a parent fails to parent the child in the way the child needs, John constructed a fantasy of his perfect father. This he based on the actor Walter Pidgeon as he presented himself in his films.

> It was television that introduced me to Walter Pidgeon. I remember, on Sunday afternoons, or in the four or five snowlit days of Christmas, how he would step with such ease into the gap my father left and sit there, in my mind's eye, smoking his pipe, reading a leather-bound book, doing something with his hands. He was always a little preoccupied, always thinking about something as if life itself were a tricky, but rather amusing puzzle. Yet when anybody needed him, he was there, all attention, good-humoured but serious, ready to offer action or good counsel . . . Walter Pidgeon was the father I couldn't find

anywhere closer to home, one of those *real* fathers who can do the impossible.

More importantly, Walter Pidgeon made decisions and stood by them, no matter what. Maybe this was what made him appear so competent. Whenever I saw a Walter Pidgeon film, I wanted to be a better person in a simple, unexceptional way: more thoughtful, more alert, less self-regarding, humbler, yet more self-assured than before. What I saw was the possibility of goodness, something more than ordinary decency. I clung to the possibility, knowing it for the fantasy it was, but needing something to aspire to. I would be walking through a garden, for example, and I would see a tree that had been so very carefully planted that it moved me. Somebody selected that tree, out of all the possible trees he could have chosen, and I would feel that *this* was a Walter Pidgeon decision, because the tree was exactly right for that spot: elegant, slender, not too dominant, it filled the space in a way that no other tree could have done. This sense of things being done right, this sense of the just act, is something a man should get from his father.[4]

In much the same way as John Burnside did, we each construct our own definition of a good person, someone who has the qualities and attributes we value. Psychologists call this set of ideas 'the ideal self', but the word 'ideal' suggests something we strive for but rarely attain completely, whereas what I am describing here as our own individual version of 'good' is a vital part of our sense of being a person. It is the person we know ourselves to be. If we do something that is not up to the standard we have set ourselves, we feel shamed and estranged from the person we know ourselves to be until we can make some kind of reparation. That might mean working harder at a task or sending flowers to the individual we feel we have failed.

However, our circumstances can persist in estranging us from the person we know ourselves to be, and then we know the greatest unhappiness. Both Tony and Siegfried knew what their 'good' self was, and made this clear in their conversation with me, just as they made clear their estrangement from themselves. When her husband left her, Mollie resisted the temptation to be angry, suspicious and resentful because these emotions were not part of the person she wished to be. Eric and Christine had worked hard to create a way of living which allowed them to be the people that they were. Perhaps the best gift they gave their students was not a training in yoga but the example that, if you are the good person you know yourself to be, you are happy.

The 'good' we identify with need not be one of the traditional virtues. Despite his Catholic upbringing, the actor Jack Nicholson is not noted for his virtue. For him 'good' is being a master of his craft of acting. When talking to an interviewer about his first job in Hollywood as a production assistant in the cartoon department at MGM Studios, he said,

> What I loved about working there was seeing movie stars on the lot. In that period, 1955 into 1957, just about everybody you could name worked there – Bogart, Marlon, Elizabeth Taylor. One day somebody asked me about being an actor, and the idea started to creep into my mind. It wasn't until I got that nudge about it that I gave it a shot. Once I got started, I loved it. I wanted to be the best actor possible. I worked very hard at the craft of it. I went to classes for 12 years. I'm a member of the Actors Studio. There's nobody successful who didn't study a lot.[5]

An exercise I have used a great many times in workshops is where I give the participant a list of the ten most common virtues – truthfulness, generosity, loyalty, courage and so on – and ask them to rank them in order of importance. Ten virtues allows for 3,628,800 possible permutations. I cannot recall any two of my workshop participants ever coming up with exactly the same list. Even when two or three people agreed on what was the most important virtue, when I asked each one, 'Why is this virtue important to you?', each person gave a different answer. This answer was linked to how the person saw himself, or wished to see himself, something which would emerge in the discussion over the whole day. The values which different people give to the common virtues explain why a person may behave badly in certain situations but not in others. A man might be unfaithful to his wife and steal from his boss, but be utterly fearless in the face of danger. Knowing that he was a liar and a thief did not trouble him, but to know himself to be a coward was unendurable. John Burnside told how, after his mother died, his father lived on his own, neglecting his health, and devoting himself to smoking and drinking with his friends. He wrote,

> Now that he was alone, and sliding down, the only person who could be bothered to help him was this daughter he had treated so badly. All his life, he had attacked her – psychologically, emotionally, physically – systematically chipping away at her self-regard, eroding her confidence, bleeding her of any faith she had in herself. When I asked her why she bothered, she gave me the same answer my mother would have given in the same place. 'He's still family,' she said. 'You can't just turn your back on your family.'[6]

There are many explanations of what Jesus meant when he spoke about the greatest sin, that of the sin against the Holy Ghost. When I lived in Lincolnshire in the early 1980s I was friends with the then Bishop of Lincoln Simon Phipps and his wife Mary Welch. They never tried to convert me to Anglicanism but we often discussed religion. One day I asked Simon what was meant by a sin against the Holy Ghost. He replied,

> I suppose it would mean absolutely basically turning your back consciously, deliberately on what you saw as what God stood for. There are lots of sins, lots of things which you might do which might be called sins, categories of ways in which we can do damaging things, but this sin against the Holy Ghost means, not so much that you do something, as you actually decide *to be* something which is totally over and against what you see God to be. I think the Holy Ghost, the Holy Spirit, is an attempt to put a name to the actual impinging upon our experience of God. Behind everything and within everything is this mystery which is personal, so that we can use personal categories about Him, but He is quite beyond our ken, infinite, and yet

He impinges on our lives. It's God in action that's been called God's spirit. And if we say, yes, but I don't want anything of that, I'm just going to turn my back on that, that's something more fundamental, isn't it, than the more peccadillo things that go against it. It's a writing of God off completely.

Simon's distinction between deciding to do something and deciding to be something is very important. We can decide to do something which we know is not in our best interests, or is illegal or immoral, but, while the consequences might be unpleasant or even very satisfactory, we can decide never to do that thing again because it was unwise or we felt somewhat guilty afterwards. But, if we decide *to be* something which we are not, we commit, for want of a better word, a sin against ourselves. We have denied the person we know ourselves to be. And that is unforgivable. Tony and Siegfried could not forgive themselves for denying who they each were. They each had a dim memory of a time when they were able to live happily and unselfconsciously with themselves. Tony blamed others for this loss of the Garden of Eden; Siegfried blamed himself.

A baby does not lie in his cot wondering if other people will approve of him. He lies there just being himself, experiencing his state of unselfconscious self-acceptance. When people like me write about how we can turn against ourselves and hate ourselves, or come to see ourselves as being bad and unacceptable, we can give the impression to our readers that these are conscious decisions, as if we say to ourselves, 'I am now going to hate myself because I am bad and unacceptable.' This is far from the case. What we experience are feelings which, although they are meanings, are difficult to put into words, though they can be described in images that can be spoken in terms of 'It felt as if . . .'. In my conversations with people I have often used the question, 'If you could paint a picture of what you're feeling, what sort of picture would you paint?'

When this question has to do with discovering that your world is not what you thought it was, and you have been betrayed, humiliated and hurt by those whom you trusted, the words which feature most frequently in people's description of the image of their feelings are: broken, smashed, dirty, disgusting, grey, and black. Something whole and beautiful has been destroyed and in its place is a sticky blackness which envelops the sense of being a person ('I felt black and disgusting inside'). Some people describe this blackness as chaos, and others as complete emptiness. Then the blackness slowly oozes out and besmirches the whole of the person's world. This experience creates an intense disgust that some people turn against themselves, while others turn it against the world. Many do both. They hate themselves and they hate their world.

Terrible though this experience is, some people manage to retain a dim memory of the time of unselfconscious self-acceptance. It is this memory which has been elaborated into the myths about some Garden of Eden from which the inhabitants are expelled. If early in our life we discover that the world is not what we thought it was, and that we have been humiliated, betrayed and hurt by those we trusted, and from then on we regard our body and the world we live in with disgust, we can create a set of beliefs based on the idea of a perfect place that transcends the world. There spiritual beings, divested of their bodily form, live in harmony. Such a belief can comfort us, but, focused on this supernatural place, we cease to care about what happens to the world and the people in it.

Those people who manage to retain a precious shred of their infant unselfconscious self-acceptance can construct a sense of being a person who is, in essence, good. Even if circumstances prevent them from being who they know themselves to be, they can envisage being able to become themselves. Moreover, they are able to construct a model of a human being, representative of all human beings, which is, in essence, good. Those who lose their hold on their unselfconscious self-acceptance, who turn against themselves and hate themselves, can find it difficult even to conceive of, much less return to, their original state of unselfconscious self-acceptance. Their model of a human being sees all human beings as, in essence, bad.

In practice it is much easier to be the person you know

yourself to be if you believe that all human beings are, in essence, good and that, unfortunately, they can learn to be bad. However, many people use the alternative model, that of a human being who is, in essence, bad. This badness has to be kept under control, either by the person himself or by others. People who see themselves as being, in essence, bad can take pride in their acknowledgement of their badness, and this pride prevents them from changing and seeing themselves as, in essence, good or even just ordinary.

It is extremely rare for a person to display what we might call equal quantities of goodness and badness. From our personal vantage point, our world divides into goodies and baddies. When we were small we knew the nice teachers and the nasty ones; who were our friends and who were our enemies. Only our parents presented us with a confusing mixture of good and bad, a necessary preparation for the confusions of right and wrong in adult life. Life is much simpler when the goodies and baddies are clearly defined. Those of us old enough to remember the Second World War can look back nostalgically to the days when the British Empire, the United States, and the USSR were good and Germany, Italy, and Japan were bad. Life was never to be as simple again.

That people never display equal and invariable amounts of goodness and badness leaves us with only two basic hypotheses. We can say that a person is born good but can be corrupted, or we can say that a person is born bad but can acquire goodness. If we use a model of essential goodness, if we see the baby coming into the world 'trailing clouds of glory', then we can deplore the effects of the world as the 'shades of the prison-house begin to close upon the growing boy', but we can hope that such essential goodness can be brought forth, led out, as our word 'education' implies by its derivation. If, on the other hand, we use a model of essential badness ('born in sin'), then we can see the effects of the world as increasing or controlling or eradicating this badness. Hope lies in expiation, redemption, and salvation.

Whichever model we use, we reveal it in the kind of statements we make about our expectations of other people. Sir Melford Stevenson, a judge renowned for the severity of his judgments, said in a BBC interview,

I have no doubt that the softening of the penal system towards the young offender has done infinite harm. I know that 'do-gooders' is a term of abuse, but they exist. They are dedicated people and they are very good people, and most of them start their work with the sincere conviction that they have a gift for work among boys and so they have, and mostly it works out quite well; but they also suffer from the illusion that a high proportion of people are capable of redemption and I don't think it is so.[7]

By contrast, Arthur Scargill, the Yorkshire miners' leader, told his BBC interviewer,

I'm a Christian and I've also got faith not only in my belief as a socialist but a tremendous belief in human beings, and I know that we can produce a society where man will not simply go to work and have a little leisure, but will release his latent talent and ability and begin to produce in the cultural sense all the things I know he's capable of: music, poetry, writing, sculpture, whole works of art that, at the moment, are literally lying dormant simply because we, as a society, are not able to tap it.[8]

Arthur Scargill, like psychologist Abraham Maslow, believed in the possibility of the person 'actualizing his potential' and one's 'full Humanness'.

Whether we hold a model of the essential goodness or the essential badness of mankind we have to decide whether our model allows for improvement. Can a person become a better person – approach, and perhaps achieve, perfection? Can the human race, or certain sections of it, achieve progress? Not everyone answers 'yes' to these questions. 'Human nature never changes' is a commonplace, while many observers of history would support Talleyrand's 'Plus ça change, plus c'est la même chose' ('The more things change, the more they remain the same'). The historian Edward Gibbon saw the causes of the decline and fall of the Roman Empire as essentially human weakness and depravity. The rise and fall of great civilisations would continue, he believed, since human nature does not change. The ancient Greeks saw neither men nor gods as perfectible. The gods, as described by Homer and

Hesiod, would deceive, steal, and commit adultery. Their intervention in the lives of men and women, for good and all, is the core of Greek tragedy. Capricious though the gods may be, there was one sin they would not forgive and that was *hubris*, spiritual pride, the seeking of self-sufficiency or perfect happiness. There are many people today who believe that to seek happiness is to invite disaster. There are others who believe, like John Calvin with his doctrine of predestination (God has pre-ordained, at the beginning of time, who it is that He will graciously save), that their lives, their salvation or damnation, are predestined. They say, 'It was meant to be.'

If our model of a person allows for improvement we then have to decide whether this improvement can come about through the person's own efforts or through some outside agency. Institutions like psychiatry and the Christian Church are divided on this issue. Psychotherapy, whatever form it takes, is based on the idea of helping the patient to discover his own power to help himself, while in chemotherapy, electroconvulsive therapy, and psychosurgery, the power to cure lies in the hands of the psychiatrists. The Christian is charged 'Be ye therefore perfect, even as your Father which is in heaven is perfect', but to achieve perfection we should 'Trust in the Lord with all thine heart: and lean not unto thy own understanding'. St Augustine argued that perfection could be achieved only by loving God with one's whole heart and soul, and, since the Fall, man has been incapable of doing this as his will is corrupted by original sin. The Christian, therefore, is dependent upon the grace of God. Pelagius argued against the idea of original sin and claimed that man could rely on his own efforts, with God's guidance, to achieve perfection. Pelagianism was condemned by the Council of Carthage in 417, and from then on it was Roman Catholic doctrine that men could not perfect themselves without special grace from God. The Protestant movement challenged the view that salvation lies in the external power of the grace of God. St Paul had written, 'If thou shalt confess with thy mouth the Lord Jesus, and shalt believe in thine heart that God hath raised him from the dead, thou shalt be saved', and so Luther argued for justification by faith and

Wesley for acceptance of free grace. William James pointed out the similarity between the mind-cure movement (now called psychotherapy) and the Lutheran and Wesleyan movement.

> To the believer in moralism and [good] works with his anxious query, 'What shall I do to be saved?' Luther and Wesley replied, 'You are saved now, if you would believe it.' And the mind-curers come with precisely the same words of emancipation. 'Give up the feeling of responsibility, let go your hold, resign the care of your destiny to higher powers, be genuinely indifferent as to what becomes of it all, and you will find not only that you gain a perfect inward relief, but often also, in addition, the particular goods you sincerely thought you were renouncing.' This is salvation through self-despair, the dying to be truly born.[9]

Relax and be successful, say the psychotherapists.

Both religious and political revolutionaries believed that progress could come suddenly, while liberal humanists saw progress in terms of incremental change. John Gray, Professor of European Thought at the London School of Economics, wrote, 'Whether they stress piecemeal change or revolutionary transformation, theories of progress are not scientific hypotheses. They are myths, which answer the human need for meaning.'[10] Myths are ideas, and ideas create actions. The waves of unrest in Europe in the nineteenth century sent adventurers to the New World and with them went the belief that man had within him the power of self-improvement and the hope that life was capable of infinite improvement.

Such ideas were handed down from one generation of Americans to another, and now the differences in the American and the European models of man and society are reflected in the differences between American and European interpretation of the theories of psychoanalysis and existentialism. Freud saw man as essentially bad, and his life as a conflict between the demands of his id and the demands of society. Psychoanalysis could benefit man by turning uncomprehending neurosis into common unhappiness, but man and society were, in the end, doomed. Such pessimism is certainly not shared by all American psychoanalysts, while the great men of psychotherapy, Erich Fromm, Carl Rogers, Abraham Maslow, and Rollo May, have at the core of their theories a model of the self that is essentially good. Nor do American existentialists and phenomenologists share the resignation of their European counterparts. William Barrett told the story of how

> Sartre recounts a conversation he had with an American visiting this country. The American insisted that all international problems could be solved if men would just get together and be rational; Sartre disagreed and after a while discussion became impossible. 'I believe in the existence of evil,' says Sartre, 'and he does not.'[11]

In 1978 the American phenomenologist Peter Koestenbaum wrote,

> Evil can and should be totally eliminated from the world, because evil does not possess the solidity and permanence of good. Evil is not as entrenched in the structure of being as is good. The proper attitude, therefore, toward evil is to struggle for its total elimination.[12]

In 2004 Lieutenant Colonel Gareth Brandl of the US Marines, who led his troops into the assault on Falluja, said, 'The enemy has got a face. He's called Satan. And we're going to destroy him.'[13] In saying this Colonel Brandl was following in the wake of his Commander-in-Chief. President Bush, speaking in the National Cathedral a year after the fall of the Twin Towers, said, 'Our responsibility to history is clear: to answer these attacks and rid the world of evil.'[14]

Evil is an abstract noun on to which we can project a wide variety of meanings. William James notes that there are people

> for whom evil means only a maladjustment with things, a wrong correspondence of one's life with the environment. Such evil as this is curable, in principle at least, upon the natural plane, for merely modifying the self or the things, or both at once, the two terms may be made to fit and all go merry as a marriage bell again. But there are others for whom evil is no mere relation of the subject to particular

outer things, but something more radical and general, a wrongness or vice in his essential nature, which no rearrangement of the inner self can cure, and which requires a supernatural remedy.[15]

If we construct a model of the human being as essentially good, and see the universe as good, or neither good nor bad but simply there, we can construe evil as 'a wrong correspondence of one's life with the environment' and so believe that we can, with intelligence and cooperation, go some way towards solving the world's problems. We can agree with Herakleitos that 'all things are beautiful, good and right; men, on the other hand, deem some things right and others wrong'.

The ancient Greek philosophers were the first to examine in a rational and systematic way the question of the origin of evil. Socrates saw evil as the result of the lack of episteme, knowledge of how to seek virtue. The Cynics saw evil as the result of the pursuit of wealth and fame. Epictetus pointed out that 'It is not things in themselves which trouble us, but our opinions of things.' In forming our opinions we make choices, and choices, said Marcus Aurelius, which are based on ignorance and thus thwart the intentions of God, lead to evil in an otherwise non-evil world.

The belief that evil is created by people and thus is curable by people is held only by those of us who enjoy a certain sense of security. Those of us whose experience of life has led us to the conclusion that life is a chancy business where the bad often, and perhaps always, defeats the good, see evil as 'something more radical and general'. In his book *The Devil; Perceptions of Evil from Antiquity to Primitive Christianity*, Jeffrey Burton Russell describes evil as

meaningless, senseless destruction. Evil destroys and does not build; it rips and it does not mend; it cuts and does not bind. It strives always and everywhere to annihilate, to turn to nothing. To take all being and render it nothing is the heart of evil. Or as Erich Fromm puts it, evil is 'life turning against itself' or 'attraction to what is dead, decaying, lifeless, and purely mechanical'.

Russell goes on to point out:

> Whether one perceives the Devil as a supernatural being, or an uncontrollable force arising in the unconscious, or as an absolute aspect of human nature is less important than the essence of the perception, which is that we are threatened by alien and hostile powers: 'Evil is terribly real for each and every individual,' Jung said. 'If you regard the principle of evil as a reality you can just as well call it the devil.'[16]

'I sense the power of evil quite often', said Billy Graham, 'Satan doesn't want me to read the Bible or to pray.' Billy Graham believed that 'Satan won't win because he's already been defeated at the Cross', but not everyone shares Billy Graham's optimism, that the forces of good will ultimately defeat the forces of evil. Many people whose lives are consumed by fear, no matter how secure their personal circumstances may be, interpret all the world's problems as evidence that the forces of good are at the point of being overwhelmed by the forces of evil.

I do not believe in a force of evil, but I do believe in human stupidity. Evil or stupidity, the results are the same. When I went to work at St John's Hospital in Lincoln in 1972 Harry Weber was the hospital chaplain. He was a man of unsurpassed goodness. I saw this not just in the kindness and patience he showed to every patient but in the fact that every week he attended the case conference which was held by the consultant psychiatrist who dominated the whole hospital. The sociologist Erving Goffman called case conferences the 'degradation ceremony', and so it was. Consultants have always defended the case conference as the most efficient way of reviewing patients – that is, it was the most convenient method for the consultant. This was not the patients' view. As a patient you went alone into a room where there could be as many as thirty people of whom you might know only two or three. The basic rule was that any of these people could ask you anything at all about yourself. Nothing about you was private. The only question you were allowed to ask had to be directed at the consultant and was, 'When can I go home?'

The other consultants at the hospital regarded their case conferences as a necessary chore to be got through as quickly and uneventfully as possible. The dominant consultant regarded his case conferences in much the same way as Louis XIV, the Sun King, regarded his court, a place to display his total power. The consultant chose a room large enough to seat around the walls his entire retinue of senior and junior doctors, doctors from other psychiatric hospitals, the full hierarchy of nurses, various social workers, occupational therapists, physiotherapists, and any students who might be visiting the hospital. On my arrival at the hospital, he made it clear to me that attendance at his case conference was my most important duty. I went for a few weeks and watched him sitting like a portly king, dispensing his judgements, homilies and witticisms. I saw the patients waiting outside the door to be called, and shaking with fear. Called inside one by one, they sat isolated as the consultant confused, humiliated or rewarded them according to his whim.

My capacity to watch, helpless, this display of power-crazed cruelty was limited. My attendance only added to the number of those witnessing each patient's shame. I felt that I could be better employed giving what support I could to individual patients when I met them elsewhere and, later, by writing about the iniquities of the psychiatric system.

Harry Weber saw the situation differently. Every case conference he was there, sitting in a prominent position, bearing witness to another human being's suffering. Those patients who knew him were comforted to know that he was their witness. I had the feeling that Harry was, in part, expiating what he regarded as the sins of his misspent youth, before he entered the Church. However, those who have suffered make the best witnesses of other people's suffering.

Sometimes the sense of badness is felt to be a force of evil which the person experiences as being as real as toothache or an icy wind. Harry described to me how,

Evil has many facets. I see evil as an influence that can take over or influence us. I think we're all having evil impinged on us in this world. I think there is holiness. In prayer and in spiritual life you are deliberately reaching out toward God. I do think there are evil influences and the world today is very much in the grip of evil. You know as well as I do that you can go to certain places which have evil associations where the atmosphere is terrible. You can go to other places which are spiritual and holy or good and full of love and friendship. I think there is an evil force and a holy force, but I think for the most part that evil forces do not take possession of a normal sort of person, though I do see some psychiatric patients as being influenced by evil. We are all buffeted by evil influences, but normally speaking we're perfectly safe. The holy influences are stronger than the evil influences. I don't think there is anything to be afraid of.

Harry spoke of combating the force of evil with prayers of healing, prayers of exorcism, and anointing with holy oil. He said,

The priesthood has a charisma. I do believe that we can touch, we can bless, heal by spiritual means. In baptism we are all blessed with the Holy Spirit. But the gifts that God gives us can be destroyed or thrown away. You are a creature of free will. The gifts that God gives us we can always throw away at our own peril.

Harry had retired by the time Trevor became a patient at St John's. Had he known Trevor he might have considered him to be a person in the grip of the force of evil. Trevor was sweet, gentle and kind. He never talked to me about his parents except in the most kindly way but, over the years I knew him, I became aware that, like most of the young people who become psychotic, he was privy to a family secret about which he could not speak and for which he took responsibility in the sense that he would not bring into the open anything which might cause his parents the distress of discovering, or revealing to outsiders, that the picture of family life which they presented to outsiders was false. Trevor never told me what his family secret was, but he alluded to it in many ways. He could not tell me explicitly because it was a secret which he knew he was forbidden to know. I can illustrate what I mean with a story about another of my clients, a woman who was extremely distressed by her husband's constant infidelities. He was a public figure well known for his moral character and philanthropic work. He cowed his wife into silence by physically abusing her when they were alone together. She pretended to her schoolboy son that the bruises on her face and arms were the result of accidents because, so she told me, she did not want the boy to think badly of his father whom she always praised for his kindness and generosity to them. Of course the boy knew what was going on, but this was knowledge he was not supposed to have. In his first year at university he became psychotic. For this young man and for Trevor, the discrepancy between the family secret and the pretence of normality which the family presented to the outside world became more and more difficult for them to straddle. University life and, for Trevor, the magic mushrooms, loosened their grip on the reality they shared with other people. They withdrew into their highly idiosyncratic internal reality in the way that introverts do when they lose all confidence in themselves.[17] Not that the psychiatrists were interested in any of this. Trevor had been to university and he had taken drugs. Therefore he was schizophrenic.

When I met Trevor he had successfully completed his university degree but after that he could not keep a job: he would drift off into a state which he called 'Nowhere Land', a lonely, empty, and very private place. Once in Nowhere Land, his perception of reality altered, and to the outside observer his behaviour could become extremely odd. At times his fear and distress were so great that one would think that Nowhere Land was a place that he would want to avoid, but I had a difficult task in trying to persuade him that it was worth keeping at least one foot in the land of ordinary, shared reality. For him Nowhere Land, which he could reach both with and without the aid of drugs or hallucinogenic mushrooms, was a land of promise and delight, and he was reluctant to give it up. But sometimes he would be unable to leave Nowhere Land and then he would discover that all other human beings suddenly appeared as dangerous, poised to attack him without warning. One day when we were talking about this Trevor said, 'I believe that we've all got this witchcraft, devil in us, all these hidden powers in our genetic code. When you take mushrooms it tends to bring them to the foreground and makes you aware of them. Normally you're not aware of them . . . It's like a closed loop system. Everything revolves around nothing. And it all revolves around nothing – nothing, nothing, zero. Everything, the whole of life around nothing. It's absolutely pointless, means nothing. This is the devil. He tortures us by making us aware of the fact that nothing is worthwhile, got no point to it. This potential to be the devil is within us. You can live a life of hell on earth – living the experience of the devil. Experiencing everything as futile. Being totally confused. End up in circular loops where everything revolves around nothing. Nowhere Land isn't necessarily where the devil is. Nowhere Land is a peaceful place to be. The devil is somewhere else. The devil lurks within us. He's there all the time and sometimes he comes forward and he can take over our consciousness. Nowhere Land is a place of rest away from the strains of reality.'

I asked, 'Last weekend, when you were in that psychotic state, were you in Nowhere Land?'

'I was partly in Nowhere Land to start off with and then I gave up and became the devil.'

Trevor dated the beginning of his difficulties from when he had first tried the mushrooms, but the more we talked the more it became clear that Nowhere Land had always been available. He said, 'As a child I was positive all the time. I had direction, a purpose. There was no need to drift off into Nowhere Land – except I do have recollections of sitting round the table with the family and drifting off into Nowhere Land.'

'When you were a child, did you have any concept of the devil?'

'No. That was not until I had those mushrooms. I was frightened at discovering the devil, but at the same time I came to the realisation of a God, a Godliness, and everything's perfection. I went through the two extremes. I could see life as being perfection or damnation. I couldn't see anything in between.'

'Where is the Godliness?'

'Inside us.'

'So you see the devil as being a person separate from us?'

'No, no. The devil is an integral part of us, of our minds. He's the way we think.'

'Is that one of the reasons – when you start to drift off into a psychotic state you get frightened of other people?'

'Yes. I get frightened altogether. The devil and all his works. There's no means of escape.'

'You can't escape your own devil and other people who look normal have the devil inside them?'

'Yes, but it might not be obvious at the time.'

'Is it the same with God? Do you see God as separate?'

'God's an integral part as well.'

'Do you see us as having a choice about God and the devil inside us?'

'No. It's all decided by conditioning, I think. In the extremes you can't control them. But there's a gradual path to the extremes – a gradual path of events that led you to that extreme, so that there's points on the scale between the two extremes. I think that circumstances lead us one way or the other. If we're in easy company we tend towards God-liness, whereas if there's a difficulty we tend towards the devil. If we're in the company of people with similar minds the two people come together to form Godliness. Whereas if you're with people you don't communicate with – that's steps toward the devil. Nowhere Land isn't Godliness – it's an escape, a retreat.'

'Is Nowhere Land always solitary?'

'Yes.'

'So no communication and so you drift toward the devil.'

'Yes.'

'What would happen if you moved right to the extreme of Godliness?'

'All the time? I don't think it's possible. If it was possible I think you'd do the same as Jesus – teach other people how to achieve the same position, the extremes of Godliness.'

'How far along the line of Godliness do you see yourself moving?'

'About three-quarters of the way.'

'And what would you be doing?'

'Most of my relationships would be kind and loving. People would communicate with me.'

'How far along the devil dimension could you see yourself moving?'

'I could see myself moving to the furthest extreme. I would hope that something would manage to get me out of it. But – death comes at the extreme of the devil, because the devil has taken over to such an extent you can't control it any more. You feel like committing suicide.'

'If you did commit suicide, what would happen to you then?'

'That would end everything between the two alternatives.'

'Do you see any existence going on after death?'

'No. None whatsoever. Life will go on as usual on the planet. I'll be just the molecules and atoms I'm made up of – eventually they'll make something else.'

Trevor tried hard to create a decent life for himself, but when you are on high doses of anti-psychotic drugs it is impossible to maintain the degree of alertness and organisation we all need to live an ordinary life. Faced with failure, he killed himself.

We each have our own individual way of interpreting good and bad, goodness and evil. All of these interpretations are fantasies. We have no way of proving that good and/or bad reside in us, or that goodness and evil inhabit the world. We can judge people's actions as being good or bad by their outcomes, but there is a multitude of theories about the cause of a person's actions. Yet we all judge people and events in terms of good and bad. Our actions follow from our judgements. If we are wise we know quite consciously what the ideas are that lead us to make certain judgements rather than others.

If you are wise you will be able to answer the following questions.

1 Who is the person you know yourself to be? What are the attributes of the person you know yourself to be?
2 Are you able to be the person you know yourself to be?
3 What for you is the most important virtue?
4 Why is that virtue important to you?

5 Do you see yourself in essence good or bad?
6 Does goodness exist as a force? If so, where does it reside?
7 Or is goodness simply a word which we use when we are talking about the wonderful things that happen?
8 Does evil exist as a force? If so, where does it reside?
9 Or is evil simply a word which we use when we are talking about the terrible things that happen?
10 And lastly – do you believe that we live in a world where ultimately good people are rewarded and bad people punished?

The Just World

Small toddlers know what 'It's not fair' means long before they are capable of uttering these words. As self-consciousness develops so does the concept of fairness applied, not yet to the world at large, but to the toddler's burgeoning sense of being a person. Fairness validates the person; unfairness invalidates it. So toddlers protest when other children take their toys. Teaching a small child to share and care is not easy.

By the time children have discovered the necessity of fairness they have come to expect a pattern to their day. For some the pattern is no more than light and darkness, awake and sleeping, while for others the pattern includes meals and walks and nursery without mother. Whatever the pattern, there is within this another pattern which helps the child predict his future. This is the pattern: if I'm good I get rewarded, if I'm bad I get punished. Even when the reward is no more than the avoidance of punishment, the child gradually comes to understand what his parent means by 'good' and 'bad'. With that understanding comes the belief that he can predict the future, and thus control his life by choosing when to be good and when to be bad in the way that his parent defines these words.

Some parents present the rule 'If you're good you get rewarded and if you're bad you get punished' to the child solely in terms of how their family life functions. Punishments and rewards are in the gift of the parent. There are no sanctions or rewards beyond the naughty step and the special treat, except the breaking of the bond between parent and child, and the expulsion of the child from the family. Many parents actually utter this threat, often intending it as a joke or a threat that the child knows will never be carried out. They do not understand that for the child the threat of expulsion can never be an idle threat or a joke. Children know how hard it is for a homeless child to survive. They recognise their dependency on their parents, no matter how incompetent or cruel the parents might be.

When their rewards and punishments and the threat of expulsion seem not to produce the results the parents want, most parents call on some higher power to provide the ultimate sanction and reward. In doing so, they introduce the child to the Just World. This is the belief that there is an all-encompassing Grand Design which governs everything that exists. This design ordains that ultimately good people are rewarded and bad people punished. *Within the Just World nothing happens by chance.* Whatever happens, it was caused either by yourself or by others. 'Others' can be other people or powers such as God, the Devil, and the forces of good and evil.

Some people see themselves as the cause of every outcome, good or bad. Some people feel that the outcome of every event is decided by God or the Devil. Some people believe that they create all the good outcomes and their enemies the bad. Some people thank God for every good outcome and blame themselves for every bad outcome. It is a choice between total responsibility, total helplessness, paranoia or depression.

All religions teach that we live in a Just World where goodness is rewarded and badness punished. Religions differ in how they define goodness and badness, rewards and punishments. Some religions have God or Allah or a range of gods handing out the rewards and punishments, while in Buddhism the rule of karma decides your fate.

The belief in a life after death necessitates a belief in the Just World. If there is a better life after death, there must be some kind of system of justice which decides which people merit this better life. However, many of the people who believe that life ends in death also believe in the Just World. They find it too painful to see the disasters and injustices they witness as random events. They cannot bear the feelings of pity and helplessness. Instead they look for evidence that the rich and famous are unhappy, the wicked receive their just deserts, and that good people are rewarded by being loved by their families. Public rewards, memorials, and the telling of the person's life story can be seen, not just as ways in which relationships between people function, but as evidence of a Just World operating in a life bounded by death.

'Chance' and 'luck' are words which refer to the inherent randomness of the universe. However, many people co-opt these words into their picture of the Just World in operation. Intellectually gamblers know that lottery operators and casinos make their money from the randomness inherent in the spin of a wheel or the turn of a card, but, rather than calculate the odds, they place their faith in, 'Someone has to win. Why shouldn't that person be me?' Many believe that there is some supernatural force which will reward them when such a reward is deserved. They may court Lady Luck in the way as children they courted their mother in the hope of a reward; they may read their star signs, or say a prayer, or light a candle, or make an offering, all in the hope that some higher power will grant them the good luck they deserve. Some people believe that they were born with a certain amount of luck which they hope will last them a lifetime. Mr G. was one of these people. I met Mr G. a few years before post-traumatic stress disorder (PTSD) was invented. Thus it was that, instead of giving Mr G. the diagnosis of PTSD and writing a report which said that Mr G's extreme anxiety was caused by a mental disorder, his psychiatrist sent him to me.

It is not uncommon for a person to suffer a disproportionate amount of anxiety after an accident. When the accident is followed by a lawsuit, then the question arises as to the motivation for this manifestation of anxiety. It was for this reason that I was asked to assess Mr G. At work in a factory, Mr G. had fallen on to a moving conveyor belt and was within inches of being crushed to death when the machinery was stopped. He had suffered little more than bruising and shock, but in the months following the accident he had become so anxious that he was unable to work or even to leave the caravan where he lived. He managed to obey his solicitor and come and see me at the psychiatric hospital. Afterwards I wrote the following report:

Mr G. arrived early for his appointment. He was very nervous about yet another examination, and later in our conversation he said that he was frightened about coming to the hospital in case he was kept there. We talked for some time but, although he was more at ease with me, as soon as we started what he quickly identified as an intelligence test he became almost too nervous to do the test. On the W.A.I.S. Vocabulary I could repeat the questions to give him time to answer, and so he was able to make an average score. On the Block Design the test instructions are precise and limited and each item is timed. Mr G. recognised that the problems should be easily solved but he could not solve them and as he berated himself for his failure he grew increasingly anxious. His score on this test was well below average. This kind of anxiety made it impossible for him to carry out complex tasks at work and so he could be employed only at work well below his intellectual level which appears to be in the average range.

On the Rorschach Mr G. showed himself to be a person who wants everything about him to be neat and complete and to fit reasonably into its proper shape and position. Many of us are like that, but to survive in this chaotic, unreasonable world we have to be efficient in bringing order out of chaos and confident in our abilities. Mr G. is neither. He sets himself a high standard to achieve, but he lacks the ability and the originality to reach this standard. When he does manage to organise something in an adequate, mundane way he immediately fears that he has not done it well enough and that other people will do it better. He seeks constant reassurance that what he does is acceptable.

Further, on the Rorschach, he showed that his ability to empathise with and relate to other adults is limited, but that his awareness of his need for affection is quite great, so problems must arise within his relationships. He must demand affection without perceiving how to return affection in the way the other person wants it returned. He is very much aware of his needs and fears, but he is unable to express them in any direct fashion. He is very much aware of what goes on around him, but again he is very cautious and controlled in his reactions. In short, some men react to pressure from their needs and fears and to outside stress by being aggressive, or by drinking, gambling or copulating to excess. Mr G. turns his painful needs and fears into bodily pain. Medical science has not yet elucidated how thought processes, many of which never come clearly into consciousness, transmute into physical pain, but such pain is felt as keenly as that caused by physical injury.

By turning fear and aggression into pain the problem of what to do with the fear and aggression may be solved and may even have the bonus of gaining affectionate sympathy, but the pain itself then raises anxiety. Such anxiety is not relieved by assurances that the pain has no physical basis. Mr G. fears that the pain is a necessary precursor of death and it is death that he fears.

When Mr G. fell on to the conveyor belt he lay there expecting to die. He said that he knew death was imminent and he thought of all the things that mattered to him, his life and his family. He was, he said, saved by luck. Now luck is something that means different things to different people. To some luck is a lady who may or may not grant her favours. To others, of whom Mr G. is one, luck is a commodity, a portion of which we are given at birth. As our life proceeds, we use up our luck and when our luck runs out we die. Mr G. sees himself as having used up a lot of his luck in surviving a long war and a serious wound. He used up more of his luck in a car crash. In his accident at work his luck all ran out and he is left with so little that he expects not to survive the next dangerous situation into which he is thrown.

He lives in daily expectancy of death. A car journey is fraught with terrors whose presence he would not have recognised before his accident. His pains and stiffness suggest cancer or a crippling illness terminating in death. For some of us, death is merely a doorway to another life. But others cannot conceive of a life after death. For them death is final. This is all the life we have. Mr G. is one of these. He describes death as loss, 'loss of life, family, friends, country, everything'.

Mr G. joined the factory before the war and returned to it after the war. He has never wished to work anywhere else. He has never wished to live anywhere other than his home town. He was married and had a home and a family. Then came his accident which left him with a greatly heightened fear of death. This was followed by a series of disagreements with his wife which culminated in his leaving. A mere eight weeks later he was divorced. He lost his family and his home. This loss appeared to him as part of death and he wonders when the other parts of death will come. He looks at his caravan home and thinks that it is too insubstantial to survive. He looks at the woman he now lives with and wonders when she will leave him. She says she will stay but how can he be sure? He wonders when his firm will discard him and he knows that he would be unable to cope with a new job. He wonders if all these anxieties mean that he is going mad. He looks at the chronic patients from the psychiatric hospital who work in his factory, and he sees that they take tablets as he now takes tablets. He fears that he will be incarcerated in this psychiatric hospital. He fears being alone in the world, unable to work. He fears living and he fears dying.

In short, Mr G. is a man of average ability who, though somewhat over-controlled and somewhat restricted in his capacity to form adult relationships, was sufficiently stable to cope with ordinary life. Then he had an experience, the effect of which no person could master with ease. To master such an experience one would need a high degree of intelligent flexibility of mind and the kind of self-confidence which sees it as just and right that one has survived. Mr G. has neither of these, and so his accident has brought him an agony of mind which far exceeds the bodily pain of which he complains.

Mr G's idea of luck as a limited commodity is analogous to the 'three strikes and you're out' system of sentencing used in some American courts, but lawcourts, being an earthly institution, allow those sentenced to appeal; but, where supernatural good fortune is concerned, we are helpless. The belief in the Just World is much more attractive because you have a chance of manipulating good fortune by being good.

Believers in the Just World each have their own image of that world, but all these images have the same underlying structure, that of a world which is governed by immutable and transcendent laws of justice and retribution. Consequently, they view life very differently from those who see it as being random, where chance and probabilities, not certainties, determine the outcome of events. Many of us who see the world in this way place great value on the freedom, opportunities and hope which it offers. Others see it as John Burnside's father did.

The Burnside family lived in Blackburn Drive, Cowdenbeath in Scotland. Their neighbour Arthur Fulton was a gentle giant greatly liked by those who knew him. When Arthur was charged with the attempted murder of a young woman, George Burnside told his wife that Arthur had probably committed the crime but he should not go to gaol for it. He said,

'These things happen. I don't suppose Arthur planned it. If he had, he'd surely done a better job.' He shook his head sadly; it seemed that what bothered him most about the incident wasn't the possibility that Arthur had tried to kill the girl, but the idea that he'd botched it so badly. 'It was probably an accident, one way or another.'
My mother didn't answer. There was no point, after all. To her, everything happened, or ought to have happened, for a reason. You made a choice, and if you chose the wrong path, it was a sin and you had to pay the penance – and it struck me, then, how odd it was that these two people should be married to one another. It wasn't just that they were different in temperament, or in what they wanted from life, or in what they believed – it was that they inhabited different worlds. For my mother, life was full of

patterns and logic; my father, on the other hand, was haunted by the irrational. Maybe that was what made him so decisive: there was a sense in which no action had any meaningful consequences for him, a sense that there was really no such thing as cause and effect. When he said that Arthur's pathetic attempt to kill the girl was an accident, he was saying something about life itself. What he meant was that it was *all* an accident: the meeting, whatever history Arthur had with the girl, whatever feelings he or she might have had, the mood Arthur was in that afternoon, the fact that he panicked. Everything that happened was an accident. The only power you had was to act decisively when the accident happened and so make your own mark on the proceedings. And the truth was that, in Arthur Fulton's place, my father wouldn't have flunked the job. He would have broken the girl's neck and left her in a ditch somewhere, then he would have gone to the pub and sat all night playing crib with his friends. I think he was disappointed that Arthur hadn't acted in the same way. The one thing Arthur had done wrong was to get himself caught. Had he been in Arthur's place, my father wouldn't have made the same mistake.[18]

Many people find the ideas of randomness and chance far too frightening. They prefer the comfort and security of believing that they live in a Just World. The Just World which Tess McGahern described to her small son John was a world of certainty, wonder and delight. John lived with his mother, his sisters and his father's mother in a small bungalow a mile outside the town of Ballinamore in Leitrim, Ireland. His father, a sergeant in the Garda, lived in the barracks twenty miles away in Cootehall. In his memoir of his childhood John McGahern said of his father,

> His upbringing was as an only child. He was religious too, but his religion was of outward show, edicts and strictures, enforcements and observances and all the exactions they demanded. In his shining uniform he always walked with slow steps to the head of the church to kneel at the front seat. [My mother] would slip quietly into one of the seats at the back.[19]

The Just World which underpinned his mother's faith was clear to the boy. As a man he wrote,

> Prayers were said every morning. Work and talk stopped in the fields and houses and school and shop and the busy street at the first sound of the Angelus bell every day. Every day was closed with the Rosary at night. The worlds to come, hell and heaven and purgatory and limbo, were closer and far more real than America or Australia and talked about almost daily as our future reality.
>
> Heaven was in the sky. My mother spoke to me about heaven as concretely and with as much love as she named the wild flowers. Above us the sun of heaven shone. Beyond the sun was the gate of heaven. Within the gates were the thrones and mansions, the Three Persons in the One God, the Blessed Virgin, the angels and saints, and beyond those mansions were the gardens of paradise where time ceased and everything entered an instant of joy that lasted for all eternity at one with the mind of God. It was her prayer and fervent hope that we would all live together in happiness with God for all eternity.
>
> Heaven was in the sky. Hell was in the bowels of the earth. There, eternal fire raged. The souls of the damned had to dwell in hell for all eternity, deprived forever of the sight of the face of God. At its entrance was a great river. Across the wide plain, naked and weeping, came the souls of the damned from the Judgement Seat, bearing only a single coin to give the boatman to take them across the river into eternal fire.
>
> Between this heaven and hell purgatory was placed. Descriptions of it were vague, probably because all of us expected to spend time there. The saints alone went straight to heaven. In purgatory, we would have to be purified in flame to a whiteness like that of snow before we could join the saints in the blessedness of heaven.
>
> Away in a silent corner was limbo, where grave-faced children who hadn't received baptism slept, without consciousness or pain, throughout all eternity. Limbo was closed to us because of our baptism. In those young years, contemplating a future hell, or at best long purifications

of purgatory, it did not seem a bad place at all, and there were times when I hoped that some essential rite had been overlooked during my baptism; but I could not communicate this to my mother.

At Easter my mother always showed us the sun. 'Look how the molten globe and all the glittering rays are dancing! The whole of heaven is dancing in its joy that Christ has risen.' When Easter arrived with overcast skies and we asked for the sun, she assured us it was dancing behind the clouds. Blessed are those who have not seen but have believed.[20]

Not all of the people who believe in the Just World behave with the same gentleness and compassion as Tess McGahern showed. Many take intense pride in belonging to a group which has been especially favoured by God because of their outstanding goodness. They feel entitled to regard those who are not members of their group as mere objects on whom they can inflict their hatred and contempt, and punish those whom they feel had been inadequately punished. It was to this group that the manufacturers of Taser guns in the USA directed their advertisement.

What does Santa bring you when you're good but the world is getting bad?
The non-lethal Taser C2 stun gun, designed for consumers' self-defence. Available in four colours, the gun shoots two probes that can penetrate up to 5 centimetres of clothing and transmit electrical pulses that affect the victim's nervous system. It has a range of 4.5 metres. (www.2taser.com)[21]

The belief in the Just World can not only provide the comfort of feeling secure in your future, special in God's eyes, and entitled to administer justice whenever there is a fault in the machinery of the Just World, but it can remove the necessity of behaving well even though no reward is on offer. My friend Petra, who taught Religious Education to Muslim boys in an east London secondary school, told me that few of her students could comprehend the idea of altruism. They told her that they acted solely in terms of reward and punishment.

Thinking is hard work. Believing in the Just World reduces the immense complexity of the world to the simple categories of good and bad, reward and punishment. Closing their eyes to the complexity of the world means that believers in the Just World create a fantasy about the world which has little connection to what is actually going on. Even though this fantasy consigns most of the world's population to the 'bad' category, believers in the Just World see the 'good' category triumphing over evil. This comforting fantasy prevents believers from seeing what evil deeds are actually being committed. At present, fundamentalist leaders in the Anglican Church are absorbed in their crusade against homosexuality; they seem to be totally indifferent to the suffering of millions in Congo, Darfur, Chad and Kenya, suffering which has been caused not by some natural disaster but by the wickedness and stupidity of men who hold political power and/or guns. The Most Reverend Peter Jensen, Archbishop of Sydney, speaking after the service of ordination of forty-eight deacons at St Andrew's Cathedral in Sydney on February 2, 2008, said,

> With regret, the Archbishop and Bishops of the Diocese of
> Sydney have decided not to attend the Lambeth
> Conference in July. They remain fully committed to the
> Anglican Communion, to which they continue to belong,
> but sense that attending the Conference at this time will
> not help heal its divisions. They continue to pray for the
> Archbishop of Canterbury and the Lambeth Conference.[22]

Undoubtedly the Lambeth Conference would be discussing Congo, Darfur, Chad and Kenya, but, if there was any discussion of homosexuality, it would not be solely in terms of it being an unforgivable sin. This is the reason why Peter Jensen and his bishops would not be attending. They are more offended by homosexuality than they are by cruelty and the suffering it engenders.

As I see it, inflicting suffering on others is wrong. No one has the right to harm others. We do have the right to restrain others who inflict suffering, and, if offenders do not learn to mend their ways, we have the right to separate them from our orderly society, but we do not have the right to

inflict suffering on them, other than the loss of their freedom. When I refer to inflicting harm as being wicked, I do
not need some transcendent power to tell me that it is so.
I know it is wrong simply because I feel pain, and so I know
that other people feel pain. To live safely in this world we
need to be keenly aware of those people who do not have our
interests at heart and who would harm us, either carelessly
or by intent. However, a dislike of witnessing other people's
suffering and the comfort of the fantasy that this is a Just
World can lead us to underestimate the kind and degree of
wicked acts being carried out by people who have no interest
in our well-being. In Germany in the 1930s most of the German
Jews could not believe that the National Socialist Party,
which had been elected to parliament, included in its plans
the extermination of all Jews. Like a great many people the
world over, they could not conceive that such monumental
wickedness actually existed. God would not allow it.

When the playwright Arthur Miller was a child just after
the First World War he lived with his family in an apartment
near Central Park in New York. Aged six, the only non-Jews
Arthur had met were Lefty, the cop, and Mikush, the Polish
janitor of their building. Most of the Jews in the building
believed that Mikush hated them. They, or their parents or
grandparents, had fled from the pogroms in Poland. Arthur
Miller wrote,

> I nevertheless had an ambiguous relationship of sorts
> with Mikush; I brought my badly bent almost-new bike to
> him after an experiment of no-hands riding banged the
> fork into a lamppost in the park. He straightened it with
> his bare hands, a memorable feat of strength that I
> imagined no one else in the world was capable of. I must
> have had some faith in his goodwill towards me, Pole or no
> Pole; my fear of him was less than total. Such a
> relationship made it understandable, a decade or so later,
> that German Jews – even those who could afford to – did
> not immediately leave when Hitler came to power. Had we
> lived in Germany, Mikush would have been the Nazi
> representative in the building, but it would have been hard
> to imagine even Mikush, anti-Semitic as he undoubtedly

was, going from apartment to apartment with a list of
names and ordering us out into trucks bound for a
concentration camp and death. After all, he straightened
the fork of my bike.[23]

But the Mikushes of Nazi Germany did go from apartment to
apartment with the list of Jews in their hands, and in France
and Italy policemen lifted small Jewish children into the
cattle trucks bound for Auschwitz.

People do evil deeds, not because they are impelled to
do so by some evil force, or by some evil gene they have
inherited, but because they want to preserve their body or
their sense of being a person. The police who rounded up
the Jews knew that they would be shot if they did not obey
orders. A great many more people, who were not in any
immediate danger of being shot, supported the Nazi programme of exterminating the Jews. Anti-Semitism was a
common theme in the popular press long before the Nazis
came to power, and many non-Jews agreed. In every society
there is always one group of people who are deemed to be the
lowest of the low. In England in the nineteenth and early
twentieth centuries it was the Irish. They were replaced by
the Pakistanis after the Second World War, and now it is the
Muslims. For white Australians it was the Aboriginal people
and anyone who did not come from British stock, but, now
that 40 per cent of white Australians have a parent born
overseas and not necessarily in Britain, and indigenous
Australians, as Aboriginal people are now called, no longer
unwillingly acquiesce to their lowly status, white Australians
feel that they must be superior to Muslims and black Africans.
This delusion of racial superiority arises from a person's
secret fear that, no matter how superior he may claim to be,
he is, in essence, bad and unacceptable. This secret is a constant threat to his sense of being a person, and so his
personal pride resorts to saying, 'I mightn't be perfect, but
I'm better than those Jews/Muslims/Irish/Pakistanis/Abori-
ginals/homosexuals/women/infidels/those not of my faith,
and so on.' People who hold a prejudice against a group of
which they are not a member will behave wickedly in a situation where they fear that their secret badness and weakness

will be revealed, or where they see an opportunity for them to express against other people the anger they feel towards themselves.

Whether they see life ending in death or going on to another life, those who want to believe that, ultimately, virtue is rewarded and wickedness punished often search for a leader or a form of government who will right all wrongs, protect the innocent, reward the virtuous and punish the wicked. They can be easily beguiled into becoming a devout follower of a guru or politician who, untrammelled by a conscience, is in search of wealth and power. Being well educated did not prevent thousands of people from being seduced by Bhagwan Shree Rajneesh. These people wanted sexual freedom, drugs, and the promise of permanent happiness, and this is what he gave them, while he took their money and their labour. The Bhagwan knew that it is easy to seduce those people who are eager to give up the hard work of being responsible for themselves and to be enveloped in the illusory comfort and safety of being in the care of some parent-like figure.

Many millions of people who survived the Second World War but who saw little hope of improving their lives were gulled into believing the promises of the Communist leaders in the USSR. My father, born in 1892, saw very clearly that most politicians and financiers had no one's interests at heart except their own. However, like many people, my father believed that 'my enemy's enemy is my friend'. The politicians and financiers whom he despised saw Communism as their enemy, and so my father looked to Communism as his saviour and friend. Like the many thousands of people outside the USSR who saw Communism as their friend, it took him many years to recognise that Stalin was a wicked man, and that the amount of evil in the world is not necessarily balanced by the amount of good.

Believers in the Just World are prone to believing that, because they are successful, or lead secure lives, they must be good. Similarly, they tell themselves that, if bad people are punished, then those who suffer must be bad. You might try to insulate yourself from the pain of pity by telling yourself that those who suffer have brought this suffering upon themselves by being bad, but in doing this you significantly reduce your capacity to empathise with others. Thus you become less than the fully human person you might have been.

Believing in the Just World does give a sense of security, but you can enjoy that only when nothing in your life goes wrong. When something does go wrong, you suffer. Since nothing in the Just World happens by chance, when a disaster befalls you and you ask, 'Why in the whole scheme of things did this happen?', you are left with only two possible answers: it was my fault, or it was someone else's fault. Of course there are disasters which are clearly someone else's fault, or clearly your own fault, but the causes of a disaster are rarely as clear-cut as this. Some people blame all disasters on others, and so they come to inhabit a world full of enemies with their mysterious plots. Such is the nature of paranoia. Good people, that is, people who believe that they are never good enough, feel that it is wrong to blame others. They must always blame themselves. Blaming yourself for the disaster that has befallen you is the way to turn the natural sadness which follows a loss into depression. Romulus 'prayed each day to a God he believed would listen to all prayers that came from a pure heart'.[24] When God did not answer his prayers that Lydia would be the fine person he wanted her to be, he could only conclude that he was wrong to believe that his heart was pure. Lydia's betrayal was his punishment for being wicked.

Some believers in the Just World do not see themselves as being good. They interpret the disasters that befall them as the punishment they deserve. They feel that they cannot accept any help that might ameliorate their plight. If you are trying to be good you must accept your punishment. Good children hold out their hands to be smacked. Good adults pay their fines. Such people might dutifully obey their doctor and keep their appointment with a therapist, but they resist the therapist's overtures and later complain that the visit was a waste of time. One such woman was sent to me because she was depressed. She had a very handicapped child about whom she talked to me a great deal. Her conversation had two themes. If the child was at home with her she would talk about how muddled she was and how she could not cope; if he was in hospital (a very good hospital, as I knew) she would complain about his care and say how guilty she felt about his being excluded from the family. At the same time she would subtly accuse me of not helping her while, in overt and covert ways, she made it impossible for me to give her even the simplest of help. One day, in desperation, I asked her if she thought she deserved to be happy. She rejected the word 'happy' – it was not in her vocabulary – but she did venture to admit that, 'I don't think I ought to be comfortable.'

If believers in the Just World see themselves as being bad, they often punish themselves, partly to end the tension of waiting for their punishment, or in the hope of showing the higher powers such contrition that mercy is given. Some people, not wanting to reveal to others their intent, injure themselves 'accidentally'. Others quite deliberately cut themselves or inflict other injuries. Suicide bombers are a relatively recent phenomenon, but in Islam and Christianity martyrs have always existed. Christians may no longer feel the need to be burnt (or burn others) at the stake, but many individuals live a life of martyrdom. Tess McGahern believed in everlasting life in heaven, but to get there she had to accept without complaint her selfish husband's cruelties and the cancer which killed her. In some religions self-punishment became a sacred ritual. Shia Muslims have a period of ritual mourning called Ashura in memory of the seventh-century imam Hussein, grandson of the Prophet Mohammed. During this ceremony men dress in black robes and parade as they whip their back with a flail and pound their chest with their hand. In Malaysia, the Hindi ceremony of Thaipusam is all about faith, endurance and penance, where the Hindus show their appreciation of one of their gods, Lord Murugan, a son of Shiva. Some of the men

> carry elaborate frameworks on their shoulders called
> 'kavidis', which have long chains hanging down with
> hooks at the end which are pushed into their backs . . .
> Many of these pilgrims are pierced with two skewers
> (or vels – symbolic spears); one through the tongue and
> one through the cheeks.[25]

When John Humphrys asked three religious leaders, Rowan Williams, the Archbishop of Canterbury, Jonathan Sacks, the Chief Rabbi, and Professor Tariq Ramadan, 'Why do bad things happen to good people?', none of them could give a straightforward, simple answer. Each answer was a fudge, something that John Humphrys decided 'would not do'. If we remove the concept of chance from our understanding of the world and see the world as a Just World, the picture we create seems to be simple and straightforward, but actually we have created a jigsaw where the pieces do not fit. From then on we live in a fog of confusion, asking questions which cannot be answered.

Beliefs which require the believer to see the world in the clear-cut terms of good, bad, reward, punishment cannot resolve the dilemma that faces us all, that of being an individual in a society. Our physiology compels us to experience ourselves as being an individual. We need to maintain our sense of being a person just as much as we must try to preserve our body by being healthy and warding off anything which might kill us. Yet, we have to live in a society because only as a member of a group can we keep ourselves in touch with the reality about which we can only guess. We need to help one another make good guesses about what is actually going on. At the same time physical survival requires the help of other people. If we identify totally with the group, our sense of being a person is swallowed up and we become a no-thing. If we live entirely selfishly we will be expelled from the group – sent to gaol, incarcerated in a psychiatric hospital, or forced to live completely alone. To survive we have to, day by day, balance these competing needs, yet at no time do we have sufficient information about all the possibilities which might affect us to be sure that we have got the balance right between selfishness and unselfishness.

Getting the balance right is not easy.

Chapter 6

TRYING TO BE GOOD

Ella

Parents want their children to be obedient but, fortunately for most children, they are rarely more than partially successful in teaching their child to be obedient. To be successful the parents have to establish themselves as the sole arbiters of everything the child does. Most parents are too inconsistent and too lazy to monitor their child every minute, and most want to enjoy the pleasure of indulging their child and granting some of his wishes. Most children know that, if they become completely obedient, they will lose their sense of being a person and become a no-thing, just as those inmates of the Lagers who were completely obedient and carried out every order unquestioningly became no-things, and perished. In the Lagers only those people who were cleverly and persistently disobedient had a chance of surviving physically and as a person. It takes great courage to be disobedient in a situation where those in charge inspire fear and demand total obedience. Not all children have that degree of courage.

Ella was a beautiful sixteen-year-old whose increasing withdrawal and isolation had worried her teachers long before her parents had noticed that there was any problem. They loved Ella dearly, but, as they each told me, they expected their children, without exception or argument, to do exactly as they were told. Their children always did obey. Ella and her sister confirmed to me that this was the case. Their parents would indulge their children if it did not run counter to their own desires, but if there was a conflict of views, then the parents' view would prevail. 'I always obeyed my parents', Ella's mother said, 'and I expect my children to obey me.' So Ella obeyed. Since both parents would get very angry when something occurred counter to their wishes, Ella learned to avoid spontaneous decisions and actions. At school she obeyed her teachers and spoke only when spoken to. She would respond only to two of her classmates, and she never joined in any social activities. At home she would not use the phone or touch the radiogram. She spent as much time as possible alone in her room. When the family were together there could be a good deal of talking and family jokes, but conversation was always about objective realities, mundane practicalities. No one ever talked about feelings. If you want to be a powerful, controlling parent you must never show any weakness. Ella's parents did not regard their anger as weakness; indeed, they saw it as a right. They could display their anger, but all other feelings which might reveal their fallible humanness were carefully concealed from their children. Ella said, 'My parents don't show how they feel. My sister never tells me how she feels, and neither does anyone else.'

One day I asked Ella how she saw the purpose of life and the nature of death. She said that these were questions that she had been puzzling over for a number of years. 'That's where I go upstairs and think. I spend a lot of my time doing that. I started to wonder whether I'm the only person who's really alive – the only living person. Everyone else is just a vision. I'm living each person's life in turn. Not just people, everything. It's there but it's not really real.' Here Ella is describing the introvert experience of how external reality, the reality of what goes on around us, becomes unreal while the internal reality of being a person remains real. This is what happens when introverts lose all self-confidence.

'The most real thing is yourself?'

'Yes. I've often thought that what I see in the mirror isn't me. I've never actually seen my face.' The image of her face in the mirror was outside her so it was not real, just as everything outside her was not real.

'Do you feel certain about yourself?'

'Yes. It's other people that are not really there. I've

thought that I've already lived their lives or I'm about to live their lives and that as I see them they're not really real.' Ella now described how she explained her experience by creating her own myth about life and death.

'Do you feel that there is any order or relationship between successive lives?'

'I'm not sure whether I would be the same person or a different person. I think everyone's basically the same, it's just different ways they act. I think when people are born they're the same people and they just develop in different ways. They don't really have any character of their own at all. They acquire it from the people they live with, the environment. I think all the qualities are there at birth – all the virtues and all the badness are there. Every person can be kind if they want to, but few people are.' That is, other people are only chimeras, and they have acquired their characteristics from the people around them. If the people around them are not kind, then they are not kind.

She went on, 'I'm the only person, but each time I live as a different person. I grow up in a different way. The way I am now is the result of the way things have been as I've been growing up.'

'Does the way you develop in this life have any effect on subsequent lives?'

'No. I forget about previous lives.'

'What will happen to you when you have lived every life?'

'I don't know. I just thought that I might go back to the beginning and live it all again.'

'How do you feel about living all these lives?'

'I never feel anything about it. I just think that's what is going to happen to me and it doesn't matter what I feel about it. I can't change anything.'

'Do you mean that the life you are living now is in some way fixed or ordained and there's nothing you can do to change it?'

'Yes.'

'When we think of our lives as pre-destined, we then have the question of how this plan got made.'

'I see it as there being a God but not outside, being in it all. I believe that everything I see is God. There's a power that made all this.'

'The totality of everything is God?'

'Yes.'

'Then you are God, or part of God.'

'Yes.'

(Completely powerless people create myths about being completely powerful. Thus they are attempting to defend their sense of being a person. However, Ella did not see herself as having the power to influence events.)

'If you're the only person, if other people are visions, then this makes you a very important part.'

'I have never thought of that. I try to look at myself as what part I play, why I am here. I haven't thought of an answer to it yet.'

'Do you feel that there must be a purpose?'

'I've often thought that there isn't any purpose. I'm just here for no particular reason at all.'

'Does that thought frighten you?'

'No. It doesn't matter whether I'm frightened or pleased or anything. That's what would happen, is happening . . . I have thought that this world is one of several worlds, not just separate planets, separate worlds altogether. There's no way I can get from this world to another world. The other worlds are similar to this one in some ways – people of some kind living in them – but as separate worlds they're completely different in the way they've developed.'

'Would they be real people like yourself?'

'Only one real person in each one. There are countless worlds.'

'Are you able to have contact with these people?'

'No. They're completely separate.'

'Do you see yourself as having power over the people you see as visions?'

'No. I feel there's nothing I can do to change anything.'

'How would your life change if you, somehow or other, gave up this idea of people being just visions and you came to believe that they were real?'

'I don't think I would change. How could I change?'

'If you did change your beliefs?'

'I don't think I would – but I always treat people as if they were people.'

'So, with people who are close to you, your family, at the back of your mind all the time you feel that your parents, your sister, aren't real.'

'I think that they're not real. They just behave like real people.'

'You don't think there's somebody inside them like you?'

'No.'

'And you don't think I'm real.'

Ella smiled. 'No.'

Ella's parents expected her not only to do what they wanted but to think what they wanted her to think. As much as she wanted to obey her parents and keep herself perfectly safe, she could not help but have her own way of seeing things. Because she was unable to share her ideas with her parents and sister, she lacked the checks and balances that other people supply. Consequently her ideas were becoming so idiosyncratic that she could not share them with others without being seen to be mad.

Peter

In my talks with Peter he often mentioned his Celtic background. When I first met him he was living in a lonely farmhouse with his wife and children. He did some casual farmwork, but he had to rely on Social Security for his family's support. When he was twenty he had begun a career as an actor, but illness had interrupted his career and so he had never fulfilled his early promise. Whenever we discussed his return to work he said that he had to decide whether he should go back to the theatre or resume his training as a social worker. These seemed to me to be two disparate ambitions, but within his philosophy this was not so.

Peter had been born into an aristocratic family which traced its origins into the mists of Celtic history. He numbered amongst his ancestors men who had guided the great British nation, who had created and administered her laws, who had led her armies in far-flung places, who had defended the flag and protected the weak, ignorant, and oppressed. This was a formidable family for a young lad to grow up in, especially when he was not particularly wanted by his parents. They made it quite clear to him that his presence would be tolerated only if he showed himself to be worthy of the family. To be unruly or noisy, to get angry, or to argue with one's superiors was to show oneself to be like the inferior races. To be a member of this family one had to assume the duties of the family which were to protect and guide the inferior people who were at the mercy of their passions. Born forty years earlier, Peter might have slipped easily into a well-defined and comfortable niche; but by the time he was born the family had gone into a decline which was hastened by the war. When Peter came of age there was no comfortable niche for him. He had to make his own way in the world, but he still carried with him the ideals of his family.

I asked him to tell me about Celtic philosophy. He said, 'I think the Celtic philosophy tends to be external rather than internal. They made very distinct separations. The outside influences have an effect on one. They were very much at the mercy of omens, external influences, the gods, the ancestors, the weather, things that were superstitious. I don't think they were very advanced in a philosophic sense. In a cultural, creative sense they were more advanced.'

'These outside influences, were they good or bad?'

'About half and half. There was a lot of the old biblical thing – though it wasn't related – that if you follow the right path and do the right things, then good things will happen to you.'

'Sort of, you can influence outside influences by being a good person yourself and if you're bad you get bad omens.'

'Yes, this is so. You create your own world. The tool you use to do this is yourself.'

'The other day you were telling me how much you hated a strong wind. When you're depressed and feel that you're full of badness, would you interpret that wind as a bad omen?'

'Yes, I think so. One tends to see it as a visitation upon oneself. I say this very cautiously because one feels the root connection with Celtic history, but I have to be careful because it included a lot of things that are a lot more modern. There is that "This is happening to me because I've done something bad." Walk on the lines and the bears jump up. I do something nasty and it's God punishing me, or one of the gods. There's a sort of instinctive feeling, "I've done something unlucky." I've been in contact with a bad omen which in some way outside myself is telling me about myself and about my future.'

We went on to talk about Peter's fearsome anger. Peter said, 'The person who suffers after a row – I know other people do, don't misunderstand me – the person who suffers extremely is myself. I get shattered. I think about it for months afterwards. I suppose in a sense I punish myself for it. I'm not sure that there aren't times when I promote anger in order to lay the stick on myself. In a sense, one sort of feels that for some reason or other it's appropriate that I should punish myself. I deny myself things on occasion. Self-denial. I think it does me good – it's like "If I don't do this God won't punish me." '

'So you punish yourself as both a reparation and a propitiation.'

'Yes, absolutely. It's curious in a sense – that, like having animals around, and I get upset when they die, on the other hand, I'm quite convinced, having other things about the place to sort of take, to be the fall guys, so to speak, protects my family and myself.'

There were always large numbers of fowls, ducks, geese, cats, and dogs wandering around the old farmhouse. Whenever I drove into the farmyard I was anxious lest I inadvertently destroyed a favourite pet or a Sunday lunch. Now I realised that I could be seen as a vehicle for a Celtic god. 'You mean', I said, 'if the animals die then somebody in the family won't die.'

'Yes, absolutely. This is an almost atavistic thing, I am sure the gods demand sacrifices and therefore if you have a lot of things around you that can be sacrificed, I mean, the chance of the closest things being sacrificed are really further removed. I know the absurdity of it, but that's not what I'm dealing with, the intellectual side – I'm dealing with the emotional side. Of course one had God in my childhood. The Old Testament, as a child, is much easier to understand and is much clearer than the New Testament. One didn't begin to understand the New Testament until one begins to understand the quality of Jesus, but the Old Testament where you behave yourself or you got punished and you were born a sinner anyway – this was crystal clear to a young mind. Because the mild side, the forgiving side, the loving side is not at all clear to a child. But you knew where you were with the gods. You knew you had to conform, you knew you deserved punishment because you knew you were a sinner and you knew the gods demanded sacrifices.'

'And that kind of picture of the gods didn't run counter to the picture you had in your home, of your family.'

'Oh, quite right. It was certainly the way my father presented himself to me: actually he was a rather mild gentleman, but, of course, he was Father with a capital F, he was an army officer, becoming increasingly senior, and he had fought one war and was going off to fight in another. He was very authoritative – a figure who had power of life and death. He was a god-like and rather frightening figure even though he wasn't a frightening man.'

Peter went on to explain that later in childhood he came to see that 'if you're allowed to make a decision, you can't expect God to protect you . . . If one looked at what Jesus was, what He became for me, what He was really showing us was what any of us could do if we managed to attain that sort of thing. What He was showing was the potentiality that existed for all people, and this became for me much more realistic and logical, so that one had the forces of good and the forces of evil which I think really cannot be denied. Of course, one realised that whatever the example of Jesus, one was nowhere near measuring up to it. So I translate God into gods; and because of the other side – there are terrible things in the darkness, aren't there – the forces of evil which one has to propitiate.'

A belief in the forces of good and evil allows a belief in magic. Peter went on, 'One believes or one very much wants to believe in magic, or I do – romance, magic are very important factors in life – the romantic and miraculous side of magic. The magic on one side is the balance against the dark forces. You can't have one without the other . . . There are still the demons, there are still the fairies . . . This is all part of one's identity. One has this thing that one would disappear if one took away the things that one feels make up, contribute to, bolster up oneself, one's importance – my ancestors came over in 1066 on my father's side and on my mother's side it's a long history of Scottish kings and nobles – this is all very irrelevant, bloody laughable, but it is there and one is frightened of dismissing it, getting rid of it, because one feels that these things are, rightly or wrongly, for good or ill, the things on which one's own identity rests, to quite a large extent.' (Here Peter illustrates how the myths we create about life and death are an integral part of our sense of being a person.)

I asked if he saw his identity continuing to exist after death.

'I do find this very difficult to talk about,' he said, 'It's a thing one doesn't talk about because it's ingrained not to. It's labelled with being a profound subject, and I don't think I'm a particularly profound person. For what it's worth, I very definitely don't see a beginning and end in terms of one's current mortal life. I think that one is surrounded so much by evidence of cycles, re-birth, in terms of things like trees and grass. I feel very strongly that we're in a similar sort of cyclical thing, where we, in some way, are developed – and there is a purpose. I would not say that reincarnation in personal, selfish terms is a possible rule, but I think in group terms, social terms, it is. I would see it as a sort of processing in rather the same way as you process steel. You put them through various stresses to refine, temper, improve. I feel that one belongs to a group, in the sense that there is probably what might be called an artistic, creative group, there is a healing group, there is probably an artisan group. You could invent permutations out of this. I feel that the group factor is probably more important than the individual factor, in the sense that one has a life, it is a thread spun off this group which probably returns to it. Am I being clear?' (Peter, like Christine, was an extravert, and thought in terms of groups.)

'You feel that you must live your present life so that the sum total of your life will meet whatever the standard is, so you can proceed to the next stage?'

'Sort of. I think one ought to do the best one can and I think one often fails to do it.'

'When you were depressed, did you feel you hadn't met the standard?'

'Yes, and I was quite unable to deal with that. It's also confused by the fact that one does not really know what the standards are. You look at someone like Jesus and whether He existed or not is probably not very relevant, because what is relevant is the Example, and these do seem to be nearly impossible standards to meet, and I think also because the standards are so high there is a great temptation to say, "I cannot possibly achieve anything like that and therefore I'm not going to make the effort." One doesn't want to be a committed Christian because it is very uncomfortable, and also if one is looking at that sort of attainment, one is being frightfully grand and really overambitious. If I can just succeed in leaving a pleasant feeling around as far as my family and people I know are concerned, maybe for me this is the most I can do.'

Peter had explained to me that being an actor meant being a responsible member of a team, just as it is to be a social worker. Either job could fulfil the conditions set by his family and could ensure his continued identity after death, an identity which had its foundations in his Celtic ancestry. His Celtic beliefs inspired in him great fear, but, as he said, 'There is a sort of loyalty factor. If I am a Celt; then I've got to pay some sort of service to the rules I believe are Celtic rules, Celtic laws: I've got to subscribe to some of those superstitions, otherwise I lose that identity with the Celtic background; then I lose contact with myself. I'd have nothing to hold on to. One does feel that because one has grown up in this sort of format, that it is valuable and that one's own identity, one's sense of self, will disappear if one removes the casing, the setting, in which one lives.'

Peter was much troubled by violent rages and abysmal despair. He said, 'If I could construct a model of me, inside it would be something in the form of a bucket which was full of broken glass which was being rattled about rather violently, and bits fly off and this is highly dangerous. And somehow that should be organised into something which has system and pattern and symmetry, but I'm not sure how to organise it and I'm not sure what the symmetry and pattern ought to be.'

When Peter first came to see me he told me that what he found hardest to bear was his fear and depression. What his family found hardest to bear was his anger. Peter and I spent a great deal of time discussing anger and exploring what were the values and implications he put on anger. For him anger was something bad, completely unacceptable. He feared his anger, and, in doing so, made it impossible for himself to come to terms with his anger, to accept it and so control it. In different contexts I would describe to him how I construe anger. To me it is a human response to frustration. It is not essentially evil, but is a facet of our vitality and creativity. Our task in dealing with our anger is to inspect critically the sources of our frustration and to develop ways of expressing our anger which are socially acceptable and creative. To this he would say, 'Intellectually I know what you mean. But in my heart I can't believe it.'

Like Tony, Peter was a man of strong opinions, and when events challenged these opinions he would be most angry and intransigent. In this discussion he explained why.

'I can identify the anger. I can say "Yes, I'm angry about this", and the reason I am angry about it is so and so – I can and I will on occasions say to myself, "Well, it's not something to be angry about", and it may make me angry, but it's an unrealistic reaction on my part because it isn't important enough. I tell myself that I can translate virtually any situation into this sort of equation and, whatever it is, life is short, it's only me getting angry over something I feel and it doesn't justify anger. And then I get frightened because I think, okay, if that's the way it is, then I'm in danger on a long-term basis, and if I spread it over the whole of my outlook, my attitudes, my behaviour, maybe I shall stop feeling. I don't want to stop feeling. I want to feel pleased about things and cross about things because I feel that, without feeling, motivation goes and I don't think I'll become a vegetable, but I'd become so bland that I'm no longer a person, and I know that's not a good argument but it's again where I come to war with myself about feelings. I would like to be serene and wise and able to take everything in my stride and that would be a lovely sort of ego thing, I tell myself, I think with my heart. But I don't feel that with my gut. My gut says that I've got to care because if I don't care about this or I don't care about that, then I cease being me. I feel that things matter and, God, one can extend this argument indefinitely. One could say, if you like, we should stop immigration on the purely practical grounds that this is a small island and there are too many people here, and the more people we get here, the harder life is going to become, the less there's going to be for me and my family, and so I should feel strongly about this because if I don't feel strongly about it, then we're going to end up in a pretty poor state, and we're going to end up like the middle of India where there isn't enough food – I know I'm using a crude extension of the argument. Now if I get all bland and accepting of this particular situation, the results could be such and such and then I'm going to feel that I haven't looked after my responsibilities and cared about the people near and dear to me – that my acceptance of the situation, if I don't feel strongly that one needs to contain problems and deal with them, then I become the instrument for inflicting unhappiness or pain or deprivation on people I should be protecting, be it my family, be it my community, be it my country.'

'What you're saying', I said, 'as a principle of living, is that there is always the danger that if you enquire into the causes of your emotions that enquiry may come up with answers which take your emotions away from you and make you into a bland person and this is the kind of person you don't want to be. Having that attitude to enquiry into emotion, this means that in the past you've not done this very often. You've not developed the habit of self-inspection, and so when later in life it's suggested to you that you ought to have a look at these things, you come up against two problems – the attitude that it's not a safe thing to do, to introspect, and also you haven't got the habits of it. Self-inspection is a mode of thought that one learns, and if you haven't learnt it, you're not very good at it.'

'Yes', said Peter, 'sort of. I don't entirely agree with you. I think in some ways I've inspected myself too closely. The fear is that if I inspect and as a result of that inspection I see that there is another line I could take, there are changes I can make which will defuse my reaction to certain things, the stumbling block comes when I look at the consequences of that defusing.' (Extraverts are quite likely to say, 'I've inspected myself too closely.' Introverts never say this.)

'When', I answered, 'you're talking about how important emotions, feelings are, you don't want to wipe them out, because if you make yourself into a bland person you won't be so aware of other people. You won't interact with them. Now when we were talking about your sense of identity and I said to you that you used other people as a mirror, you rejected that image and you said no, it's interaction. This ties back to now, when you talk about the importance of your emotions because it's through them that you interact with other people, and if you become a bland person, then you wouldn't have these interactions with other people and you would lose your sense of identity.'

Peter said, 'I would accept that as a fair evaluation. If I became passive and didn't have an active part in life, then I would see consequences which I would see as very dangerous, very threatening.' Thus he could not afford to give up his anger.

Time passed. Peter thought about our conversations and, with the great support of his wife Diana, he returned to work. Peter told me how he no longer set himself such impossibly high standards. 'If I can just succeed in leaving a sort of pleasant feeling around as far as my family and the people I know closely are concerned, maybe for me this is the most I can do. I am back to functioning much more as I did some years ago – more placidly – a lot more of my humour has come back – a lot more of the fun. And what you call my mythology – I'm able to laugh at it. I'm able to diminish its importance. It's still there, but I'm able to take far less notice of it now. It doesn't have the importance, it doesn't have the threat. I'm openly able to recognise that it's a bit silly, it looks smaller and less real and more ephemeral. This is a change in the basics. The house is not so haunted. There's glass in the windows. When we first talked about structure – I can't remember whether we talked about it or whether it's just what happened in my mind – but I do remember I had an image of a house, and at the time, I remember it very clearly, almost too clearly for comfort, the house was sort of stone. It was big, it was forbidding, it was greenish, it was swathed in mist, the floors were all uneven, the stairs didn't exist, or if they did you couldn't find them, there was no glass in the windows, it was bloody cold. I had quite a clear physical picture and this structure remains, again quite clearly, but now it's got glass in the windows, it's got stairs, it's much smaller than it seemed, it's been polished up and painted, but the basic structure, in picture terms, is there still, but vastly altered both in appearance and in effect on me.'

Julie

Many parents teach their children that, if you do not have a purpose in life, a goal, then, not only would something bad happen, but there would be something wrong with you as an individual. A child who accepts this doctrine wholeheartedly may make something of himself, but he can never just be – just live accepting himself and his world. In all our lives there are times when we can follow a path of striving and achievement, and times when we can do no more than live within the cycle of the rising and setting of the sun, in the cycle of the seasons. In some of our activities, such as to be close to another person, to love, to make love, the essence is just to be and not to try to achieve. In trying to win or to be the best, the person is seeking to gain control and power. This is incompatible with the development of a loving relationship between equals. For the child who learns to see life as a series of goals to be achieved, the ultimate goal must be some kind of perfection. It then becomes a hard lesson to learn that life, in this world at least, never admits of perfection. Moments of bliss are possible, but perfection always eludes us. Parents believe that they are acting in the child's best interests when they stress the importance of having goals in life. However, when we give a young child advice, whether it is 'Work hard at school and pass your exams so you'll get a good job', or whether it is 'Have a good time while you're young', we are implying something about the fundamental nature of life. Our advice carries a metaphysical implication – perhaps that in this world hard work is rewarded or that pleasures must be snatched in a world where life is transient. We cannot know what implications a child will read into our advice.

A young woman, called Julie, who came to see me, said that she had been depressed from the age of sixteen. She described to me how, through all her childhood, and especially at school, she did everything 'well', and, oh, the scorn she put into that word 'well'. She said, 'I've been conscientious all my life. When I was a little girl at primary school I got reports where I was "conscientious, serious and hardworking".' Now she feels that her parents have betrayed her trust. As she said to me, 'I think they used me. They saw me as an extension of themselves. I felt exploited by many people, by the school, by them.'

Parents often do try to get their children to achieve in areas where they themselves have wished to achieve and failed, and this may have been the case with Julie's parents. They certainly had advised her of the desirability of gaining educational qualifications, but they may not have realised that in doing so they were, in Julie's ears, making her a promise. As Julie said to me one day, 'I really hate myself for being so depressed. It's so pathetic. It does make it worse that I think we should be happy all our lives. I feel really bad that I'm unhappy. I'd always expected to be happy. My parents built me up. They used to pay me a lot of attention and say, "You're going to have a great time." I just thought I would. I thought everything was going to come to me and I wasn't going to have to do anything. I had one hell of a shock.'

Some parents, wanting to protect their children from the cruel truths of this world, paint for their child a picture of a sunlit, joyous land, where evil is always punished and virtue always rewarded. If the child identifies himself with virtue, then he may sail through childhood and adolescence secure that his reward will come, but if, like Julie, he thinks that his reward will follow like night the day and that he does not have to work for it, then he is in for a rude awakening when the vicissitudes, the random bad luck of the big world, crash in upon his small world. On the other hand, if he doubts that he is one of the virtuous and that he has the guile to avoid his just deserts, then he feels helpless in the face of the future his parents have created for him. Some high achievers are plagued by the feeling that they are imposters and that one day they will be exposed and shamed. Parents who determinedly create such a sunny picture, a world where 'everything happens for the best in this best of all possible worlds', are often protecting not merely their child but themselves as well. They find it intolerable that life contains so many random events, the ground that suddenly shifts beneath our feet, the clot of blood that appears and blocks an artery, the two aeroplanes on converging paths. The randomness of happiness perturbs them just as much, since, as happiness can come, so it can go. Unable to deal with the uncertainty of life, they fail even more to deal with life's most certain uncertainty, death.

Children learn early in life of the existence of good and evil. Goodness is pressed upon them by the adults in their world, and evil (even when disguised as naughtiness) is punished. A child may learn to see evil in William James's terms, as 'only a maladjustment with *things*, a wrong correspondence of one's life with the environment', or he may learn that evil is 'a wrongness or vice in his essential nature, which no rearrangement of the inner self can cure, and which requires supernatural remedies'. A psychotherapist, lacking a supernatural remedy, has to do battle with the patient's idea of having a 'wrongness or vice in his essential nature'. Julie once put this into words when she said to me, 'When I was a child my mother used to tell me I was critical even before I knew what critical meant. Mother's always irritated me. I don't know why. She said it's because I just wasn't a lovable sort of child. She makes me tyrannise her. Because of this I have this vision of me as a little devil – just unlovable – that I will destroy anybody who comes near me.' We discussed this little devil and I asked her how much this little devil interfered in her relationships with other people. 'Almost totally', she said. 'People shouldn't get near me because I'm just going to destroy them. I feel like I'm standing with a dagger in my hand. I'm a dangerous person, or rather, that's the feeling she's given me.' I asked her how she destroyed people and she said, 'In the way I destroy my mother, by tormenting her because she irritates me constantly. But with other people I'm not a tyrant. I'm very unassertive. I suppose that's because I'm afraid that if I assert myself I'll destroy them, and it makes me very timid with people.' And then later she said, 'If I get feedback from somebody that they don't think I'm unlovable and horrible, I just think they must be stupid because I am. I don't believe anything people say. While I've been coming to see you I've been listening for things which I could twist like that, but you haven't said anything.' The word 'yet' hung unspoken in the air.

Many daughters would understand only too well what Julie meant when she said, 'My mother is very unselfish and as a consequence I'm constantly guilty.' The guilt aroused in this way made Julie very angry but, as she said, 'It's exhausting being angry, but if you subtract the anger there's nothing there.'

Many people see the Just World as an accounting system, where the amount of our goodness is balanced against the amount of our badness. Julie said, 'I feel as though I don't have a right to be here ... I feel I've been running up a shopping bill for seven years and I've got to pay for it all before I can go on, instead of paying for it day by day or not paying it at all. I don't know who I'm in debt to, but I do feel in debt. I think this is the basic idea of having to suffer. You'll only gain if you suffer ... I think I'm totally plastic. I just don't feel like a human being. I don't feel three-dimensional. Like a sort of cardboard cut-out. If you look at it from the front it looks perfectly normal, but if you look around it, there's no form to it.'

Julie described her depression in the image of 'just me in a desert. Other people don't exist but I do.' Try as she might, she could not people that desert. One day I posed her that problem of being respected or liked. I asked her, 'Suppose you were faced with a situation where you could act only in one of two ways. If you acted one way people would like you, but you wouldn't respect yourself, and if you acted the other way people wouldn't like you but you would respect yourself. If you were faced with that, which would you choose, respecting yourself or other people liking you?'

Julie answered immediately, 'Respecting myself. That's

one of my standards. I realised that at university. One thing about depression, it does make you independent because you don't care about popularity. You just function without other people anyway, so it doesn't really matter about other people. I suppose you just live like an observer, observing people, the way they live, and just get a bit cynical. I'm very scornful of people who do things just to be popular. I analyse myself and other people constantly, and "honesty and integrity" is the byword. All the time I'm scorning myself because of that attitude – it's totally ridiculous. I can't live up to my standards, so nobody else could really, could they?'

'Why is it important to be honest?' I asked.

'Well, my aim is to be able to communicate to the outside world what I feel on the inside, not just about myself, I mean generally, and I think it is important to be as honest as possible. That way you get a clearer picture of things that are going on around you, and I think it's important to be clear. It's better than living in a fuzz. What I really mean is that you can keep channels of communication better if you're being honest with yourself and other people are being honest with themselves. Actually, that sort of honesty you arrive at only once in a blue moon. The rest of the time I'm just miserable because I don't find it. I suppose I live in a fuzz now. This is a fuzz. I can't communicate anything at all. I feel so impatient. I've got such a struggle to establish some kind of clarity. There's something propelling me on all the time. I've got to struggle to get out of this . . . I think that when you die your body decomposes but maybe your spirit remains behind. Maybe spirits return in other forms through the years. But I do believe you have to concentrate on the here and now. I've no beliefs in the hereafter at all. I don't believe in heaven or hell or anything like that. I feel really angry that I've wasted seven years being unhappy. I feel I should be happy all my life – which is just another tremendously high standard which is impossible to achieve . . . I do have the sort of feeling that there is reincarnation. I don't see how your spirit can be totally snuffed out. I have this feeling that we kind of inhabit our bodies and it's up to us to make our body work.'

'And are you failing at your task because you haven't been making your body work?'

'Yes. This is what I mean by clarity. I don't mean that I want everything cut and dried. I want to be able to express myself. That's the biggest task, the most important. You've got to struggle to express what is within you to express. I feel that if you fail you've wasted your life.' (Julie said this without knowing that in the ancient secret Gnostic gospels Jesus is reported as saying, 'If you bring forth what is within you, what you bring forth will save you. If you do not bring forth what is within you, what you do not bring forth will destroy you.')

Yet she hung on to her depression. One day she described to me how she had never learned to swim because she would not relinquish the kick-board. She did not believe her teacher when she said that Julie could stay afloat without it. 'I also feel', she said, 'that my depression is something I've grown out of long ago which I cling to for support.' Julie's depression was even more than a kick-board that kept her afloat. It was a vocation. 'In a way I see life as a big problem which we have to solve. At some stage in your life most people seem to have some terrible problem they've got to solve. Or if you don't, you tend to lead a two-dimensional life.' Thus Julie's depression was something she could put aside only when she felt that she had completed the task of solving the problem of her life, becoming a developed person, capable of formulating and communicating her message with utmost clarity.

Kerry Packer

When the Australian media mogul Kerry Packer had recovered from a massive heart attack during which he virtually died, he told his friend Phillip Adams, 'I've been to the other side, and let me tell you, son, there's fucking nothing there. There's no one waiting for you. There's no one to judge you, so you can do what you bloody well like.'[1]

However, Kerry Packer did not need a God in heaven. He had had one on earth, one who towered over him and terrified him for all of his life. His god was his father, Frank Packer.

Frank had inherited his thriving newspaper business from his father, Robert Clyde Packer, who had been described in an obituary as 'the pattern of the modern newspaper boss ... innovative, cynical, thriving on hard work, inspiring loyalty as well as enmity, politically influential, but chiefly concerned with commercial advantage'.[2] This description could equally be applied to his son Frank and to his grand-son Kerry.

In his biography of Kerry Packer, Paul Barry said of Frank:

> For nigh on four decades he used the [*Telegraph*] for his own personal soapbox from which to harangue politicians, attack his rivals or declaim on whatever subject had lately caught his eye. He had strong views about socialism, the need for stable government, the goodness of America and the divine right of royalty, and was ever keen to voice them. An old-fashioned newspaper baron in the Hollywood tradition, his view of the world was entirely black and white. There was right and there was wrong: there were friends and there were enemies; there was nothing in between. Neither he nor his papers left anybody in doubt about where they stood in relation to this great divide ... The rules of fair play rarely restrained him ... Among the *Telegraph* staff, Frank Packer was jokingly referred to as 'God'. And in his own limited universe it was perhaps only a mild exaggeration. Thanks in part to his temper and in part to his physical appearance, he was viewed with a mixture of fear and awe. He was a huge man, built like the heavyweight boxer he had been in his youth ... He was a man with great presence and, if he cared to bestow it, great charm ... He appeared to have difficulty in making relationships on anything but a master–servant basis ... Although he was capable of great generosity, he was extraordinarily suspicious and a great hater. In his eyes, people were generally regarded as guilty until they had proven themselves to be innocent.[3]

In all, Frank was not unlike the fearsome God of the Old Testament. When the interviewer Michael Parkinson enquired of Kerry, 'Can I ask you, can you name anyone you most admire?', Kerry replied, 'I hold no one in higher regard than my father.'[4]

Kerry was the second of two sons. His brother Clyde

appeared to be much brighter than Kerry whose dyslexia had been unrecognised by either his parents or his teachers, and it was Clyde who was expected to inherit the family business. Each boy had an unhappy childhood, but their unhappiness divided them rather than brought them together. They saw little of their father who was fully engaged with his business interests. 'Not only was Frank an absent father, he was also harsh and unrelenting and the two boys bore the brunt of it.'[5] Kerry's mother Gretel devoted herself to her husband and to the social life their wealth brought them. Kerry was first looked after by a nurse, and at five was sent as a boarder to Cranbrook, a private school not far from the Packer home in Bellevue Hill in Sydney. With the threat of invasion by the Japanese army in 1942 Kerry was sent to stay with an aunt in the southern tablelands of New South Wales. There he contracted polio during the epidemic of the disease in 1945, and spent nine months in an iron lung. When he left hospital his parents sent him to Canberra to be looked after by a nurse. Later he called this 'a lonely, difficult period'.[6]

Kerry's illness and many changes of school meant that he was well behind his classmates when he returned to Cranbrook aged nine. As an adult he distanced himself from his suffering and said it was 'a very tough period for a kid. It was probably the hardening of a shell because kids are very unkind to kids.'[7] He defended himself by displaying what Barry called 'an ostentatious lack of interest in learning'.[8] He was bigger than most of his classmates and he used his size to try to dominate the other boys. Barry wrote,

> Kerry, according to one boy who knew him well, wanted to be at the centre of things: 'he tried to be like his father, he wanted to be the leader . . . to run the pack.' The trouble was he was something of an outsider. He couldn't run the pack because he wasn't in it.[9]

Frank never recognised how his sons suffered at his hands. As far as he was concerned, his father had been very hard on him, and so he was very hard on his sons. His father beat him, and so he beat his sons. Many children learn that they can separate themselves from the pain of a beating and then tell themselves, 'It didn't hurt.' Denying your own pain can be an effective defence, but refusing to have any sympathy for yourself when you suffer can reduce your capacity to recognise other people's suffering and pity them. In adult life they say, 'I was beaten as a child and it didn't do me any harm.' Thus Frank became 'a great believer in the benefits of corporal punishment, and his two boys came in for a fair few beatings, as Kerry has told a number of interviewers.' Michael Parkinson asked him, 'Was he a very strict man with you?'

Kerry replied,

> Yes, he was very strict. But he was very fair. He used to sentence me to going upstairs and waiting for him where he used to come and er . . . he used to use a polo whip very well. I got a lot of beltings, because I wasn't a very good child, but in all the times I can remember that I got a belting from him I never got one that I didn't deserve, and there was quite a few that I didn't get that I should have got.[10]

Here Kerry is unknowingly revealing the process through which most children learn to see themselves as being bad and unacceptable.

The punishments adults inflict on children take many forms, of which physical punishment is just one. When a small child finds himself being punished for something he has not done, or receiving a punishment which is hugely out of proportion to what he has done, the meaning he gives to that situation is, essentially, 'I am being unjustly punished by my bad parent.' This is the truth of the situation, but the child quickly realises that he cannot afford to stay with and acknowledge that truth. He knows that he is in a situation from which he cannot escape, and that he is dependent on the adult who is punishing him. So he proceeds to do what most people do when they find themselves in an intolerable situation from which they cannot escape. They reconstrue the situation. They give it another meaning. This meaning might be a lie which they tell themselves, but it is a lie which at the time allows them to have some hope of survival. In such a situation the child changes 'I am being unjustly punished by my bad parent' to 'I am bad, and am being justly punished by my good parent.'

For many children the unjust punishments are limited in number and the child simply learns to see himself as being, in essence, bad and unacceptable. Thus he becomes good. Good people believe that, as they are, they are bad and unacceptable, and that they have to work hard to be good, where 'good' is how the punishing parent defines 'good'. However, for some children the unjust punishments are harsh and frequent. On each occasion the truth of the situation threatens to break through into the child's consciousness, and so he pins the lie in place with another reconstruction, namely, 'I am bad, and am being justly punished by my good parent, and when I grow up I shall punish bad people in the way I was punished.' Thus the child learns to identify with his torturer, and to be cruel. Through this identification he comes to believe that he is good in the way that his torturer is good.

Moreover, he begins to take pride in the way he can identify bad people and punish them. He tells himself he can do this because he is good. This is the kind of thinking that drives the actions of those people who disfigure and kill Muslim women who fail to cover themselves sufficiently, or who torture prisoners in America's secret gaols, or who attack abortion clinics and murder the staff, or who beat up and sometimes kill homosexuals, or people from a different ethnic group, and so on. In order to deny their fear that they are, in essence, bad, they tell themselves the lie, 'Because I belong to the most superior religion/race/gender/nationality I am good, and therefore have the right to punish bad people.'

Children who do not identify with the adult who punished them are able in their adult life, if they so choose, to recognise that their belief that they are bad and unacceptable is an idea, not a reality, and that they are free to change it to an idea with which they can live comfortably. They can see themselves as being, like all people, simply human. If they have identified with the adult who punished them, they are unable to look critically at that adult and question his or her actions. Kerry certainly identified with Frank. The long list of similarities between Frank and Kerry included being unsuccessful at school, being convinced that making money was the highest good, being not concerned with what others thought, presenting a façade of moral rectitude behind which their business practices were sharp and ruthless, including their methods for avoiding paying tax, being sexually rapacious, and using other people's weaknesses to advance their own interests. However, when people identify with the adult who punished them, they can feel that their parent always knows what they say, think or do, even when the parent is not present or dead. Thus Frank seems always to have been with Kerry, watching him, still calling him 'Boofhead', and telling him that he would never be the man his father was.

Kerry seems never to have stood up to his father. When Clyde, in his late thirties and a competent journalist and manager director of Channel 9, opposed Frank over a clear-cut issue involving the then prime minister Bob Hawke and felt obliged to resign, his father disinherited him and made Kerry his successor. Kerry 'would never dare defy his father'.[11]

> Even though he was thirty five or more, Kerry was still not seen to challenge him. Someone setting up a deal with Frank in the early 1970s remembers a number of meetings when father and son were present. 'When we discussed business, Kerry didn't speak. If Sir Frank left the room, Kerry would have an opinion. If Sir Frank came back, he would shut up completely.' The son would always stand with the rest of them when his father came back into the room.[12]

In an interview with Michael Parkinson in 1979, Parkinson said, 'You live very much in his shadow, don't you?'

'I hope so.'

'Why?'

'I think he was a very great man. There are people who create things . . . Perhaps fifty or a hundred every generation. I'm not one of those. He was. I'm very proud of him.'[13]

If only Kerry had heard and understood that wise advice that the therapist Sheldon Kopp gave the world, 'If you have a hero, look again. You have diminished yourself.'

The most damaging lies we can ever tell are the lies we tell ourselves. If we lie to other people, these people can examine what we say and confront us with our untruthfulness, but when we lie to ourselves there is no one to tell us that we are lying. One lie that can do a lifetime's damage is the one that the small child tells himself, 'I am bad, and am being justly punished by my good parent.'

This is the lie that Kerry Packer told himself and kept on telling himself for the rest of his life. He may have told some friends that his father's death came as a relief to him, but, when we identify with our image of our parent, that parent lodges inside us and does not die until we die. Barry wrote,

> Kerry would say years later, in a Pollyanna sort of way, that he had been a lucky child – lucky to have been born with all the advantages, lucky to survive his illness, lucky to have had so many good things happen to him, lucky to have had such fantastic parents. Defiantly, almost, as if saying it would make it so, he said that he had a stack of happy memories, marred only by one thing, the loneliness of his childhood.[14]

When I am trying to understand how an individual experiences his sense of being a person I often ask, 'If you could paint a picture of what is inside you, at your very essence, what picture would you paint?' Sometimes just in conversation people will reveal their image of their essence. Once when Kerry and Phillip Adams were discussing astronomy and black holes, Kerry said, 'That's what I have: a black hole inside me.'[15]

This is the image of immense loneliness, sadness, and self-disgust. There was no way that this black hole could be filled with solid light and joy. The lie that Kerry told himself about his father pinned the black hole in place. The lie did not let him see that his loneliness, sadness and self-disgust followed from his father's neglect, injustice and cruelty. Kerry told himself that all he needed was for his father to give him his unquestioned and complete approval. This approval need not be of everything the child has done: it is the approval which says, 'You exist, and I rejoice in this.' Such approval validates the child's existence. Alas, a great many people go through life believing that they have to earn the right to exist. They have learned from their parents, and from the religion they were taught, that they must be grateful for being born, and that they must show their gratitude by being good. Such people have never experienced their parents' joy at their mere existence. As Kerry discovered, but would not admit he had discovered, when a man has set himself the goal of being tough, ruthless, and winning every contest, no matter what the cost, he is unlikely to have the generosity of spirit to stand aside and let his son win the competition. Frank did not possess such generosity of spirit. Generosity of spirit is based on self-acceptance, and men who cannot bear to lose any competition lack such self-acceptance. Some men, self-accepting or not, recognise the importance of showing their son that they are proud of him, but many men do not. They thus inflict on their son a grievous wound. Some wounded sons retire from the race, and others go on striving to win. But the race is unwinnable, as Kerry found. No matter how much money he made, there was no amount of money that would fill that black hole.

Other people's unconditional love could have gone some way to filling that black hole, but, if we hate ourselves, we come to hate other people. Kerry did not like people. He told Parkinson, 'When I meet people, I don't expect to like them.'[16] Kerry loved his children James and Gretel but, as Barry wrote, 'There was more than a hint of the old-fashioned Packer methods in the way he had gone about it. Like his father, Kerry was a great believer in not spoiling his children, which meant, in James's case, that he rarely praised him.'[17] Thus James's love for his father must have been more than tinged with his fear of his disapproval, and Kerry's many sexual liaisons, about which his wife could not have been ignorant, ensured that his family did not give him their free and unconditional love. Kerry was never close to his brother, and he could never be sure that the many friends and acquaintances he gathered around him would have been there had he not been rich.

Kerry's identification with his father prevented him from knowing just who he was as a person. Perhaps he would have understood what Sarah Kane, the brilliant playwright who killed herself when she was twenty-seven, meant when she wrote the penultimate line of her last play *4.48 Psychosis*, 'It is myself I have never met, whose face is pasted on the underside of my mind.'[18]

Kerry may have died an extremely wealthy man, and he may have sampled many of the great pleasures which wealth can bring, but, in striving to be good in the way his father defined 'good', he never became the great man he could have been.

Chapter 7

HOW WE ACQUIRE
OUR BELIEFS

If there were no death there would be no need for a religion. We would have beliefs about how we should live our life but there would be no need for a religion which promises, as all religions do, to overcome death with some kind of eternal life. What all religions promise is that, even though our body dies, our sense of being a person will continue on as a soul or spirit, or by being reborn in another body. If you are good, whatever that may be, your body might die but you as a person will continue on. If you are bad, even though you as a person might continue on, you will not be happy.

So fond are we of our sense of being a person that all of us, including those who see death as the end of their existence, cannot imagine our non-existence as a person after our death. When I talked with my clients and in the workshops which I ran for counsellors and mental health professionals, I found that, though many people are reluctant to talk about death, if asked to say whether they would prefer burial or cremation, they can immediately state a preference. An indifference to the fate of our corpse seems to be rare. The preference seems not to be related solely to the practicalities of disposing of the body in that particular locality, but rather to what the person wants, in some way, *to see being done* to his body. Sometimes this is expressed as a lack of trust of other people – that they may not have noticed or they may have maliciously ignored the fact that the person is not really dead. For some people the thought of being conscious as one's coffin slides into the flames holds the greatest horror; for others it is the thought of scratching on the coffin lid as the clods of earth fall down to cover it. Stories, perhaps apocryphal, are often told of coffins being dug up and opened to reveal the marks of frenzied fingers on the inside of the lid. Cremation leaves no mark of the person wrongly consigned, but the dread of the flames of hell is burned into the minds of many of us brought up in the Christian faith.

On the other hand, we may have no doubt that we shall be well and truly dead at our own funeral, but other matters can be important. We may want to ensure that we are properly remembered by the placing of a suitable memorial, or that we are cast to the winds and the sea and forgotten. It is as if some vestige of our consciousness must be there to witness the fate of our mortal remains and sometimes, even, to share the experience of what happens to them. I used to live in a Lincolnshire village where the churchyard was large and beautiful. In winter the snow lay heaped where the villagers had been buried since Eagle was, as its old Saxon name (*ac Leah*) declared, a clearing in the oak forest. The forest had long since gone, but in spring the daffodils nodded over the graves and in summer the swallows swooped under the lime trees and the long grasses blew among the headstones. Whenever I walked through the churchyard I would think about what a nice place it would be to be buried in – to be part of the cycle of those birds and flowers and trees. Such a thought created in me a feeling of tranquillity (though I hoped that this ultimate pleasure would be a long time in coming), unlike that in Dr Johnson whose dread of death often caused him to repeat Claudio's words,

> Ay, but to die and go we know not where
> To lie in cold obstruction and to rot;
> This sensible warm motion to become
> A kneaded clod, and the delighted spirit
> To bathe in fiery floods.[1]

Harry Weber said,

> I have a horror of being buried alive and suffocating. I have a horror of it! When I die I want to be comfortable and sort of go to sleep – that's death. But this thought at the back of my mind – you know Rachmaninov's *Piano Concerto* – that one where there's supposed to be somebody alive,

knocking on the coffin. This is the thought that horrifies me. But apart from that, I think that death is something to look forward to.

When we feel secure, heaven can seem to be a pleasant place, but when we are depressed, as Dr Johnson often was, the horrors of hell can seem to be very close.

In day-long workshops the participants usually return from lunch somewhat tired and dispirited, but I found that posing the question, 'When you die, do you want to be buried or cremated?', was an effective way of waking people up. In a workshop for a group of psychologists who had no religious beliefs, all of them in answer to my question became lively and argumentative. One person said she wanted to be buried because 'it was natural, returning to the earth'. 'Oh, no', said another, 'I want to be cremated. I like the idea of turning into smoke – all that marvellous freedom.' One woman who had listened silently all day said very firmly, 'Burial's to do with religion and I want none of that. Cremation is me, just me. I'd like my ashes scattered over the sea.' 'Not at all', said a man on the other side of the room, 'cremation's so clinical and there's nothing left. But with burial, there's a gravestone. There's something there –.' 'I think burial's disgusting, horrible', broke in another woman, 'I couldn't face being eaten by those maggots.' 'But the thing about burial', argued another, 'I've always thought that if they've made a mistake and I find I wasn't dead – I'd be able to attract attention. I'd have a chance of getting out.' 'If they had made a mistake', said one woman in a tone to end the argument, 'with cremation at least it's over quicker. You don't have a slow, lingering death.'

All of these psychologists had grown up in a Christian society. Had they been, say, Muslim or Hindu they would not have had a choice as their religion allows only one mode of disposing of a body, burial in the case of Muslims and a funeral pyre in the case of Hindus. Those of us who do have a choice can no longer enjoy a simple personal preference. We need to take into account the future of the planet. Burials encroach on much needed land, but in a biodegradable setting, as is now allowed in special woodland cemeteries, bodies can perform a useful purpose. The land requirements of crematoria are limited, but, in their own small way, crematoria add to global warming. Do you want to see your remains being disposed of in an environmentally friendly way?

Our preference concerning the disposal of our body is a matter which concerns us only when we are alive. Dead, we are beyond caring. Funerals are for the living to allow them to express their love and grief, or satisfaction at still being alive. Near-death experiences do not reveal what actually lies beyond the grave. Reports from those who have been on the brink of death reveal that, as in life, we see what we expect to see. Christians see God or Jesus, Muslims Paradise, Hindus one of their many gods. If God were a humorist He would arrange for bigots to see the object of their bigotry. Anti-papists would see the Pope, and members of the Ku Klux Klan the smiling face of Martin Luther King.

* * *

In writing this about near-death experiences I know that I will offend many of those people who hold their religious beliefs most tenderly. Some of us are very matter-of-fact about our beliefs about the nature of death and the purpose of life, but there are others who guard their beliefs as being something sacred. The conventionally godly assume an air of self-importance while the more mystically inclined confide to listeners, 'I'm very spiritual', in a tone which implies, 'I am especially virtuous.' These people are easy to offend, and when offended they attack with words and sometimes with violence.

Whenever we react disproportionately to an event and become very distressed, or anxious, or angry, there is something in that event which we see as being a threat to our sense of being a person. Our friends can tease us about one aspect of our behaviour and we laugh along with them, but tease us over something we guard tenderly and we do not find this funny. We might be offended, or angry, or even cry. We can laugh at those aspects of ourselves about which we harbour no doubts. We accept these aspects of ourselves as being our idiosyncrasies, indeed, our strengths. We become defensive about those parts of ourselves we suspect are not quite right, but we are attached to them and do not want to give them up, in the way that a child does not want to give up the comfort blanket he has outgrown. These are aspects of ourselves which derive from our primitive, personal pride which defends our sense of being a person but without taking into consideration the nature of the situation in which we find ourselves. A common example is the man who has all but lost his hair and who carefully plasters a few long strands across the top of his head and assumes that no one will notice that he is bald.

If we react angrily when our beliefs about life and death are criticised, we reveal that we have not examined our beliefs and carefully tested them against what we have learnt about life, and come to the conclusion that our beliefs are as sound a philosophy as we can create. We may fear to examine our beliefs because we believe that, if we examine them, they will disappear and we shall immediately be quite unable to be good in the way we have been taught to be good. (I have often been told by believers that without a religious belief people will have no morals. Whenever I hear this I immediately check that I have a clear path to an open door lest this believer suddenly suffers a loss of belief and immediately falls to plunder, rape and murder.) Or it may be that we have been taught from our earliest days that to question your beliefs is to doubt God's word, and for that you would be punished. Or it may be that our family and friends seem so necessary to our survival as a person that we do not want to differ from them in our beliefs. Or it may be that our beliefs are a defence against the emptiness inside us or a sense of aloneness and sadness which we feel would overwhelm us if we brought to mind clearly what our beliefs actually were.

In these cases our beliefs are no more than a magical comfort blanket which we hope will protect us from the terrors of life. We want our beliefs to defend our sense of being a person and to ward off the fear of death, but we have not faced up to the fact that our beliefs, like all beliefs about life and death, are imperfect defences. There is no belief about the nature of death and the purpose of life which can give us complete security and comfort. All beliefs have advantages and disadvantages. For example, knowing that God is watching over you can be comforting, but do you really want God to see everything you do? Believing that you live in a Just World might make you feel secure and protect you from the pain of pitying those who suffer, but it also means that, when you do something wrong, you cannot escape the punishment that follows. Moreover, when you or the people you value suffer disasters, you cannot see this as merely random bad luck. It must be the work of enemies. Hence, conspiracy theories flourish in the USA, while in Muslim countries every adverse event can be blamed on the USA.

To feel secure in our beliefs we need to recognise what disadvantages are attached to our beliefs, and accept them rather than deny them. We need to recognise that life and death are mysteries, and that our beliefs are fantasies aimed at containing our fear and giving us hope. When we lack the courage to acknowledge what we know about the limitations of our beliefs, we become frightened and angry when our beliefs are criticised.

When we are sure that our beliefs are conclusions drawn from a careful assessment of our experience of life, we do not react with fear and anger when our beliefs are criticised. We are open to any evidence which might lead us to modify our beliefs because we know that our beliefs are hypotheses or theories about life and death. They cannot be absolute certainties. One person might tell us that they are absolute certainties and another person tell us that they are not, and there is no way we can set up an experiment to see who is right. Evangelical Christians often dismiss Allah as being a false god, while Muslims believe that Allah is the only God. If advertisers tell us that Brand A washing powder washes whiter than Brand B we can test this, but there is no test which can show which is the only true God. Understanding this, we can be happy to debate our beliefs with others, provided they do not fall to personal abuse and unseemly behaviour such as trying to kill us. When we respond to criticism of our beliefs with fear and anger, and then we attack our critics, what we are attacking is that part of ourselves which secretly or openly doubts and criticises our beliefs. We project on to others those parts of ourselves which we see as being bad, and, seeing our critics as being bad, we attack them. We might try to kill them, or force them to confess their sins and seek salvation, or, if we are among the well-mannered godly, we try to humiliate our critics by patronising them. A member of the well-mannered godly, offended at something I had said, stood looking down on me and, with an I-know-best smile, said, 'Jesus loves you.'

If we respond to criticism of our beliefs with fear and anger we should ask ourselves, 'What exactly is it in me and in this situation that leads me to feeling fearful and angry?' It might be that you tell yourself that you never doubt your beliefs when in fact you sometimes do. Even the Archbishop of Canterbury has his doubts about God's universal benevolence. The liberal wing of the Anglican Church recognises doubt as part of what it is to be human, whereas the fundamentalist wing, like all fundamentalist religions, condemns doubt. You might fear to admit your doubt to yourself, just as militant atheists can be reluctant to admit to themselves that when life is difficult they have been tempted to believe in a benevolent God who answers prayers, or in a hell where those you hate can be consigned. Or it might be that the roots of your anger and fear go back to when you were a small child being taught to be good. You had to bury your rage with those who punished you, and your sadness when you had to relinquish those parts of yourself which you valued. Are you expressing against your critics your secret rage against your good parents?

Alas, many people are reluctant to undergo such self-examination. They might believe that inside them is something so terrible that they must keep it hidden, or they might believe that, if you analyse something, you destroy it, just as some actors believe that, if they analyse their acting skills, they will destroy them. Science is concerned with analysis; hence many people reject science. I notice that amongst my friends and acquaintances who reject science none of them reject the products of science which they find useful. They use their computer to write articles deploring science. They might eschew allopathic medicine for alternative medicine, but they have apparently not noticed how much the various complementary therapies are using in their advertisements 'biobabble' derived from science. But then, in our fantasies we do not have to be consistent.

The belief that analysis destroys comes from a real experience. As small children all of us would lose ourselves in fantasies which we explored and elaborated in our play. Childhood fantasies are tremendously important. In them we experiment with our experiences: we try out different characters and scenarios; we express and master our emotions; we build up our courage and hope. So one day there we were, lost in our fantasy, and in came some crass, stupid older child or adult who scorned what we were doing. Our fantasy was left in shreds around us. The humiliation and loss threatened to destroy our fragile sense of being a person. To recover from such a blow our immature self had to struggle to put itself together again. In adult life the conscious residue of this event can be a fear of doing anything that would cause a treasured belief to fall apart. From this kind of experience most of us learned to keep our fantasies private, but some of us concluded from this experience that to analyse anything is to destroy it.

Those people who are afraid to enquire into themselves can be very pleased when their religion tells them not to think, but to take what their teachers tell them on trust. They must have faith. Not to do so is a sin. Thinking is indeed hard work, but, if we do not look critically at what our leaders tell us, and if we never enquire into our emotions, we will find ourselves being swept along by our emotions and acting in ways which we later regret. It may be that you joined a Pentecostal church when you were young and looking for a direction and meaning in your life. Pentecostalism is about experiencing emotion, and not about understanding it. It has little time for intellectual endeavour. In our teens and twenties we live in a tumult of emotions, and in that part of our life we often make big mistakes. For some, these mistakes are irreparable, but others of us manage to emerge from our twenties older and wiser. Pentecostal congregations tend to consist largely of young people, with many young people joining while older ones leave. Youthful enthusiasm is likely to wane with the discovery that matters like abortion and homosexuality have personal implications which cannot be dealt with simply by regarding them as sins, and that a relationship with Jesus does not necessarily make you rich. The older people who stay in the church usually see advantages in membership beyond the expression of religious enthusiasm. However, when you are older and wiser it is better to writhe in embarrassment at the memory of being saved and talking in tongues than to carry the burden of guilt for having murdered people for no better reason than that their religious belief or nationality was different from yours. Believing that those who do not share your beliefs will be damned and punished by God can have some very nasty consequences.

Emotions may be wordless, yet if we pause and think we can translate the meaning which each emotion has into words. A careful and truthful inspection of our emotions and an equally careful and truthful inspection of our life, looking not just at events but at how we interpreted those events, allows us to know who we are. Our face is no longer pasted on the underside of our mind. We no longer need to pretend we are someone that we are not. We can be ourselves, at home and comfortable with ourselves.

In writing the above paragraph I have tried not to use any words which are akin to psychobabble because I do not want to imply that therapists are the only people who can describe the process of gaining wisdom. Life forces all of us to reconsider our beliefs. Most people do this and become wiser as they get older. Those who do not include those, like Kerry Packer, who are in thrall to their parents and teachers, those who, like John McGahern's mother, look solely to their religion as the source of their courage and hope, those who are so frightened of their religious and political leaders they dare not think for themselves, and the intellectually lazy who acquired an unexamined set of beliefs early in life and never questioned and changed them.

* * *

A very important part of our inspection of our ideas is working out how we came to create our beliefs about the nature of death and the purpose of life. If your beliefs are as rock solid as you believe they are, working out how you acquired them will not change them. Remember, too, that the only person who can change your beliefs is you. Other people can present arguments but you decide whether to accept or reject their arguments.

My grandmother disapproved but my mother did not object when, aged fourteen, I decided to leave St Andrew's church to go to the local Methodist church which my friend Betty attended. Perhaps my mother decided that her mother's disapproval was easier to bear than my increasingly vociferous reluctance to continue attending what I found to be a cold and unfriendly church. Picnics and parties were much more acceptable to the Methodists than to the Presbyterians. The Presbyterians were of the opinion that we were not put on this earth to enjoy ourselves. Nor did they need salvation as the Methodists did because they were sure that they had been born as the Infallible Elect. The Methodists saw themselves in need of salvation, and so at frequent intervals young men training to be evangelical preachers conducted services there. I got saved several times. I tried very hard to believe in God but, as much as I told others that I believed, I knew it was not true. Quite by chance, I came across Lin Yutang's book *The Importance of Living* where I discovered that I was harming myself by trying to believe what I knew was not true. However, I could not have been a Christian no matter how much I tried. I had arrived at my moral and religious beliefs much earlier in my childhood, and they were at the centre of my being.

In my first five years of life I would rarely have heard my parents refer to God except perhaps in moments of extreme frustration or anger, and then never in the hope that God would intervene in any helpful way. My father has no religious beliefs and saw the Church and State as the two great powers engaged in repressing working-class men and women. My mother's strongest attachment was to her mother, Isabel Snedden, who, like her husband Andrew, was a God-fearing Presbyterian. My mother never attended church because she was frightened of anyone who was not a member of her family (all her family were frightened of her), but she made sure that I was christened in the Presbyterian Church, and, when I was about seven, she sent me every

Sunday to St Andrew's church to attend Sunday School and church. My sister willingly attended St Andrew's because she found companionship there, but she disdained to have anything to do with me. So every Sunday I set off alone on a long walk and tram ride to St Andrew's.

Sunday School was held in the rather dreary basement of the church. There I listened to stories about Jesus. This was a different Jesus from the one that Pentecostal churches like Hillsong celebrate with their Prosperity Gospel. The Jesus I learnt about was a man who was very like my father. He loved children, he was kind and generous, and he was a good friend to outcasts and the lowly. He shared my father's view that money had no value in itself and should be seen as no more than a means of trade of goods and services. When a rich young man asked him how he could be saved, Jesus said, 'Sell what you have, give your money to the poor, and follow me.'

Throughout my childhood I read everything I could find, whether I understood it or not. Books were scarce, so I read newspapers and magazines, and listened to my teachers and to the radio. I came to understand that historical evidence showed that there was once a man called Jesus, a rabbi, who lived on the shores of Lake Galilee, and who was killed by the Romans in Jerusalem. On this historical truth I imposed my ideas that Jesus was a kind, generous and loving man who believed that all people were equal and that wealth should be used for the good of all. People like this are always a threat to those in power, and so Jesus, like such people before and after him, was destroyed by those in power. I used fantasies to help me deal with the hurts and disappointments in my life, and so I could understand why Jesus' followers needed to construct a fantasy that Jesus rose from the dead and went to heaven, just as Siegfried as a boy constructed fantasies that his beloved uncle had not been killed in the war. In my family it was considered most reprehensible to expect to be praised, while self-praise was nothing but sinful pride, yet in church there were endless prayers and hymns praising a god whose wrath would be upon the heads of those who failed to praise him. Moreover, I could not worship someone who arranged that his son be tortured and killed to achieve something which God could have simply decided to do. He could have just said, 'I forgive you all.' My father would not have allowed such a fate to befall his daughters.

My experience of my fellow Presbyterians taught me something else. The minister and the elders must have seen that I was alone and shy. Not one of them befriended me. I listened to the minister's sermons where a favourite theme was Paul's 'faith, hope and charity' where the greatest of these was charity, which the minister explained meant love. I wondered why no one there ever showed me love. When I heard the parable about how it was as difficult for a rich man to get into heaven as it was for a camel to get through the eye of a needle, I was sure that Jesus meant the eye of a needle and nothing else. Yet at St Andrew's I was given the explanation that what Jesus had actually meant was the smallest gate in a wall surrounding a city. It was called the Eye of a Needle and was the last gate to be closed before sunset. A camel driver who needed to get his camels into the city before dark could with some difficulty push his camels through this gate, and the well-off Presbyterians at St Andrew's could likewise squeeze into heaven. When I was told, as I was often, that only those who believed in God would go to heaven, I would wonder why God had condemned all those millions of people born more than 2,000 years ago, or who in the last 2,000 years had no chance of hearing God's message. Why, I wondered, when our species first appeared on this planet, didn't God put a big notice up in the sky for all to see? A series of pictures could have easily explained what God would do to unbelievers.

When I learned the word 'hypocrite' I saw it as being a part of being a Christian. In later years I met many fine, truth-loving, decent people who were Christians, but it was clear that they were people who would have been fine, truth-loving, and decent whatever the nature of their religious beliefs. I continued to meet people who believed that, as they were Christians, they were superior to those who were not Christians. With some notable exceptions, I found that, if I accepted an invitation from some Christian group to give a talk, I would not be offered a fee, and I would be paid expenses only if I made a point of asking for them, and I would have to fend for myself and not expect to be treated like a guest. All this was in great contrast to the people in the non-religious mental health charities who, though with little income, would make sure that I was not out of pocket and that I was well looked after.

My mother's family, the Sneddens, might not have been keen church-goers but they enjoyed the knowledge that their views on everybody and everything were right, infallibly so. Anyone who did not agree with them was wrong. In the 1970s when Ian Paisley began his rants against the Pope, the Catholic Church and the Irish Republicans, I knew him and all that he stood for in the way that only experience acquired in childhood can let us know anyone. Paisley could have been a Snedden, except that, when he was in his early eighties, he changed, and agreed to talk in a most friendly way with his erstwhile enemies. No Snedden would do that. If anyone ever offended a Snedden, that Snedden never spoke to that person ever again. They did this to one another. Two of my uncles fell out some years before I was born. Whenever Uncle Bob drove up to his mother's house, my Uncle Jack, who lived at home, went out the back door and stayed down the yard until Uncle Bob had left. Whenever my mother was offended with one of her family, she retired to her bedroom where she sulked. Her sulks could last many months.

I would like to think that I would never do such things. I have spent much time trying to understand why people can be cruel, or greedy, or power-seeking, or why they display a meanness of spirit towards those they do not know. I can understand why friends might need to put their own concerns before mine. However, when someone whom I regard as a friend betrays and humiliates me and then denies all wrongdoing, even chiding me for being so sensitive, the affectionate connection I have with that person withers and dies. I have always thought of friendships as being ongoing conversations. When an affectionate connection withers and dies, for me the conversation is at an end. If I meet the person again I do not refuse to speak, as my mother would have done. I converse politely, but my spirits do not lift as they do when I meet a friend.

My concepts of human decency, generosity of spirit, conversation and the end of conversation are at the very centre of me, as is my inability to believe in some deity or supreme power. To pretend otherwise would be shameful. Even if I was presented with irrefutable scientific evidence of the existence of God, it would be impossible for me to trust him. I learned very early in my life not to trust those who should have taken care of me, so I could not expect that a god would be any different.

It is often said that we create our deities out of our experience of our parents. Indeed this is the case, but it is a very subtle process whereby we create a deity out of a selection of the characteristics of, not only our parents, but anyone who was a dominant figure in our childhood. There are stages in the development of our beliefs, but it is not inevitable that we all pass through every stage and in the same order. However, we all start out in the same way.

In his apology to the Aboriginal people for the treatment they had received at the hands of white Australians, the Australian prime minister Kevin Rudd told the story of Nanna Nungala Fejo, a stolen child of the 1930s.

> Nanna Nungala Fejo was born in the late 1920s. She remembers her earliest childhood living with her family and community in a bush camp just outside Tennant Creek . . . then sometime around 1932, when she was about four, she remembers the coming of the welfare men. Her family feared that day and had dug holes in the creek bank where the children could run and hide. What they had not expected was that the white welfare men did not come alone. They brought a truck, two white men and an Aboriginal stockman on horseback cracking his stockwhip. The kids were found: they ran for their mothers, screaming, but they could not get away. They were herded and piled into the back of the truck. Tears flowing, her mother tried clinging to the side of the truck as her children were taken away to the Bungalow in Alice, all in the name of protection.
>
> A few years later, government policy changed. Now the children would be handed over to the missions to be cared for by the churches. But which church would care for them? The kids were simply told to line up in three lines.

Nanna Fejo and her sister stood in the middle line, her older brother and cousin on her left. Those on the left were told they had become Catholics, those in the middle Methodists, and those on the right Church of England. That was how complex questions of post-reformation theology were resolved in the Australian outback in the 1930s.[2]

We are all lined up and told what religion we now belong to. We are born into a particular family and told that we are a Presbyterian or a Shia, or a Greek Orthodox, or a Buddhist, and so on. We have no choice in the matter, just as we did not have any choice in who our parents would be, though there are some people, like the followers of Rudolf Steiner, who believe that before we are born we are in some region where we choose our parents in terms of the lessons we need to learn in the next life that follows. For these people, we chose both our parents and our religion. If these prove to be unsatisfactory, we have only ourselves to blame.

Whether we chose our parents and thus our religion, or not, when our parents took us to their synagogue, church, mosque or temple, our first encounters with religion were no more than a phantasmagoria of impressions. Arthur Miller remembered at four years old being with his great-grandfather in the synagogue. He wrote,

From where I sat, on my great-grandfather's lap, it was all a kind of waking dream; the standing up and the sitting down and the rising and falling of voices passionately flinging an incomprehensible language up into the air while with an occasional glance I watched my mother up in the balcony. Even my inability to ever find out what was happening seemed inevitable and right, every question of mine being greeted with a holy and violent 'Shhhh!' lest God turn an impatient eye my way. I shut up and invented a religion of my own composed of close-up views of beard roots, eyebrows, nostrils, backs of hands, finger nails, and longer shots of the Torah scrolls being sometime touched or lifted out of their Ark and carried around the congregation for everyone to kiss, for they were the law, the heart of hearts, that which the earth kept trying to hurl away into space so it could fly apart and die of its sins, but could never let go of. Without fear, of course, there can be no religion, but if one small life in the 114th Street synagogue means anything, the transaction called believing comes down to the confrontation with overwhelming power and then the relief of knowing that one has been spared the worst.[3]

We learn to see the world in the terms our parents used to describe it. We learn not only about everyday things like houses, streets, cars, birds and trees, but about unseen things. My father scorned religion, but, when the thunder rolled in the black clouds behind Mount Sugarloaf, Dad would tell me, 'That's Jim McMahon rolling his stones.' I never discovered who Jim McMahon was and why he was rolling his stones, but imagining this big man with his big round stones dissipated any anxiety I might have had about the approaching storm.

Aboriginal children growing up in the bush listen to the stories of the Dreamtime that the elders tell, and through these stories they form a bond with their land. Children in other countries and other religions hear stories about spirits, gods, angels and devils, and learn to see their world peopled with these. We learn that other people do not have to be physically present for them to be part of the world we live in. When our parents tell us stories about our grandparents who are dead or our cousins who live far away, these people become real to us, and thus inhabit our world. Similarly, if our parents talk about God who is watching over us, being pleased or angry with us, God becomes part of our world. Some of the figures in our world, whether physically present or not, become very important to us. We identify with aspects of these people, and thus our idea of these people becomes part of our sense of being a person. Thus our parents never die because they are always inside us. In the same way many people identify with some aspects of the God that they have learned about, and this image of God becomes part of them. From then on, they cannot not believe in their God. The man Jesus whom I have described became one of my internal objects, not as a god but as a good man whose qualities I would try to emulate. When I hear of certain actions by a devout Christian, such as George Bush saying that waterboarding, the process of near-drowning a prisoner, is not torture, I say to myself, 'I wonder what Jesus would have thought of that', knowing full well the man Jesus would not have approved. On the other hand, I did not make an internal object of the deity the Presbyterians worshipped, an irascible, unreliable, irrational god who demanded constant praise and who placed his followers in unbearably difficult situations. I have heard a Christian leader say that the fact that God stopped Abraham from sacrificing his son showed what a benevolent god he was. A truly benevolent god would not have put Abraham in that situation in the first place, nor would he have allowed Isaac to experience being so close to death at the hands of his father.

Xenophanes, the ancient Greek philosopher, noted that Ethiopians say that their gods are snub-nosed and black while Thracians say that theirs are blue-eyed and red-haired. He added that, if horses and oxen had hands and could draw pictures, their gods would look remarkably like horses and oxen. *New Scientist* reported that,

> Nick Epley at the University of Chicago has been exploring the assumptions that believers make about their god. He asked religious volunteers – mostly Christian and Jewish – to give their views on issues such as the death penalty and abortion, and also to say what they thought God believes on the subject. Sure enough, people tended to assume that the beliefs of their God tallied with their own.[4]

Thus, if you are a woman who is secretly offended that homosexual men prefer male sexual partners, or if you are a man who is scared that someone might discover that you have experienced sexual feelings towards another male, you might try to deny your feelings by hating homosexual men. You want to believe that you are right in doing this, and so you believe that your God hates homosexuals too.

Ask different people to describe the God they believe in and these descriptions will be as variable as the description each person would give of his parents. In his study of those particular experiences that might be called spiritual, Edward Robinson asked his subjects to say whether their image of God was based on their experience of their parents. In answer, one woman wrote:

> I think my earliest ideas of God must have been derived from what my parents were. They were the rock and anchor of all existence; they knew everything, were all-wise, all-powerful, always there. So what could God be but someone a little more powerful and wiser? Only He could not be seen. I think I must have been early teenage when I suddenly realised my parents were not all-wise, and not perfect, and they could go away, or die, so God was not a super-parent.

Not all parents allow the child to develop the idea of God as a super-parent. Another person wrote, 'I think that my early ideas about God were drawn largely from certain characteristics in my parents. The idea of an impassive observer, rarely giving help or hindrance except at indefinite and often illogical times, very much like my parents.' Another wrote, 'Yes, my early idea of God was derived from what I saw in my parents, but it gave me a wrong idea of God, i.e., not as a God of Love.' One man replied, 'Not at all. My father seemed either asleep or out.' Some people would say that this is the perfect description of God.[5]

For some people their God is remarkably similar to their father. In a family where the father is a wrathful father, always dispensing his form of justice, then the God the children are likely to believe in will be a wrathful and justice-dispensing God. In this kind of family, if the mother is kind and compassionate, some of the children might project these attributes on to the God they believe in. However, what children project on to the God they believe in are not the attributes which other people see in the parents but the attributes which each child sees in the parents. Thus, while two siblings might believe in a wrathful God, one sibling might see their God's wrath being directed at their enemies, while the other sibling sees God's wrath being directed at himself.

When we listen to a story which contains a number of

characters we find ourselves identifying with one character rather than another. Religious myths might have one main character, but there is usually a cast of other characters, one or two of which might be more appealing than the main character. The ancient Greeks had what was a kind of extended family of gods which allowed every human drama of parents and children, husbands, wives and lovers, siblings, cousins and friends, to be enacted by the gods. Moreover, since there was no holy writ, no Bible or Qur'an, story tellers and dramatists created a plethora of interpretations of every story. Hindus believe that their god Brahman created everything, but he left the tasks of creating, maintaining and destroying the world to three gods, Vishnu, Shiva and Brahma. These, along with a host of lesser gods, offer a wide range of characteristics which individual believers can see as desirable in the particular god they worship. For Catholics whose God is somewhat remote and unpredictable, the Virgin Mary becomes an important figure because she can seek God's mercy for the believer. The Archangel Gabriel plays an important part in Judaism, Christianity and Islam. In the Book of Daniel in the Hebrew Bible he appeared in a vision to the Jewish leader Daniel, while in the Talmud he was the destroyer of the hosts of Sennacherib. In the New Testament Gabriel foretold the birth of John the Baptist, and he visited Mary to tell her of the impending birth of Jesus. In Islam the Archangel Gabriel or Jibreel was the messenger through whom God revealed the Qur'an to the Prophet Mohammed. In these patriarchal religions the believer is urged to be 'God-fearing'. If you fear your God, you cannot be close to that God without feeling anxious that you might provoke his anger. Hence you can decide that one of the lesser gods is your best friend. A Serbian psychologist told me that most Serbian families had their own special angel. His family's angel was the Archangel Gabriel. Once, at a very difficult time in his life, he was in a foreign city he had never visited before and, too anxious to sleep, he went for a walk. He rounded a corner and there in front of him was a church called St Gabriel's. He took this as a sign that the Archangel was assuring him that everything would be all right. From Amanda Lohrey's account of the three teenage Hillsong girls (see p. 12), it seems that Jesus is their best mate, while Jesus' dad hovers dimly in the background.

We encounter the unseen beings which our family calls God, or Allah, or Vishnu, or Gabriel in our early years when we are discovering that our parents are fallible human beings. Even the very best of parents can fail to be there when we need them. The great appeal of a religious belief is that it assures us that we are not on our own. Someone, somewhere, is watching over us. It takes a great deal of courage to accept that we are on our own and we have to look after ourselves. Most of us would rather believe anything, however improbable, rather than take responsibility for ourselves. However, if we do not take responsibility for ourselves, we cannot be ourselves. We remain children, clinging to the coat-tails of an adult whose actions we find impossible to understand. If God is benevolent and all-powerful, why do the good suffer and evil flourish like the green bay tree?

We create our image of our family's God or gods over the same space of time that we learn how our family defines 'good'. Thus our religious beliefs and our moral imperatives become enmeshed, so that the knowledge, 'Mummy will be annoyed if I don't wash my hands before dinner', becomes, 'God will punish me if I am unclean.' God and gods are very keen on cleanliness. Christians wash away their sins with baptisms and christenings. Muslims wash before praying. Hindus bathe in the Ganges. Arthur Miller told the story of how,

My mother's father, Louis Barnett, once instructed me never to walk under a large lighted cross overhanging the sidewalk outside a Lennox Avenue church; if by accident I did, I must spit when I realised what I had done, in order to cleanse myself. There was a certain mild fear of that particular cross after this, but mainly that it might break loose and fall on me. Nothing of the history or theology behind such admonitions was ever mentioned, leaving them in the realm of superstition or in a kind of immanent symbolism of menace.[6]

Non-believers wash regularly for the sensible, practical

reasons of being healthy, avoiding infections, feeling comfortable, and not disgusting those nearby with your appearance and smell. Ancient religious leaders who were concerned with the health and well-being of their flock would have encouraged them to wash. A way of making sure that everyone did so would be to incorporate washing in the ritual of worship. We learn by simile, seeing how something we know relates to something new. If sin can be seen as dirt, then sin can be disposed of in the same way as dirt by washing. Then the simile becomes a metaphor, and then something sacred, and the believers lose all sight of the sense of the ancient priests, mullahs and rabbis who ordered their people to keep clean.

Sacred metaphors let loose from their practical beginnings become dangerous weapons or targets. As I write, women in Basra in southern Iraq are being murdered because they have ventured out without a headscarf. The same is happening to women in Afghanistan who fail to wear the burqa. In Turkey whether women who wear a headscarf should be allowed to attend university has become a bitterly fought-over political issue. Meanwhile, some of the scientists who study earthquakes have found that they can predict where in Turkey earthquakes will happen. They cannot predict just when the next earthquake will occur, but they have predicted that the next one will be a strong one and it will be in Istanbul. Nothing can be done to prevent such an earthquake, but there are things that can be done to mitigate its effects. But this would be a major task full of uncertainties. How much easier it is to argue over headscarves!

In all this the history of the headscarf has been forgotten. The writer and artist Mordechai Beck pointed out that there is a tradition in Judaism of women covering their heads when outside their home. He wrote,

> It is unclear how widespread or popular this custom was, but there is rabbinical tradition that suggests that the covering of the face/body extended well into the first century of the Common Era. In the Mishna, edited around 220CE, a custom is recorded of Jewish women in Arabia walking about with veiled faces, while ladies from Mede

sported large, body-covering garments (Tractate Shabbat 6:6) . . .

Ironically, it may be that both Judaism and Islam share an older tradition current among the peoples living in the ancient Middle East. Covering the face, body and even the eyes would be a natural response to the ravages of the sand-carrying winds. Protecting your complexion would be crucial, especially if you were a woman. But as sometimes happens in great religious traditions, when practical necessity is transformed into a 'higher' spiritual value, the obscure origins of the custom are forgotten.[7]

The real world where we all live is full of things that can delight and comfort us, and things which can terrify us. When we people the real world with gods, angels, spirits and demons we add immensely to what can delight and comfort us, and to what can terrify us. Moreover, parts of the real world can take on added meaning, a symbolism of menace or of comfort and reassurance. People who have lost all confidence in themselves and feel that their sense of being a person is falling apart can see in certain ordinary artefacts messages for them alone, often messages of menace. Consequently, hallucinations and delusions, which are re-workings of the person's memories of certain past experiences, are often expressed in religious terminology and symbolism.

Adults use a number of different methods in teaching religious beliefs to children. These methods usually include memorising parts of the sacred texts. In Jewish and Islamic schools children often sway backwards and forwards when they are memorising. This kind of movement seems to aid learning a text off by heart, but it does not increase the child's understanding of the text. Those of us who were required to reproduce the contents of a history book or our teacher's notes in an examination usually became very adept at this task, but what we memorised usually vanished the moment the examination was over. In his memoir, Mike Marqusee told how he took 'twice-weekly Hebrew lessons for my bar-mitzvah'. However, 'within weeks of my bar-mitzvah every word of Hebrew vanished from my head'.[8] Parts of what has been memorised are not forgotten, but they are those parts that have a special resonance for the child.

Throughout their history, Catholicism and Protestantism have relied on terrifying children into belief. Often the fear remains after the belief has vanished. My friend Frank Flanagan once told me that his wartime experiences had led him to abandon his Catholic beliefs. He said, 'I couldn't keep up the pretence of believing any longer. I decided that the following Sunday I would not attend mass. I didn't go – but I didn't go outside all day, just in case God threw a thunderbolt.' I found that many of my depressed clients who had been brought up Catholic might have abandoned their religion but, in the depths of their depression, they still feared the hand of God coming down from heaven, picking them up like a flea off a dog's back, and flinging them out into infinity. In contrast, my Protestant depressed clients, even if they had abandoned their beliefs, could not escape from the cold, implacable, endless torture of a Calvinist conscience.

St Andrew's Church which I attended offered children two kinds of belief, that of the good friend Jesus to whom we were taught to pray, 'Gentle Jesus, meek and mild', and that of the heavenly Father who had every attribute you would not want in a father. Since that time, many churches, both Protestant and Catholic, in their teaching of children, have eased the God of the Old Testament out of the picture. The Good News is all about how simple it is to be saved, with little mention of what happens to you if you are not saved. The biblical stories which might have aroused the children's fears have been sanitised, as Tim Dowling found when he visited Little Walsingham.

Sundays present a special dilemma for shrines. As holy places they must feel particular pressure to Keep Sunday Special, but Sunday is also a very big shopping day for them. If you build a shrine, the pilgrims will come, and they will want ice cream.

The village of Little Walsingham in Norfolk has been a place of pilgrimage since 1061, when Lady Richeldis de Faverches had her first vision of the Virgin Mary, so they've had plenty of time to sort this dilemma out. Here the church bells and the shop tills ring in harmony all Sunday long. It's a great place to pick up all manner of holy souvenirs, spiritual aids and devotional bric-a-brac. This is where I found, and subsequently purchased, the My Little Bible With Cuddly Puppy Gift Set, not because I wanted it, but because I needed some change in a hurry. In Little Walsingham the Lord's Day brings no respite from the holy obligation of Pay and Display.

The connection between the Bible and the cuddly puppy is not an immediately obvious one. The cuddly puppy is not a traditional religious icon, after all. There are no cuddly puppies in the Bible, at least not in the King James's version. In fact I happen to know that there are only 15 references to dogs in the whole of the KJV, three of which are to dead dogs, and two which involve dogs returning to their own vomit for metaphorical purposes. Nothing cuddly about that. I can see no reason to package a cuddly puppy with a Bible in a gift set, except to mitigate the disappointment a child might feel at being given a bible as a present.

Taken on its own, My Little Bible In Pictures by Kenneth N Taylor is an undemanding version of God's word, with an illustration on every other page, how-well-did-you-read questions at the end of each passage ('What are these people doing? Why is it bad?') and some bowdlerised versions of Old Testament Highlights: 'These two women are fighting over a baby. Each says the baby is hers. God made Solomon know which woman was really the baby's mother. He gave the baby back to its mother. Then everyone thanked God for giving them such a wise king.' Scene missing or what?[9]

For those who do not know the Bible well, this is the story of two harlots (at St Andrew's we children were not told about the women's occupation), each of whom had given birth to a baby. When one of the babies died during the night, both women claimed to be the mother of the living child. They came to King Solomon and asked him to adjudicate in their dispute. The unexpurgated King James's Bible goes on:

And the king said, Bring me a sword. And they brought a sword before the king.

And the king said, Divide the living child in two and give half to the one and half to the other.

Then spake the woman whose living child was unto the king, for her bowels yearned upon her son, and she said, O my lord, give her the living child, and in no way slay it. But the other said, Let it be neither thine nor mine, but divide it.

Then the king answered and said, Give her the living child, and in no wise slay it: she is the mother thereof.

And all Israel heard the judgment which the king had judged; and they feared the king: for they saw that the wisdom of God was in him, to do the judgment.[10]

When I was told the King James's version of this story at St Andrew's Church (minus the harlots) I doubted Solomon's wisdom. I knew that my Auntie Doff would never have allowed me to be cut in half but I was not too sure about my mother. A cuddly puppy as a present along with this story would not have solved my problem.

Tim Dowling's skill as a writer is to show us how ridiculous we can be when we let our vanity and irrational hopes override our good sense. We can fail to see that every shrine, church, mosque, temple and synagogue is a business as well as a place of worship, and that these businesses can trade very profitably on our superstitious and sentimental ideas. Moreover, we might want to protect our children from the harsh reality of life, but, if we lie to our children in our efforts to protect them, our children will not thank us when they discover the truth. Indeed, such a discovery can lead to a loss of belief.

Elizabeth described how she lost her faith in Jesus.

We were brought up Anglo-Catholic. I started school at three, and I remember the priest coming in in his robes. What they put over to us was that God loves every child. He watches every little sparrow that falls. So long as you're good, the only thing you have to do if you're in trouble or afraid, have little problems, you ask God or Jesus to help you. And of course you believe all this. You sit starry-eyed listening. I used to be a very sickly child, and in our house – if you were ill my parents were extremely angry. Well, it was winter and I knew I was going to have quinsy. My throat was so sore. I was about six, a little puny kid, and they'd sent me home from school, but I tried to dawdle, waiting for the other children to catch up, because if I arrived home early my parents would demand, 'Why are you home early?' and they would see immediately that I wasn't well. So I prayed. I remember I stood at a lamppost praying, 'Please, Jesus, don't let me be sick. Let me be well when I get home.' Of course, I fiddled around in the cold and got worse, I suppose, and arrived home with my brothers. Unfortunately, there was celery for tea. I normally liked it, but I couldn't eat it because I couldn't swallow. It was all quiet – we didn't talk much at tea – and suddenly my mother noticed and she said, 'Why aren't you eating?' and I said, 'Um-um', and she said, 'God, she's sick again. Are you?' and my sister said, 'Yes, she was sent home from school', and she said, 'Why didn't you come home? Off to bed!' I thought, 'That's Jesus off my list.' He wasn't paying any attention to me. And then as we got older I was quite off Him. I didn't like saying all the prayers. And I think I suggested once to one of the teachers, rather about the sparrows than about me. I said, 'What if one sparrow He missed, or one child?' And then the answer came that the child or the sparrow must have met with His disapproval.

* * *

Thus far I have talked about the way our religious or philo-sophical ideas grow out of our interpretations of what we have been taught as children, and how these ideas might evolve over time. However, many people can describe certain special experiences that illuminated, or confirmed, or even changed their beliefs. Alister Hardy, founder of the Religious Experience Research Unit,[11] began his study by asking people to give him accounts of experiences which he had described as 'a deep awareness of a benevolent non-physical power which appears to be partly or wholly beyond and far greater than the individual self'.[12] Hardy was followed as director of the unit by Edward Robinson who had noticed that, when people talked about their experiences, they often talked about childhood events where they experienced something of what Wordsworth had described.

> There was a time when meadow, grove, and stream,
> The earth, and every common sight,
>   To me did seem
>   Apparelled in celestial light,
> The glory and the freshness of a dream.
> It is not now as it hath been of yore –
>   Turn wheresoe'er I may,
>   By night or day,
> The things which I have seen I now can see no more.[13]

Thus Wordsworth described the special vision of childhood, where the world comes to us new, vivid, and immediate. Not everything we saw was beautiful. Some of the original perceptions of childhood are indescribably horrible, but whether beautiful or horrible, or simply intriguing, what the child sees conveys a reality and knowledge that say to the child, 'This is what the world is.'

Some of our childhood perceptions are particularly heightened and real. They comprise what Edward Robinson called 'the original vision'. Robinson reported that, 'Some 15% of all our correspondents (they now number over 4,000) started by going back to events and experiences of their earliest years.' His subsequent research led Robinson, a botanist, not a psychologist, to be somewhat contemptuous of the psychologist Piaget. He wrote, 'The starting point of all Piaget's thought about childhood is the incapacity of children to see the world as adults see it ... Piaget is in fact continually setting children an exam in a subject that adults are good at and children bad.' Robinson concluded that there were some perceptions which showed the child to be wiser than the adult. He wrote,

> I believe that what I have called 'the original vision' of childhood is no mere imaginative fantasy but a form of *knowledge* and one that is essential to the development of any mature understanding ... I believe that many of these

childhood experiences are *self-authenticating*: they have in themselves an absolute authority that needs no confirmation or sanction from any other source. I believe that they are also self-authenticating in another sense: they bring to the person who has them an awareness of his true *self* as an individual, with identity, freedom and responsibilities of his or her own. I believe that his vision can only be understood, either by the person who has it or by the outside observer, in *purposive* terms: there seems to be no substitute for the old-fashioned word 'destiny' – which must, however, be clearly distinguished from 'fate'.[14]

'Destiny', as Robinson uses it, seems to encompass the person who we know ourselves to be, included in which is the knowledge of the life that we must live if we are to be and become ourselves. Much of our unhappiness stems from our inability to be ourselves. Many people are busy trying to be good, often in the way that their religion demands that they be good. Many people do not trust themselves sufficiently to be themselves. Many people live a life they feel is that of an imposter, but they also believe that they cannot change their circumstances. Yet, if we cannot be ourselves, who can we be?

From about the age of seven I knew I was a writer, not just that I wanted to write but that I was a writer. The writers I read (and that was pretty much anyone who came my way) gave me a validation and a goal which no one in my family or at school gave me. Writers, or at least my idea of these writers, became, as we now say, my mentors and my role models. Everything about writing I loved. I was never more myself than when I was writing, but none of the adults around me encouraged me. My teachers punished me for my bad spelling and handwriting, and, in high school, for having ideas of which they disapproved. If my mother and sister came across any of my writing efforts, they found them most amusing. Years passed. When I was forty-seven I was living in a little village in Lincolnshire. I returned home late one night, having been in London to deliver the manuscript of my first book to Michael Coombes at John Wiley and Sons. I was standing in my living room, feeling too tired even to decide whether I would get supper or go straight to bed, when the thought came to me as clear as a bell, 'From now on my life will be different.' This thought was not, 'I wonder if . . .', or, 'I hope that . . .', but, 'It will be.' And it was. This was not a spiritual experience showing me something of the transcendental, but something as, or even more, powerful. It gave authenticity to what I knew myself to be. From then on I could live my life as myself.

In the following account, one of Robinson's correspondents speaks of 'an intensest joy and indescribable longing'. As a child alone in the bush I often felt that joy and longing, but I related it to writing while this person related it to God.

On the first occasion (aged 8–10) I was in the garden, muddling about alone. A cuckoo flew over, calling. Suddenly, I experienced a sensation I can only describe as an effect that might follow the rotating of a kaleidoscope. It was a feeling of timelessness, not only that time stood still, that duration had ceased, but that I was myself outside time altogether. Somehow, I knew that I was part of eternity. And there was also a feeling of spacelessness. I lost all awareness of my surroundings. With this detachment I felt the intensest joy I had ever known, and yet with so great a longing – for what I did not know – that it was scarcely distinguishable from suffering . . . The second occurred a good while after the first. It was an absolutely still day, flooded with sunshine. In the garden everything was shining, breathless, as if waiting expectant. Quite suddenly I felt convinced of the existence of God; as if I had only to put out my hand to touch Him. And at the same time there came that intensest joy and indescribable longing, as if of an exile, perhaps, for home. It seemed as if my heart were struggling to leap out of my body. How long I stood, or would have gone on standing, I do not know; the tea-bell rang, shattering the extra dimension into which I had seemed to be caught up. I returned to earth and went obediently in, speaking to no one about these things.[15]

Such experiences are not rare. David Hay interviewed a random sample of Nottingham residents to find how many had had 'the experience of being aware of, or influenced by a presence or power, what this experience had been like, when it happened, what it meant to the person'. Some 62 per cent of those interviewed claimed to have had such an experience, double what had been predicted on the basis of national surveys of religious experience. Hay reported that 'the largest group of experiences was those referring to an awareness of the presence of God' and that three-quarters of these felt that their experience had changed their outlook to some degree. The kind of changes could be categorised as 'confirming or intensifying my beliefs, making me more optimistic, giving me insight into life, encouraging moral behaviour'. A young married woman told the interviewer, 'I feel God's always with me; it's confirmed and strengthened the things I've been brought up to know; given me will-power to go on.' A factory charge-hand said, 'Well, I've certainly been a lot happier. I've been able to mix with people more. More at ease with life.' A twenty-four-year-old graduate revealed, 'It completely changed my viewpoint, my philosophy of living. Instead of thinking that everything could be decided on the basis of reason, I realised that the deeper things were intuitive.'[16]

Not all people describe these experiences in religious terms. In Robinson's book *Living the Questions* a young woman told of an experience one snowy winter's night in a birch wood. She said,

> . . . like recognizing that someone has given you a gift of some sort, something that is a true gift . . . I felt so much standing there that I had to hug the birch tree . . .
> Sometimes I feel I've lost my bearings and I'm very depressed about something or other, or wonder if there's any meaning to life or anything, and I can't get in touch with it, I can think back mentally, think of the birch trees, and be assured that it really did happen even if I can't feel it at the moment. And that makes me feel better, it makes me feel more alive . . . My father had died . . . when I was about fourteen . . . I really felt that after that everything had peeled away, you know, all your assumptions about justice and what should happen in the world that you're taught when you're little: that if you're good, good things

> happen to you, and if you're bad, bad things; when all this
> is peeled away . . . the feeling that when everything has
> gone there's still something left, that's what I got from the
> birch tree thing. Before that, everything was gone, but
> after, I realized that no matter how much in your personal
> life is torn away, there's always something left.[17]

These studies and others like them show that many people, perhaps a large percentage of the population, have experiences which can only be described in words like 'religious', 'intuitive', 'numinous', 'revelatory', and which exert a profound and often beneficial effect on their lives. Psychologists and psychiatrists interested in why people change should not ignore these kinds of experience, nor should they attempt to belittle or invalidate them. A client of mine, after she had known me long enough to have some trust in me, told me of an experience which she kept secret in case people thought she was mad. Some years before she had developed a kidney stone of such dimensions that it could not pass from her body and she was admitted to hospital for an operation. The pain was so intense that she needed regular doses of morphine, but even then, when she was conscious, all she could do in her agony was to cry out, over and over, 'God help me'. The day before the operation she was lying in a drugged sleep, when suddenly she awoke to sharp, full consciousness and turned her head and saw, just beyond her, the face of Christ looking on her. She was terrified, thinking that she was about to die. She did not. Instead she drifted back to sleep. When she woke she found that the pain was gradually abating. The next day she could get out of bed. The kidney stone had gone, and no operation was necessary. In a Catholic hospital this may have been counted a miracle, but where she was, miracles – except those performed by surgeons – were not allowed to happen. Instead, the doctors told her that she had been hallucinating. What she had seen was no more than the effect of the morphine. They did not attempt to explain why the kidney stone had gone and they did not pause to consider that by explaining her experience in this way they had destroyed a gift which could have supported her through the years that followed. When she was referred to me by her general practitioner she was suffering from extreme anxiety which made her feel that she was losing her mind. Although she believed in God and prayed to Him, she did not draw on her experience for strength and security. Not being a Christian, I could not assure her that she had been a recipient of God's grace, but I did, drawing on Hardy's work, show her that other people had had experiences like hers, and that these experiences suggest that the world contains mysteries that are beneficial and not terrifying.

When we are small children and gradually becoming aware of our sense of being a person we have an implicit trust in our sense of being a person. Lacking self-consciousness, we take our sense of being a person for granted, and we concentrate our attention on what is around us. We look at the world with intense curiosity. However, the adults in that world soon make us self-conscious. Soon we find it very difficult to retain that trust in ourselves because the adults are busy teaching us to be good in the way they want us to be good. This means they are telling us that, as we are, we are not good enough. If we take this to heart and believe that we are, in essence, flawed, perhaps irreparably so, we lose the trust we had in ourselves. With this trust gone, and beset by life's difficulties, we can lose all self-confidence, feel ourselves falling apart, and then resort to one of those forms of defences which psychiatrists call mental illnesses. The 'cure' for such 'mental illnesses' is the recovery of trust in oneself. Some people achieve this by talking things over with a compassionate but challenging listener, and by engaging with their surroundings in an increasingly active way, while others achieve this simply by letting go of certain ideas. Often the latter occurs in situations that could be described as revelatory.

In my book *Beyond Fear* I have told the story of Val, a vicar's wife, who was deeply depressed when we first met. Some time later, when she was no longer prepared to be the downtrodden wife and mother, she talked to a television interviewer about what she had learned. She said,

> In my experience of depression I feel as though I'm falling into a bottomless pit and, if I let go, I shall just disappear

into the bottom of this pit. But I felt a love reaching out to me like a pair of hands. I want to let go and disappear into that black hole, but somehow the hands won't let me go. I used to think I would find nothing inside me, but I've come to realise as my depression lifted, that if you let go, you don't fall into a bottomless pit, and that the hands that I thought were beyond and outside me reaching out to me in love are actually within me and supporting me from within, and, if I let go, I fall into these hands that hold me in love.

Val had been brought up in the Anglican Church and had heard innumerable sermons about God's love. Her great discovery, so she told me, was that God's love was the same as loving herself. Loving oneself is not a matter of vanity but a matter of being the person you know yourself to be. She said, 'I have changed from feeling that I have to suffer by trying to be perfect to earn God's love to a feeling that I only have to be still and be myself to the . . . I suppose the soul centre you might call it, and find God there.'[18]

It is not necessary to explain these kinds of experiences in terms of some supernatural power because a supernatural explanation explains nothing. Explaining, say, electricity as the work of the Almighty will never lead you to discover how electricity can be controlled in order to boil a kettle. What is needed is a scientific explanation of what electricity is and how we can use it for our benefit. Explaining these experiences in terms of how we operate as human beings is much more complex, but, from this, we can learn a great deal about ourselves. Here are three ways in which these extraordinary experiences can occur.

The first concerns how, at every moment of our life, we are creating meanings. Some of these meanings are in words, some in wordless emotions, some in images, some in bodily feelings. Every meaning brings in its train a host of associated meanings. Every moment we are creating not just one meaning but a torrent of meanings, only a few of which become conscious. It seems that our frontal cortex has to work very hard to create some order out of the chaos of all these meanings. Even when we are awake and functioning well, our conscious train of thought is less like an orderly train and more like a thousand coloured beads sloshing around on an endless roller-coaster. If our frontal lobes relax in sleep, or under the effects of alcohol or drugs, or cease to function efficiently because of injury, or illness, or extreme exhaustion, meanings that at other times would never make it into consciousness become conscious. If they become conscious not in words but in images we have consciously to interpret them. How we do this depends on our past experience. We see what we expect to see. One of Alister Hardy's correspondents wrote,

After the death of a four and a half year old son I found no comfort in anything or anyone, the Church seemed powerless to help me as did the medical profession. I could not go out of the flat I was living in at that time and although I tried hard I could not see anything but blackness and an intense longing to die. One morning I was dusting – tidying, the usual household chores when I smelled the most wonderful garden flowers, it is difficult to describe the smell I mean – rather like a garden after rain, being of a rather practical mind in such things I looked around for the source of the smell, there was no flowers in the flat, certainly none outside, no perfumed polishes or toilet things in use, then I sat down and for the first time since my son died I felt peaceful inside. I believe this was God's comfort, my son felt near and I was no longer alone.[19]

Secondly, it seems that one of the important functions of sleep is to allow our brains to do some filing and sorting of the meanings we have created during the day. Many of us have discovered that, if we have a problem to solve, such as one of those situations where we have to decide whether to do this or that, a good plan is to think about the problem as we prepare to go to bed, not in terms of 'I must solve this now', but in terms of just setting out what the issues are, much in the way we might lay out our clothes for the next day before we go to bed. When we get into bed we do not think about the problem, and we go to sleep. It is not unusual to wake up in the morning with the solution to our problem clear in our mind. We can solve very complex, personal problems in this way. One of Hardy's subjects wrote,

> Gradually I became psychotic, and attempted suicide. I had done something which I considered utterly dreadful, and I was being driven to self-destruction because of an intense feeling of guilt. I had only one desire – to be forgiven . . . I was visited by the psychiatrists, my husband, my brother and the hospital chaplain, but I was unable to communicate sensibly with any of them. Then quite dramatically the whole picture changed overnight. The weight of guilt had been lifted and I was myself again, quite rational and ready to go home again. This recovery was not due to any medical aid at all. Both psychiatrists and clergy were at a loss to understand this sudden change, but it was quite simple to me: I believed that God had forgiven me . . . It was not a temporary healing. I never needed treatment since that time. Looking back I still know that there was a divine intervention in my life at that point.[20]

There is another way in which we can have extraordinary affirming experiences. Those who practise meditation call what goes on in our conscious minds 'chatter'. To learn to meditate you have to learn how to still the chatter. Most of this chatter has to do with the past and the future. Not much of the chatter is about what is happening in the present moment. Buddhists have always talked about 'mindfulness', and now some therapists have taken this up and shown that, by paying attention to the present moment, we can find peace of mind. However, you do not have to be a meditator or a Buddhist to have that wonderful experience of suddenly focusing on what is in front of you and feeling yourself become part of what is there. This usually happens when we are away from the man-made environment, on our own, and quietly looking at the world around us. These experiences occur more frequently in childhood than in adult life. One of Robinson's correspondents wrote,

> My first remembered experience of the numinous occurred when I was barely three. I recall walking down a little cul-de-sac lane behind our house in Shropshire. The

sun was shining, and as I walked along the dusty lane, I became acutely aware of the things around me. I noticed a group of dandelions on my left at the base of the stone wall. Most of them were in full bloom, their golden heads irradiated by the sun, and suddenly I was overcome by an extraordinary feeling of wonder and joy. It was as if I was part of the flowers, and the stones, and the dusty earth. I could feel the dandelions pulsating in the sunlight, and experienced a timeless unity with all life. It is quite impossible to express this in words, or to recall its intensity. All I now know is that I knew something profound and eternal then. Now I am deeply conscious that my human failings have taken me far from my childhood understanding of a greater reality.[21]

Many of us find these kinds of experiences so extraordinary and wonderful in themselves that we do not need to believe in some supernatural power. We might find that we lack a language to describe these experiences to other people and so we fall back on the language of the religion we were brought up in to describe them. We are not describing these experiences in order to prove the existence of God. We can feel that to do so is to diminish the importance of these experiences. They are wonderful experiences and should be treasured for that.

* * *

However, there are many people who feel that they cannot survive as a person if all they have is the world and other people. They want something more, something that will make them feel special, and will take from them the burden of being responsible for themselves. They feel that, since their own parents have failed them, they must have a supernatural parent. If their supernatural parent is proving to be a bit forgetful, they look for some person whom they can see as embodying great wisdom, someone who can carry out certain rituals and make God do what they want. They are looking for a guru.

Over the last twenty years or so, many people whom I have met have told me how helpful my books have been to them in sorting out some personal problems. This is very pleasing. At least I have not been wasting my time. However, I have reached a point in my career where some people will tell me, often at length, about what an extraordinarily wise person I am. I know that this is not the case. I have discovered nothing that someone else could not have discovered. I am not a nuclear physicist making discoveries in distant space, nor am I a medical scientist finding the causes and cures of dread diseases. There is nothing in my books that has not been said by many people before me, down all the centuries that our species has existed. I think that the reason people like my books is because they discover in them things which they did not know they already knew. However, I can now see how easy it would be to set myself up as a guru, surround myself with grateful disciples, and make a lot of money. None of this would involve any suffering such as being martyred or having to live with the poor. Many therapists, preachers and political leaders have done this. All they have to do is to surround themselves with gullible people who feel inadequate and who want someone to appear to take responsibility for them, and promise them that everything will be all right. They will be happy, rich and live for ever. If everybody in the world were prepared to take responsibility for themselves, these would-be gurus, preachers and leaders would not be able to find a single follower.

The belief in a god who is a father to his children keeps believers from growing up. In contrast, many people believe in some great transcendent power, who could be called God; they know themselves to be part of this power and everything that exists; they also know that they have to take responsibility for themselves. Taking responsibility for yourself means knowing that, while you can learn from examples set by other people, including the power in which you might believe, ultimately you make your own decisions and are responsible for the outcome of those decisions. However, such a set of beliefs does not fit the dogma of those religions where the leaders want their flock to act as unquestioning, obedient children.

In this book I have written a good deal about Christianity because I know Christianity. It is the myth that is in my bones. Its concepts are part of the framework of how I see the world. However, I know about the other religions, and I can see how very alike all religions are. Religions try to overcome our fear of death, and they tell us how we ought to live our lives. They also feed our pride. We want to be special. When we were children we wanted to be the child our parents loved the most. Our parents disappointed us, and so we want to be God's most beloved.

For Jesus' followers it was not enough that he understood the plight of the poor, the downtrodden, the outcasts. It was not enough that he told them it was of prime importance that they loved one another, and they did to other people what they would want done to themselves. They wanted, they expected something more, much more.

Perhaps they expected that Jesus would overthrow the Romans and force them to leave, but he did not. The Romans killed him in the way they killed slaves who revolted. The scholar Geza Vermes, in his book *The Resurrection*, tabled the events following the crucifixion as they are told in the four gospels, Matthew, Mark, Luke and John, and in the Acts of the Apostles. There are a number of contradictions in these stories, but, allowing for these, two questions emerge. The first is, why didn't the disciples and the followers of Jesus expect that Jesus would rise from the dead? Vermes's answer is that Jesus had not told them that he would. He wrote,

> The most significant peculiarity of the resurrection stories is that they nowhere suggest that the rising of Jesus from the dead was expected by anyone. In Matthew, Mark and John the resurrection complex is presented as falling straight out of the blue, a complete surprise. Luke mentions Jesus' earlier announcement of his rising that was either misunderstood or forgotten (!?!) by his disciples. . . . The cross and resurrection were unexpected, perplexing, indeed incomprehensible to the apostles. When Jesus was captured in Gethsemane, his apostles abandoned him and fled, at least according to the Synoptic evangelists. Peter even denied that he had known Jesus.[22]

The women who reported that the tomb was empty and that Jesus had risen from the dead were disbelieved by the male disciples. 'Female testimony, flippantly called nonsense (*lêros*) by the apostles in Luke, did not count in Jewish male society.'[23]

The second question is what happened to turn frightened fugitives into apostles who would proclaim the gospels. Vermes's answer is that,

> Within a short time the terrified small group of the original followers of Jesus, still hiding from the public gaze, all at once underwent a powerful, mystical experience in Jerusalem on the Feast of Weeks (Pentacost). Filled with the promise of the Holy Spirit, the pusillanimous men were suddenly metamorphosed into ecstatic spiritual warriors. They proclaimed openly the message of the Gospel, and charismatic potency, imparted to them by Jesus during his ministry, which had enabled them to preach, heal and expel demons, burst into life and manifested itself in word and deed.[24]

In the time they had spent with Jesus they had taken him into their hearts. Jesus lived inside them. In modern day parlance, they had identified with him, and so they could act as he had acted. Vermes concluded,

> The conviction of the spiritual presence of the living Jesus accounts for the resurgence of the Jesus movement after the crucifixion. However, it was the supreme doctrinal and organisational skill of St Paul that allowed nascent Christianity to grow into a viable and powerful resurrection-centred world religion.[25]

Christians call the resurrection a miracle. Here is another miracle. Babies are born knowing how to imitate. In antenatal classes parents learn about this, so that now in maternity wards there is likely to be a father holding his minutes-old baby up, face to face, and sticking out his tongue. The baby, watching closely, imitates his father's gesture and sticks out his tongue. This is the first step in learning how to identify with another person, to take that person inside you, and behave in the way that person behaves. When children identify with their parents, what they take in is not so much what their parents say as what their parents do. Actually, they identify with their interpretations of what their parents do. For instance, a parent might not feel particularly courageous, but if the child sees the parent behaving courageously in a difficult situation, the child can identify with what he sees as his parent's courage and in later life be able to call on this courage when he feels afraid. So extraordinary is this process that we could well call it miraculous.

Alas, the perpetually dissatisfied with this world will brush this second miracle aside. It is merely human and has no value. The perpetually dissatisfied persist in ignoring the simple wisdom that, if you ignore the treasures that you have and always yearn for something more, you cannot help but be unhappy.

Jesus was a remarkable man, just as Mohammed, the Buddha, Lao Tsu, Confucius, and all the men and women of whom we know nothing were, all of whom had an understanding of the human condition that the people around them lacked. Their ideas and their example could have been the basis on which their people could build a framework of ideas about how to live in this uncertain, wonderful world as adults who know how to take responsibility for themselves, and who would pass this knowledge on to their children. Those people who could have done this were outnumbered by those who wanted to feel special, those who were not prepared to take responsibility for themselves, and those who saw that, by claiming that a fantasy was an absolute reality and that they could do magic, they could become rich and powerful.

As a result, there are many people who reject what they actually have, a wonderful world and one another, in favour of a fantasy that indulges their personal pride, a pride that takes no account of what actually goes on. The reality is that life can be difficult, rewards and punishments do not come automatically to those who deserve them, death exists, and in the end we all die.

There are only two possible meanings for death. Either it is the end of your identity, or it is a doorway to another life. You choose one of these two meanings, and from this meaning you determine the purpose of your life. These meanings become your religious or philosophical beliefs. On the basis of your beliefs, are you entitled to believe

1 That you, and the people with beliefs similar to yours, are superior to those who do not share your beliefs?
2 That, because you hold these beliefs, it automatically follows that you are virtuous?
3 That, on the basis of your beliefs, you are entitled to force other people to share your beliefs, and, if they do not conform, kill them?

Chapter 8

THE CONSEQUENCES OF OUR BELIEFS

When we are faced with a disaster, we have a choice. We can see the disaster as it is, or we can create a fantasy about it that aims to protect us from the full horror of what has happened. When the disaster we face is the death of someone we love, the circumstances of that person's death might allow us to create the fantasy that the person has not died. We might tell ourselves that the person who gave us the news had been given the wrong name, or that the loved one had failed to catch the plane that later crashed, and so on. Bereavement counsellors see the creation of such fantasies as the first stage of the grief process, and call it 'denial'. This fantasy gives us time to recover from the immediate shock and to gather our strength and courage to face the reality of what has happened. However, some people cannot let their fantasy go. They hang on to their fantasy, and as a result they alienate those who cannot share this fantasy, just as Alberto's mother alienated Primo Levi when she insisted that Alberto was alive and well, and Primo knew that his dearest friend was dead.

Our own death is a reality which we can be reluctant to face and, because we do not know what exactly death is, we have to create a fantasy from which we develop our religious and philosophical beliefs. These beliefs are focused on ourselves. We can fail to see that the beliefs we hold have implications for other people.

In researching for her essay *Faith, Money and Power*, Margaret Simons encouraged people to talk to her in some depth about their religious beliefs. She met Bev Campbell who had gone through a severe crisis when she was twenty-eight years old and a mother. Simons did not disclose in full what had led to this crisis, but she did say that part of this involved the Billy Graham crusades in Melbourne in the 1950s. These crusades caused a tremendous stir in Australia. I remember seeing newsreels showing people screaming and fainting and behaving in ways the like of which were never seen amongst the Presbyterian and Methodist congregations that I had known. Graham was very challenging as well as charismatic. This led many people, including Bev, to question the traditional Christian beliefs they had held all their life. Bev's description of what she experienced sounds very much like the turmoil many people go through when they discover that there is a serious discrepancy between what they thought their life was and what it actually is. She said,

> I was laying on the bed, feeling that something was trying to take me over on the inside, and it was like something was fighting it from the outside. It was like this voice was screaming inside my head, 'You haven't done anything, you needn't make any kind of commitment, this has pushed you over the edge, go back to where you were, you were a nice person, go back, go back, go back.'

Bev could have interpreted this voice as the voice of reason, telling her that she had been caught up in the emotion of Graham preaching. But she did not. She decided to interpret the voice as being that of Satan, trying to intimidate her and turn her from God. She said,

> I felt I was a little thing floating up and down, in the water in a storm, and I thought, I can't hold on, I can't hold on, and I had this picture of me being locked in a padded cell in an insane institution somewhere, with this thing in me, taking control of me, and I couldn't let anyone know what it was like and I was laying there, just feeling my mind slipping away, and I said to God, 'With my last sane thought would you remember that I said I loved you, no matter what happens, no matter what I say or do, will you just remember,' and it was like the voices ceased and the whole thing just ebbed away. And it had just taken such a toll, not being able to eat, or think, and the house was in chaos, you know.

The crisis was resolved after a visit by the local Anglican minister who was a charismatic and powerful person. He performed some kind of exorcism. Bev gradually recovered, and felt that she had discovered 'the true Christian path'. Simons described her as 'the sort of person who wants the best for others – both in a literal and spiritual sense. Today she spends time counselling and comforting others who struggle with life and identity. She accepts and loves all kinds of people, including those who strain her own ideas about morality.'

This was one woman's story. However, over the three weeks of this crisis one witness was her ten-year-old son David. Now a man, he told Simons how he remembered her 'being very scared and scary, going around smashing things that looked evil'. This lasted for three weeks, a long time in a ten-year-old's life. His mother may have resolved her crisis, but the way she did this determined what David's life would be until he decided to take responsibility for himself. Simons wrote,

> David became a Christian himself, going to church groups,
> seeking solace in them for the troubles of adolescence. He
> carried the Bible to school, despite the teasing, but, as he
> grew older, the doubts began to grow. As a young adult
> he wanted to live his own life, and of course he wanted sex.
> On the other hand, he still believed. He was rebelling, yet
> it remained inconceivable that his mother might be wrong.

David told Simons that by the time he had married young and was working, 'I had the feeling I was kind of waiting for something to happen, that this wasn't my real life. I probably just wrote that off in the old days as something that didn't matter, because the real life is the afterlife. But over time I had come to the realisation that this is it, this is the life, and I wanted to live my life.' He had 'flashes of freedom, realising that I didn't have to believe. That I have a choice.' David's wife was a Christian and could not accept David's loss of belief. They divorced and David went through a wild period, catching up on the things he had not done when young, but by the time he talked to Simons he had settled down. He said, 'The major regret I have in my life is getting involved with the church. There are a lot of stupid things that I have done, but this is the one that I regret the most. If there were one thing I could go back and change, it would be that.'

David's daughter Andrea was by now a young woman. She told Simons that the big trauma in her life was when she was eleven and her father left home. She believed that this was what turned her to God. She said, 'When Dad left, Mum lost control and when she crumbled I crumbled too, because I didn't know how to be strong without Mum.' Her mother left the church Bev attended, and she and Andrea went to an evangelical Baptist church where Andrea discovered that she could speak in tongues. People at her church told her that she had a gift of intercession, which meant hearing messages from God intended for other people. Andrea passed these messages on. Simons wrote,

> Andrea suffers with shyness and anxiety but God, she says, has pushed her into places and situations she would never have had the courage or desire to go for herself. 'Without God I would be a cowering little person, with no confidence. I would have let people walk all over me. He has taken the veil off my eyes.'

Here Andrea was saying that she did not see herself as being capable of doing what most of us do, that is, learning to be self-confident as we get older and more experienced. She could not achieve anything: everything she did was God's achievement.

Andrea said that she loved her father but added, 'Dad is like a big oxymoron, he is the most unselfish person when it comes to giving, but the most selfish person when it comes to understanding how his actions affect other people.' Simons wrote, 'The challenge of her life – and she prays for help – is to understand and forgive him, to grow closer to him, to find a way of respecting him.' However, Andrea wanted all this on her terms. She seemed not to understand that we can be close to another person only if we accept that person as he is. When she said to her father, 'I love you but I want you to accept Jesus into your life', she was in effect saying, 'I reject you because you do not live up to my standards.'

Andrea worked in a nursing home where, she said, she tried to work in a Godly way. However, this did not include doing anything to improve the world. She said, 'I don't believe in fighting for peace and justice, because I don't believe that it is ever going to happen. The only time it will happen is when Jesus returns.' She told Simons that she wanted to be a missionary. She said, 'I have a real heart for people who are oppressed and that are persecuted.' But her heart did not extend so far as to try to bring oppression and persecution to an end. 'I admire people who fight for those sort of things, but the only thing I would fight for is for people to have a relationship with God.' Simons commented, 'Here, I think, is the true implication of the evangelical religious revival. It discourages activism for anything other than a personal relationship with God.'[1]

It is not God but ourselves that ensure that the sins of the father are visited on the children. The effects of the decisions we make are felt first by our children and then by their children, and so on. If we focus only on ourselves we make ourselves blind to what is happening to those around us. Bev could have decided that, even though her new beliefs were the best solution to her predicament, she would not force her beliefs on her son, but let him have the life of an ordinary Australian boy. She chose not to do this because she believed she knew what was best for him.

It is impossible to know for certain what is best for other people. Each of us lives in our own world of meaning and no one else can enter that world. No one else knows exactly how we each see our world. It is extremely difficult to predict with any degree of accuracy what choices other people will make. In certain situations we can feel that we have knowledge and experience which the other person lacks. We have a choice. We can offer our advice framed as, 'This information you might find useful. You decide what to do with it', or we can say, 'I know what's best for you. You must do so and so.' If Bev had said to David, 'I find my beliefs very helpful and you might too, but it's up to you to decide', David would have been able to weigh the joy of pleasing his mother against the discomfort of being teased by his schoolmates, and make a decision that seemed right for him. Later he might have regretted his decision, but he would have had to accept that it had been his decision. A great disadvantage of being responsible for yourself is that the number of times you can blame your misfortunes on other people is very limited. Bev, however, chose to see herself as knowing more about David than he knew about himself. He could not choose for himself or be himself. He did eventually achieve being able to be himself, leading the life which he knew was right for him, but he had to endure the knowledge that his daughter looked down on him and pitied him.

People who see themselves as being superior can only pity those whom they see as their inferiors. They cannot feel compassion, because we feel compassion only when we see those who suffer as our equals. They are fellow human beings. The word 'compassion' comes from the Latin 'com', meaning together, and 'pati', to suffer. We suffer together. 'Pity' comes from the Latin 'pietas', piety, devotion to religious duties and practices. If you are suffering and people offer you comfort you have no difficulty distinguishing compassion from pity. With the first you are your comforter's equal; with the second the comforter is looking down on you as their inferior. Compassion strengthens and pity diminishes us, both as a recipient and as a giver.

There is no place for pride in compassion because we all suffer together, whereas pity is all about pride. All religions have a tradition of compassion. Karen Armstrong pointed out that, 'Each tradition developed its own formulation of the Golden rule: do not do to others what you would not have done to you.'[2] However, religious people are not immune from pride, and this is expressed in the second tradition of all religions, the belief that believers in that particular religion are superior to all other people. Such superiority saves believers from having to feel compassion towards non-believers, and allows believers to be cruel to non-believers. Within each religion there are people who hold fast to the tradition of compassion and reject pride and all its trappings; there are those who secretly are very proud but talk the language of compassion; and there are those who eschew compassion and feel entitled to punish those who do not share their beliefs.

On the basis of your beliefs, are you entitled to believe that you, and the people with beliefs similar to yours, are superior to those who do not share your beliefs?

The Australian scientist Tim Flannery, in his essay 'Beautiful Lies', told of the first meetings between the marines of the First Fleet under Governor Arthur Phillip and members of the Eora tribe on whose land the city of Sydney now stands. One of Phillip's officers was Watkin Tench who was

the author of two highly readable and compelling accounts of Australia's first four years. He was widely acknowledged as 'the most cultured mind in the colony', and such was his enlightened and humane outlook that, despite the prejudices of his time, by the end of his sojourn among the Aborigines he could profess that, 'Man is the same in Pall Mall as he is in the wilderness of New South Wales.'

What Tench's account gives is

a confirmation of the common humanity of all people – as strong a confirmation as you could wish for of the absolute necessity of living by a humanist or at any rate a humane creed. The reason I say this is because the two peoples who met on that momentous day in 1788 – the Aborigines and the Europeans – had been separated from one another for longer than any other human cultures on our planet. For 60,000 years – perhaps half the span of our species' tenure on earth – they had been cut off from one another, living on isolated and very different landmasses at opposite ends of the globe. They had developed separate languages and cultures, different skin colours, gene frequencies and facial features. But despite it all, recognition and understanding were immediate, so strong is our common bond that 60,000 years of separation melted away in a moment. A smile was a smile. An uncertain glance, an act of friendship, a shout of hostility or fear, a sexual overture – all were instantly comprehended.[3]

Stories of such instant comprehension abound in the written records of explorers and travellers. However diverse in race, culture, language and religion, when people meet face to face they recognise the common humanity they share. The only way a person or a group can feel superior to other people is to keep themselves totally separate from those they wish to despise.

Flannery wrote,

> In Phillip and the marines we have some of the highly sensitive minds that come out of the culture of the European Enlightenment. Indeed, like Lieutenants William Dawes and Watkin Tench we find spirits whose humane attitudes and understanding of the nature of Australia were not to be met again in the Antipodes for two centuries.

When these men left the colony they were replaced by men who saw the Aborigines not as their inferiors but as an inferior species of animal. Animals cannot own the land on which they live. 'The nation of Australia was founded on a lie, that of *terra nullius*, the myth of the empty land, whose Aboriginal inhabitants of some 47,000 years' tenure had, under British law, no rights to their land whatever.'[4] Claims of being superior to other people are always based on lies, and it is these lies that those wanting to claim superiority use as their excuse for inflicting cruelty on those they despise.

The lie that Aborigines were an inferior species was not openly questioned until the second half of the twentieth century, and, even today, many white Australians cling to that lie. When we lie, we are denying a truth that we know. Here white Australians are denying the truth they know, that Aborigines are people like themselves. To keep their lie in place and strengthen their denial of the truth, they have to condemn utterly any measure of compassion shown to the descendants of the first inhabitants of Australia. To deny the common humanity of all human beings is shameful.

Primo Levi understood this. When he looked back at his time in Auschwitz, he found that,

> Few survivors feel guilty at having deliberately damaged, robbed, or beaten a companion: those who did so blocked out the memory; but by contrast, almost everybody feels

guilty of having omitted to offer help. The presence at your side of a companion who is weaker, or less cunning, or older, or too young, hounding you to death with his demands for help or with his simply being there, which is itself an entreaty, is a constant in the life of the Lager. The demand for solidarity, for a human word, even only a listening ear, was permanent and universal but rarely satisfied. There was no time, space, privacy, patience, strength; most often, the person to whom the request was addressed in turn found himself in a state of need, of credit.

I remember with a sense of relief that I once tried to give courage (at a moment when I felt I had some) to an eighteen-year-old Italian who had just arrived, who was floundering in bottomless despair on his first days in the camp: I forget what I told him, certainly words of hope, perhaps a few lies, acceptable to a 'new arrival', expressed with the authority of my twenty-five years and my three months of seniority [of being in the camp]; at any rate, I made him the gift of a momentary attention. But I also remember, with disgust, that much more often I shrugged my shoulders impatiently at other requests.[5]

The Nazis tried to turn their Jewish prisoners into non-humans, and, from this experience, Primo Levi was later to write what are perhaps the best accounts ever written of what it is to be a human being. Surely such an understanding could never be lost? Yet it was by many Israelis and their supporters. How did this happen? Through pride in being superior, and the lies that such pride needs to maintain it.

In his memoir *If I Am Not for Myself*, Mike Marqusee described his comfortable childhood as a middle-class Jewish-American boy. He had been born in 1953 to parents who had always been involved in issues of social and racial justice, often putting themselves at risk. Those were the days when America's great enemy was Communism, and the House of Representatives Committee on Un-American Activities and the FBI investigated thousands of Americans and charged many of them with being a Communist. Once before the committee, the person was pressured into giving the names of friends and colleagues who held Communist views. Failure to do so meant that the person was sent to gaol, they were blacklisted so they could not work, and their passport was seized to stop them leaving the country. Terrible indeed, but at least they were spared being sent to Guantanamo Bay.

To his everlasting shame, Mike Marqusee's father went before the committee and named names. Afterwards, in an attempt to expiate his guilt, he threw himself into the struggle in the 1960s for black Americans to gain their rights. Marqusee was proud of his parents. From them he learnt that,

> Judging people by their colour or their religion was wrong. Racism – making a generalisation about a whole people, stereotyping a whole people – was wrong. Taking over other countries, even if they had attacked you, was wrong . . . Among the shibboleths I was brought up on was that the belief 'my country right or wrong' was wrong. No one liked to insist more than my dad that if you loved your country you criticised its flaws. Surely that also applied to religion, and 'my religion right or wrong' must also be wrong.

As a schoolboy Marqusee attended a Reform synagogue and there,

> I felt at home. We all did. We were the most comfortable Jews that ever walked the planet. Not for us the longing of exile, the pain of dispersal. We were Americans in America . . . From an early age I conceived of myself as a rationalist and though I made spasmodic efforts at belief, I never felt the divine presence . . . Here [at the synagogue] the absolutes were kept in the background. God was there, mentioned in prayers, but he had been discreetly updated and denatured. No one seemed overly concerned with his judgement.
>
> So what was the creed we were taught in Sunday School? It was not about God. It was about the Jews. A singular people who had given wonderful gifts to the world and whom the world had treated cruelly. A people who were persecuted. A people who had survived. A people who

triumphed. Despite the Holocaust, we were not a nation of losers, of victims. There was a redemptive denouement. There was Israel, a modern Jewish homeland, a beacon to the world. A shiny new state with up-to-date, Coke-drinking people like us. Liberals, like us. Bearers of civilisation, making the desert bloom. A little America in the Middle East.

Israel was both our own cause, a Jewish cause, and a moral cause. Like America. A land without people for a people without land . . .

As always, the Jews had enemies. Israel was menaced by the Arabs (not Palestinians, a word never used in our synagogue). They were not exotically attired Bedouin – people who did not have or did not want a home. In our Sunday school texts, they appeared swarthy, coarse, ignorant, duplicitous. For no reason at all, they hated us.

In the Six Day War in 1967, the Israeli army attacked Egypt and succeeded in occupying Sinai, the West Bank, the Golan Heights and Gaza. At Sunday School there was great triumph. No one mentioned an occupation. A few months later an Israeli soldier came to talk to the Sunday School class.

He told us that the Arabs had planned a sneak attack but had met more than they bargained for. They were bad fighters, undisciplined soldiers. And they were better off now, under Israeli rule. 'You have got to understand these are ignorant people. They go to the toilet in the street.'

Now something akin to this I had heard before. I had heard it from the white southerners I'd been taught to look down on. I had heard it from people my parents and my teachers described as prejudiced and bigoted. So I raised my hand and when called upon I expressed my opinion, as I'd been taught to do. It seemed to me that what our visitor had said was, well, racist.

I felt the eyes of the teacher and the other kids turn on me. They were used to me spouting radical opinions but this time I had gone too far. Angrily, the teacher told me I didn't have any idea what I was saying and there would be no discourtesy to guests in his classroom. The young Israeli ranted bitterly about Arab propaganda and how the Israelis treated the Arabs better than any of the Arab rulers did.

Marqusee found the reaction of his teacher and classmates puzzling, so he decided to tell his parents about what had happened. He had always been encouraged to raise anything that troubled him with his parents. He was not prepared for his father's reaction.

For some time I remained unaware that my father was listening to me not with approval but with rising fury. When he barked, 'Enough already!' the shift was disturbingly abrupt. Like my Sunday School teacher, he made me feel I had said something obscene. Then he drew breath and seemed to soften. 'I think you need to look at what you're saying,' he said, and then the softness vanished. 'There's some Jewish self-hatred there.'

Marqusee felt

deeply and frustratingly, misunderstood. My motives had nothing to do with self-hatred or any feeling about being Jewish. Nor did they have anything to do with compassion for a people – the Palestinians – about whom I knew nothing. I was merely following, as best I could, and in typical fourteen-year-old fashion, what seemed to be the dictates of logic.

In his synagogue Marqusee would have been told that the Jews were God's Chosen People. He probably was not told how many other groups of people have believed that they were God's Chosen People. Nor was he told that the lands along the eastern coast of the Mediterranean have been occupied for almost as long as there have been humans on this planet. A land without people for a people without land is a *terra nullius* lie told by people who wish to believe that they are superior to other people and therefore entitled to do whatever they want.

At the end of his memoir, Marqusee wrote,

I used to enjoy the old joke: 'Jews are like everybody else, only more so.' Now it strikes me as self-aggrandisement disguised as self-effacement. The truth is that we are like everybody else, only at the moment many of us have made ourselves less so, less human. 'They hate us not for what we do but who we are.' No, they hate us for the way we use who we are to justify what we do. What is done in our name.[6]

Ignoring the fact that Jesus and his disciples were Jews, Christians persecuted the Jews and blamed them for Jesus' death. You might ask, if God planned Jesus' sacrifice, why blame the Jews for being, like Pontius Pilate and his soldiers, instruments that God used to achieve his purpose? But that is a fourteen-year-old's question. Logic has nothing to do with the need to feel superior in order to hide your own weakness and inadequacy. Christians needed to feel superior, and the Jews were at hand to feel superior to. Giles Fraser wrote,

> At times of tension or division, there is nothing so uniting as the 'discovery' of someone to blame – often someone perfectly innocent. For generations of Europeans, the Jews were cast in the role; in the same way women have been accused of being witches, homosexuals derided as unnatural, and Muslims dismissed as terrorists. The crucifixion turns this world on its head. For it is the story of a God who deliberately takes the place of the despised and rejected so as to expose the moral degeneracy of a society that purchases its own togetherness at the cost of human suffering. The new society he called forth – something he dubbed the kingdom of God – was to be a society without scapegoating, without the blood of the victim. The task of all Christians is to further this kingdom, 'on earth as it is in heaven'.
>
> Yet, for all his years in office, it is hard to think that President Bush has done anything to make this kingdom more of a reality. Instead he has given us rendition, so-called specialised interrogation techniques, and the blood of many thousands of Iraqis. Given all this, how can George Bush call himself a Christian?
>
> Easter is not at all about going to heaven. Still less some nasty death cult where a blood sacrifice must be paid to appease an angry God. The crucifixion reveals human

death-dealing at its worst. In contrast, the resurrection offers a new start, the foundation of a very different community that refuses the logic of scapegoating. The kingdom is a place of shocking, almost amoral, inclusion. All are welcome, especially the rejected. At least, that's the theory. Unfortunately, very few of us Christians are any good at it.[7]

It can be very difficult to give up the pleasure of feeling superior. Pride is seductive, and, in seducing us, it can take many forms. Perhaps the most popular form of pride is to pretend to be humble, perhaps by claiming to be a sinner. To this claim there comes an unspoken rider, 'I might be a sinner, but I am a better person than you because you, an unbeliever, don't recognise how bad you are. Therefore, because I am a believer, I am good.'

On the basis of your beliefs, are you entitled to believe that, because you hold these beliefs, it automatically follows that you are virtuous?

The Writers' Festival in Melbourne in 2008 was held at Abbotsford Convent. Here for over a hundred years the closed order of the Sisters of the Good Shepherd cared for fallen women and orphaned and abandoned girls. After the convent closed in 1975 it became an arts centre. The organisers of the centre were faced with the difficult task of making such forbidding buildings appear warm and friendly. The stone buildings are set around three courtyards, but the buildings are solid and heavy, the windows and doors rather narrow, and the courtyards comparatively small, in one case little more than a yard. However, the joy and grace of the convent are the gardens that were established around 1902. Here the lawns undulate down to the winding Yarra River, amid magnificent trees and colourful shrubs and flowers. The centre provides places for learning, creativity and relaxation, while families picnic and children play in the gardens.

I gave my talk at the festival and afterwards I sat at a table in one of the courtyards to sign copies of my books. A middle-aged woman put her copy down in front of me and said, 'Can I tell you what happened to me today?' I nodded, and she went on, 'When I bought my ticket for today I didn't know where the Abbotsford Convent was, but when I got here and walked around I recognised the place. This was where I was when I was a child. And then I found something else – the gardens. I never knew there were gardens here. I couldn't believe it when I saw them. The nuns always kept us children in the courtyards.'

Let me contrast that story with a story about my friend Jacqui. She suffered a long, drawn out death from cancer. She had time to draw up plans for her funeral. She wanted to be buried in a biodegradable coffin somewhere where there were trees, flowers and grass. Had it been possible, she would have been buried in the beautiful garden she and her partner Craig had created. Jacqui was not a Christian, so the Anglican Church would not allow her to be buried in the consecrated ground of a church graveyard. However, the vicar in Jacqui's village decided otherwise. She said that Jacqui could be buried in the churchyard of the village church, in a place overlooked by trees and not far from the paddock where the horses sometimes grazed. So we gathered around Jacqui's grave for a humanist funeral, and the vicar left the church open in case any of the mourners wished to say a quiet prayer.

In the Catholic Church nuns vow obedience to God and thus to the Church hierarchy. Obedience has always been a prime virtue. At Abbotsford Convent, if the Bishop (there was a Bishop's Room at the convent) or the Mother Superior decreed that the children should not go into the garden, then the nuns could feel virtuous as they carried out that order. Any nun who found herself thinking about how she, as a child, enjoyed playing in a garden would need to repent of such a sinful thought. In contrast, the vicar would have been well aware that some of her clergy colleagues would have sternly criticised her decision and felt very virtuous in doing so, but to her it was the decent thing to do for someone who lived within the bounds of her parish. In short, the nuns were concerned with themselves and their virtue; the vicar was concerned with the welfare of a fellow human being.

Christians often talk about the Christian virtues. Moderate Muslims often speak of the virtues of compassion, peacemaking and charity found in the Qur'an, while fundamentalist Muslims condemn godless Westerners for their wide variety of sins, and, by implication, praise their own virtues. Jews who support Israel's policies toward Palestine take great pains to emphasise Jewish virtues. Yet, if you drew up a list of Christian virtues, Muslim virtues and Jewish virtues, these lists would be identical. No religion has its own special virtues, much less are the virtues of a particular religion superior to all other virtues. They are simply human virtues.

When we list the virtues, we use abstract nouns – truthfulness, kindness, generosity, loyalty and so on. Abstract nouns are no more than words. They do not refer to a real thing. You do not have a lump of compassion in you, tucked behind a lump of gratitude, and superimposed on a lump of intelligence, overhung, say, by a lump of depression. The reality is that you feel compassion towards someone, you are grateful to someone, you behave intelligently, and you feel sad and hopeless. Behaving intelligently and feeling hopeless and sad are not regarded as being examples of virtuous behaviour, but behaving compassionately and showing gratitude are. We can behave intelligently or feel sad and hopeless without regard to other people, but the exercise of a virtue always involves other people. You may or may not regard being obedient as a virtue, but such behaviour is always in relation to the person who is being obeyed.

Virtues concern our relationships with other people, and relationships with other people are always complicated and rather unpredictable. When psychologists want to find out if the people answering their questionnaires are being truthful, they cunningly include one or two questions that are likely to show whether the person answering the questions is capable of lying. As a simple example, two questions might be:

1 How often do you tell a lie?
2 How often do you keep a promise?

The choice of answers is: always; sometimes; never.

Anyone who answers 'never' to the first question and 'always' to the second is considered to be lying. The truthful answer to both questions is 'sometimes'. No matter how virtuous we might be trying to be, there are always situations where we lie, and where we break a promise. No set of religious beliefs prevents such situations from arising. To say that this is not so is to delude yourself. Such self-delusion arises from pride, the pride which people can take in feeling virtuous.

The Easter of 2008 came early, at the end of March, thus incommoding those who, having given up alcohol for Lent, could not celebrate St Patrick's Day with a drink or two. Moreover, this meant that, in the way that schools divide up the years into terms so that teachers and students are not overstretched, and public examinations can be accommodated, there was a gap between the end of Easter and the start of the school holidays. Not only was this inconvenient for parents but, for everybody, Easter was not a celebration of spring but of the continuing misery of winter. Unfortunately, Easter, the seasons and school terms cannot be sensibly aligned. It is not beyond the wit of people to achieve this, but we always need to remember that God is tetchy about being praised. According to the BBC website,

> The exact method of calculation of the date of Easter was a hot topic for the early Christian church. It was felt that to celebrate Christ's resurrection on the wrong day would be blasphemous, so it was very important to get the day right. The general rule was agreed at the Council of Nicea in 325 AD. It was many hundreds of years after this that a working algorithm was devised. This was perfected in the 16th Century by Aloysius Lilius at the same time that he devised the Gregorian Calendar, which is still used today.

If you want to work out when next Easter will be, the algorithm is available on the BBC website.[8]

What made Easter worse for many people was the sight of various individuals, some of them Members of Parliament, their mouths pursed tight with pride in their virtue, declaring that their conscience would not allow them to support the government's human fertilisation and embryology bill. Evidently their consciences were more important than the suffering of fellow human beings. Cardinal Cormac Murphy-O'Connor, the leader of the Catholic Church in England and

Wales, declared that the passing of the bill would lead to 'Frankenstein monsters'. No matter that all the bill was allowing was for scientists to use the empty shells of animal eggs 'in which to implant purely human DNA for fourteen days, to derive stem cell lines which model a particular disease to be studied in the lab'. Spare human eggs are always in short supply, and animal eggs will do just as well. No animal–human hybrid could possibly be born from such a technique. This technique allows research into 'Alzheimer's, Parkinson's, motor neurone disease, and muscular dystrophy, as well as cancer, diabetes, strokes and infertility'. There had been considerable public consultation, and the bill had been passed by the House of Lords. There was strong support 'from the Medical Research Foundation, the Royal Society and the Academy of Medical Sciences, as well as Cancer Research UK and the British Heart Foundation'.[9]

Taking pride in one's virtues destroys compassion, and, when compassion disappears, cruelty follows. The Catholic Church and the Baptist George W. Bush are united in their fight to prevent women from having access to abortion and contraception, despite the fact that, when women have access to affordable, reliable contraception they do not need abortion. George Monbiot wrote,

> When the Pope tells bishops in Kenya that they should defend traditional family values 'at all costs' against agencies offering safe abortions, or when he travels to Brazil to denounce its contraceptive programme, he condemns women to death. When George Bush blocks aid for family planning charities that promote safe abortions, he ensures, paradoxically, that contraceptives are replaced with back street foeticide. These people spread misery, disease and death. And they call themselves pro-life.[10]

On the basis of your beliefs, are you entitled to force other people to share your beliefs, and, if they do not conform, kill them?

Even if you take pride in your beliefs and feel superior to non-believers, very likely you would reject the idea that you would kill. But what if your circumstances change? For instance, in the next forty years or so, climate change will mean that increasing amounts of land will become uninhabitable. The countries that border the Mediterranean will become more arid, while countries such as Bangladesh will be engulfed by the ocean. If you were living in Morocco or Bangladesh, where would you go? Obviously to countries which might be less affected by climate change, such as Britain, or to wealthy countries like America and Australia. If your home is in Britain, America or Australia, will you welcome this influx of thousands of people? Or will you try to keep them out? Will you say, 'I am entitled to hold on to my land because I am a superior person because I hold these religious beliefs'? Will you say, 'God gave me this land because I belong to his Chosen People'? Will you feel entitled to kill the unbelievers who look for a home in your home?

History shows that many religious people have had no difficulty in answering 'Yes' to this question, particularly when they feel that they are part of a great movement charged by God with the task of saving the world. The religions with the largest numbers of followers are Christianity and Islam which, as John Gray wrote,

> are militant faiths that seek to convert all humankind. Other religions have been implicated in twentieth-century violence – the state cult of Shinto in Japan and Hindu nationalism in contemporary India. But only Christianity and Islam have engendered movements which are committed to the systematic use of force to achieve universal goals.[11]

The belief that your religion is the only true religion and that it is your task to convert everyone to your religion is a belief saturated in pride. As I began to discover as a child when I went to St Andrew's Presbyterian church, every religion is divided into two parts: the compassionate and the judgemental. Even Buddhism, outwardly so compassionate, has the implacable Karma which cannot be escaped from or mollified. The compassionate by its very nature has no pride, but the judgemental is in essence a statement of pride. Believers might praise the compassionate and talk in its language, but they are drawn to the judgemental because it allows them to be self-righteous. Moreover, in the judge-mental they then have the power to vent all their anger, resentment and envy for the slights and humiliations they have received over their lifetime on those who do not share their religious beliefs, the people they feel entitled to des-pise. The judgemental in all religions brings out the very worst in us.

The worst of the worse of us was brought out by the Nazi doctrine which, with Hitler as its god, bore many of the characteristics of a religion. Nazi doctrine replaced com-passion with sentimentality, which is itself a form of cruelty. Whether the Nazis were trying to annihilate their prisoners' sense of being a person or waxing sentimentally over their blond, blue-eyed children, they were denying who the pris-oners and the children were, individuals in their own right and not merely projections of the Nazis' hatred or desire. Primo Levi wrote,

> Neither Nietzsche nor Hitler nor Rosenberg were mad when they intoxicated themselves and their followers by preaching the myth of the Superman, to whom everything is permitted in recognition of his dogmatic and congenital superiority; but worthy of meditation is the fact that all of them, teacher and pupils, became progressively removed from reality as little by little their morality became unglued from the morality common to all times and civilisations, which is an integral part of our human heritage and which at the end must be acknowledged.[12]

Pride in our superiority unglues us from reality, and we become capable of committing the worst of all crimes, geno-cide. When believers dream of wiping out the infidel in a holy war, or of rising up to heaven while below the unbelievers perish, they are, in their imagination, committing genocide. If Paul taught that the thought is as evil as the deed, he might not have meant that imagining going shopping would put groceries in your cupboard, but that imagining with pleasure carrying out an evil deed implies that, given the opportunity, you would commit it.

Writing about those who had committed genocide, Ray-mond Gaita said,

In their failure, so radical in its nature, to acknowledge a common humanity with their victims, in their arrogant assumption that they are entitled to decide which peoples are fit to inhabit the earth, the perpetrators of genocide offend against their victims, as individuals and as members of the target group. But their crime is also against the constituency of humankind. The concept of a crime against humanity expresses the belief that those who commit this crime offend against the moral constitution of humanity itself – humanity as we mean it when we say that justice will only be served when we acknowledge a common humanity with all the peoples of the earth.[13]

No religious belief entitles us to force our beliefs on other people, or to be cruel to them, or to kill them.

In choosing our beliefs, we should be very careful because what we believe has enormous implications for ourselves and for other people. When I speak of choosing our beliefs I expect there will be people who will say, 'I didn't choose my beliefs. My beliefs chose me.' No doubt such people will be offended if I say that such a statement is analogous to that of the man who beats his wife, or sexually assaults a child, and then excuses himself on the grounds that 'a red mist came over me'. (During my career as a clinical psychologist, I have occasionally been asked to write a report on a wife batterer or a sexual abuser who excused his actions to me on the ground that he had been overtaken by 'a red mist'.) The claims of being overtaken by a red mist or by a belief are examples of how we can do something which we know is not for the best of motives – say, we want to do something that allows us to give vent to our anger, or to believe something that appeals to our pride – but we do not want to take responsibility for our action or our beliefs. So we say something came over me, something robbed me of my will. The more angrily we argue that what happened was not of our volition, the more we reveal our shame or our weakness at having behaved in a way we know we should despise. Choices are made in a split second about whether to take out our anger on someone who cannot resist, or to believe what meets our needs whatever the evidence. Our decision derives from how we have interpreted our situation.

When people say, 'I don't know why I did that', they are either trying to escape the consequences of their actions, or they do not want to examine the reasons for their actions in case they discover something which frightens or discredits them. Often people know very well the reason for their action, but they do not want to reveal this to their questioner. This can be wise, because, when we reveal the reasons for our actions, we also reveal a good deal about ourselves. Whatever the situation, the questioner with whom we should always be truthful is ourselves. We should not try to lie to ourselves because we know that we are lying, and the conflict between the lie and the truth will inevitably cause us trouble.

The idea that we can act and not know why we act flies in the face of the religious belief that we have free will. Free will is an essential part of religious dogma that is concerned with judgement and punishment. If we were compelled by some external or internal force to do what we do, we should not be punished for what we do. The idea that we have a totally free will does not stand up to examination, as many philosophers and theologians have shown, but we do have a kind of free will. We have very little control over what happens to us, but we have complete control over how we interpret what happens to us. We always have a choice. We often claim that, 'I had no alternative', but, actually, we had a number of alternative interpretations available but all of these except one we found to be unacceptable. We always have a choice, even if sometimes it is only between 'It is' and 'It isn't'. Our interpretations are drawn from the ideas we have acquired from our past experiences. How large a choice we have in interpreting what happens to us depends on the store of ideas we have acquired over our lifetime. Children are greatly disadvantaged in choosing how to interpret what happens to them because their experience is so limited. Many adults are disadvantaged by their meagre opportunities for education. Then there are those people who deliberately limit the freedom they have to choose because they have chosen a world-view that is mean, cramped, and bounded by high, impenetrable walls. These walls might be the walls of religion, or nationalism, or racism, or classism, or sexism, but, whatever they are, they make the person less than he might have been.

If we make ourselves less than we might have been we can never be the person that we know we are. We always know when we are less than the person we know ourselves to be, and this knowledge undermines our self-confidence more deeply and more insidiously than all the insults other people can load on us. It might be that we are less than we might have been because we have never been let be the person we know ourselves to be. We might have been brought up by people who are so self-absorbed that they see us as little more than objects that they own; or by people who were trying to cope with disasters and loss and had little of themselves in terms of love and understanding left over to give to us; or by people who imposed their ideas of what it is to be good on to us and forced us to concentrate so completely on what we ought to be that we lost sight of who we were.

In this state we cannot help but be frightened. We cast around for something we can cling to. When a religion offers to care for and protect us, and to give us pride and status, we can grasp it eagerly in the hope that it will banish our loneliness, take responsibility for us, and make us feel loved. With such gifts in the offing, we might sacrifice even more of what we know ourselves to be, but, no matter what we are offered, underneath is still that lonely, frightened person for whom religious belief is a defence and not part of who we know ourselves to be. Our religion might teach us to despise nonbelievers, but claiming to be superior does not make us superior, any more than a child climbing on to a chair and claiming to be king of the castle actually makes himself taller.

Some of us are fortunate enough to discover that, to become ourselves, we have to abandon the weak reed of religious beliefs used as a defence, and set out to find ourselves, and with that our own understanding of the nature of death and the purpose of life.

How can you tell whether your religious belief is a defence

to protect yourself or is an essential part of the person you know yourself to be?

A defence always needs to be defended. If you become offended and angry when your religious beliefs are criticised, and if you feel impelled to convert others to your beliefs, then your religious beliefs are a defence of the frightened, seemingly inadequate person who has not yet become the person you know yourself to be. If your beliefs are your creation and thus part of the person you know yourself to be, then other people's criticisms are of no importance to you. They have their beliefs and you have yours. You do not hold your beliefs as absolute, immutable truths because you know that your beliefs are guesses which you hope to improve as your understanding of life increases. You know that you are responsible for your beliefs, just as you are responsible for yourself. Being responsible for yourself means being who you are. It is only by being who you are that you can give that fragile structure of ideas which is your sense of being a person a strength and solidity which can endure unpredictable and unhappy events. Moreover, you know that each of us has our own individual beliefs about the nature of death and the purpose of life, and that we express these beliefs in imagery drawn from our past and from the world we live in. Some people use imagery drawn from religion and some imagery drawn from nature, but neither can capture completely and exactly what it is to be a human being and how extraordinary and wonderful that is.

Your beliefs are yours alone. You might express them in words that other people use, but you have given these words their own individual meanings. Whatever your beliefs are, they do not make you superior to anyone else, nor do they make you intrinsically virtuous. Your beliefs do not confer on you the right to force your beliefs on other people, nor to treat other people badly, nor to kill them. If you are wise, you choose your beliefs carefully, making sure that they do not denigrate you, or require you to create suffering for yourself or other people, but that they confirm the person that you know yourself to be, and that from them you can draw courage and optimism.

NOTES

Preface

1. Primo Levi, *If This Be a Man*, trans. Stuart Woolf, Everyman's Library, London, 2000, p. 105.
2. Arthur C. Danto, *Mysticism and Morality*, Penguin, Harmondsworth, 1972, p. 24.
3. *Guardian*, March 18, 2008.

1. Religion in the twenty-first century

1. *Guardian Weekly*, February 15, 2008, p. 30.
2. *Sydney Morning Herald*, January 4, 2008.
3. Peter Herriot, *Religious Fundamentalism and Social Identity*, Routledge, New York, 2007.
4. www.timesonline.co.uk (21 December 2007).
5. Christopher Hitchens, *God is Not Great*, Atlantic Books, London, 2007, p. 203.
6. Herriot, op. cit., pp. 2, 12.
7. Keith Stuart, 'Death, Where Is Thy Sting?' *Technology Guardian*, September 20, 2007.
8. Karen Armstrong, *The Battles for God: Fundamentalism in Judaism, Christianity and Islam*, Harper Perennial, London, 2000, p. xiii.
9. Herriot, op. cit., p. 96.
10. Stephen Bates, *God's Own Country*, Hodder and Stoughton, London, 2007, p. 271.
11. Ibid., p. 59.
12. Ibid., p. 7.
13. Ibid., pp. 3, 6.
14. Ibid., p. 81.
15. Amanda Lohrey, 'Voting for Jesus', *Quarterly Essay*, issue 22, 2006, p. 43.
16. Margaret Simons, *Faith, Money and Power*, NOW Australia Series, Pluto Press, Melbourne, 2007, p. 16.

17. Lohrey, op. cit., p. 21.
18. Ibid., p. 22.
19. Simons, op. cit., p. 62.
20. Ibid., p. 65.
21. David Millikan, 'God, Power and Money', *Sydney Morning Herald*, March 3, 2008.
22. Sean Carroll, *The Making of the Fittest*, Quercus, London, 2008.
23. *Guardian Weekly*, February 22, 2008.
24. January 2008, p. 29.
25. Gordy Slack, *The Battle over the Meaning of Everything*, John Wiley and Sons, San Francisco, 2007, p. 95.
26. *New Scientist*, January 5, 2008.
27. Tom Parfitt, 'The Battle for the Soul of Chechnya', *Guardian Weekly*, January 4, 2008.
28. Reproduced in the *Weekend Australian*, December 29–30, 2007.
29. *Sunday Telegraph*, December 30, 2007.
30. http://en.wikipedia.org (26 December 2007).
31. *Guardian*, December 24, 2007.
32. Tom Bower, *Gordon Brown: Prime Minister*, Harper Perennial, London, 2007, p. 6.
33. Hitchens, op. cit., pp. 28, 30.
34. Richard Dawkins, *The God Delusion*, Black Swan, London, 2007, p. 34.
35. Ibid., p. 49.
36. Ibid., p. 31.
37. Daniel Dennett, *Breaking the Spell*, Penguin Books, London, 2006, p. 21.
38. Hitchens, op. cit., p. 5.
39. Ibid., p. 24.
40. Ibid., p. 7.
41. Gordy Slack and Mark Richardson (eds) *Faith in Science: Scientists Search for Truth*, Routledge, New York, 2001, p. 120.
42. John Humphrys, *In God We Doubt*, Hodder and Stoughton, London, 2007, p. 139.
43. Ibid., p. 141.
44. J. L. Mackie. 'Evil and Omnipotence', in *The Philosophy of Religion*, ed. B. Mitchell, Oxford University Press, Oxford, 1978, p. 242.
45. Humphrys, op. cit., pp. 143–5.
46. Ibid., p. 152.
47. Ibid., p. 308.

2. What it is to be human

1. Chris Frith, *Making Up the Mind: How the Brain Creates our Mental World*, Blackwell, Oxford, 2007, p. 40.
2. Ibid., p. 169.
3. *New Scientist*, January 5, 2008, p. 42.
4. Jean-Paul Sartre, *Words*, Hamish Hamilton, London, 1964, pp. 65, 91, 133.
5. Raimond Gaita, *Romulus, My Father*, Text Publishing, Melbourne, 1998, p. 167.
6. Ibid., p. 8.
7. Ibid., pp. 51, 101, 148.
8. Ibid., pp. 104, 105.
9. Ibid., pp. 117, 120.
10. Ibid., p. 121.
11. Ibid., p. 126.
12. Ibid., p. 122.
13. Primo Levi, *The Drowned and the Saved*, trans. Raymond Rosenthal, Abacus, London, 2005, p. 53.
14. Ibid., p. 20.
15. Dawkins, *The God Delusion*, op. cit., p. 320.
16. www.guardian.co.uk/science/2007/nov/16/sciencenews.g2

3. 'Hemmed in a closed cirque of our own creating'

1. Robert Conquest, '1944 and After', *Forays*, Chatto and Windus, London, 1979, p. 46.
2. J. Keegan, *The Face of Battle*, Jonathan Cape, London, 1976, p. 24.
3. Mark Twain, 'Reflections on Religion', *The Outrageous Mark Twain*, ed. Charles Neider, Doubleday, New York, 1987, p. 31.
4. G. Steiner, *The Death of Tragedy*, Faber, London, 1974, p. 45.
5. Dorothy Rowe, *Choosing Not Losing*, Fontana, London, 1988, pp. 100–28.

4. Very different points of view

1. Dorothy Rowe, *The Successful Self*, HarperCollins, London, 1993; *Beyond Fear*, 3rd edn, HarperCollins, London, 2007; *Dorothy Rowe's Guide to Life*, HarperCollins, London, 1995.
2. William James, *Varieties of Religious Experience*, Longmans, Green and Co., London, 1903, p. 53.

5. Being good and the Just World

1. John Burnside, *A Lie about My Father*, Vintage, London, 2007, p. 181.
2. Ibid., p. 45.
3. Ibid., p. 134.
4. Ibid., p. 89.
5. *Weekend Australian Magazine*, January 19–20, 2008.
6. Burnside, op. cit., p. 227.
7. Interview in *The Listener*, July 12, 1979.
8. 'I don't like losing', *The Listener*, August 9, 1979.
9. James, *Varieties of Religious Experience*, op. cit., p. 64.
10. John Gray, *Black Mass: Apocalyptic Religion and the Death of Utopia*, Allen Lane, London, 2007, p. 2.
11. William Barrett, *Irrational Man*, Heinemann, London, 1972, p. 56.
12. Peter Koestenbaum, *The New Image of the Person*, Greenwood Press, Westport, Conn., 1978.
13. Paul Wood, 'Hunting "Satan" in Falluja Hell', BBC News, November 23, 2004.
14. September 14, 2002, quoted in Gray, op. cit., p. 28.
15. James, *Varieties of Religious Experience*, op. cit., p. 134.
16. Jeffrey Burton Russell, *The Devil; Perceptions of Evil from Antiquity to Primitive Christianity*, Cornell University Press, Ithaca and London, 1977, pp. 23, 32.
17. Dorothy Rowe, *Beyond Fear*, 3rd edn, HarperCollins, London, 2007, pp. 555–629.
18. Burnside, op. cit., p. 101.
19. John McGahern, *Memoir*, Faber and Faber, London, 2005, p. 47.
20. Ibid., pp. 10–11.
21. *New Scientist*, December 1, 2007.
22. http://www.kendallharmon.net/t19/index.php/t19/article//9751/
23. Arthur Miller, *Timebends*, Minerva, London, 1990, p. 27.
24. Gaita, *Romulus, My Father*, op. cit., p. 167.
25. http://www.bbc.co.uk/religion/religions/hinduism/holydays/thaipusum.shtml

6. Trying to be good

1. Paul Barry, *The Rise and Rise of Kerry Packer – Uncut*, Bantam and ABC Books, Sydney, 2007, p. 428.
2. Ibid., p. 3
3. Ibid., pp. 76, 84, 85.
4. Ibid., p. 20.
5. Ibid., p. 92.
6. Ibid., p. 97.

7. Ibid., p. 97.
8. Ibid., p. 97.
9. Ibid., p. 98.
10. Ibid., pp. 98, 99.
11. Ibid., p. 106.
12. Ibid., p. 135.
13. Ibid., p. 153.
14. Ibid., p. 99.
15. Ibid., p. 168.
16. Ibid., p. 167.
17. Ibid., p. 494.
18. Sarah Kane, *4.48 Psychosis*, Methuen, London, 2000, p. 43.

7. How we acquire our beliefs

1. Shakespeare, *Measure for Measure*.
2. *Sydney Morning Herald*, February 14, 2008.
3. Miller, *Timebends*, op. cit., p. 37.
4. Ada Brunstein, 'You're So Vain', March 22, 2008, p. 35.
5. Edward Robinson, *The Original Vision*, Religious Experience Research Unit, Manchester College, Oxford, 1977, pp. 71, 72, 75.
6. Miller, *Timebends*, op. cit., p. 25.
7. 'Face to Faith', *Guardian*, March 15, 2008.
8. Mike Marqusee, *If I Am Not for Myself*, Verso, London, 2008, pp. 56, 57.
9. Tim Dowling, *Suspicious Packages and Extendable Arms*, Guardian Books, London, 2007, p. 62.
10. 1 Kings 4: 23–8.
11. http://www.lamp.ac.uk/aht/Home/home.html
12. Alister Hardy, *The Spiritual Nature of Man*, Clarendon Press, Oxford, 1979, p. 1.
13. 'Intimations of Immortality', *The Albatross Book of Living Verse*, Collins, London, 1947, p. 304.
14. Robinson, op. cit., pp. 9, 10, 16.
15. Ibid., p. 45.
16. David Hay, *Exploring Inner Space*, Penguin, Harmondsworth, 1982, pp. 131, 133, 153, 154.
17. Edward Robinson, *Living the Questions*, Religious Experience Research Unit, Manchester College, Oxford, 1978, pp. 33–6.
18. Rowe, *Beyond Fear*, op. cit., p. 370.
19. Hardy, op. cit., p. 43.
20. Ibid., p. 60.
21. Robinson, *The Original Vision*, op. cit., p. 49.
22. Geza Vermes, *The Resurrection*, Penguin Books, London, 2008, pp. 106, 86.
23. Ibid., p. 111.

24. Ibid., p. 150.
25. Ibid., p. 152.

8. The consequences of our beliefs

1. Simons, *Faith, Money and Power*, op. cit., pp. 24–35.
2. Karen Armstrong, *The Great Transformation*, Atlantic Books, London, 2006, p. xiv.
3. *Essays on the Australian Story*, Quarterly Essay, Schwartz Publishing Pty Ltd, 2006, pp. 233, 234.
4. Ibid., pp. 231, 224.
5. Levi, *The Drowned and the Saved*, op. cit., p. 59.
6. Marqusee, *If I Am Not for Myself*, op. cit., pp. 50, 51, 52, 59, 60, 293.
7. *Guardian*, March 22, 2008.
8. http://www.bbc.co.uk/dna/h2g2/A653267
9. Polly Toynbee, *Guardian*, March 25, 2008.
10. *Guardian Weekly*, March 3, 2007.
11. Gray, *Black Mass*, op. cit., p. 71.
12. Levi, *The Drowned and the Saved*, op. cit., p. 84.
13. 'A Breach of Trust', *Quarterly Essay*, Issue 16, Black Inc., Melbourne, 2004, p. 38.

INDEX